D0563741

INJURED HONOR

INJURED
HONOR

THE *CHESAPEAKE-LEOPARD* AFFAIR
JUNE 22, 1807

SPENCER C. TUCKER

FRANK T. REUTER

NAVAL INSTITUTE PRESS   ANNAPOLIS, MARYLAND

LIBRARY OF CONGRESS CATALOGING-IN-PUBLICATION DATA

Tucker, Spencer, 1937–
    Injured honor : the Chesapeake-Leopard Affair, June 22, 1807 /
Spencer C. Tucker and Frank T. Reuter.
        p.   cm.
    Includes bibliographical references and index.
    ISBN 1-55750-824-0 (acid-free paper)
    1. Chesapeake-Leopard Affair, 1807.   2. Chesapeake (Frigate)
3. Leopard (Ship)   I. Reuter, Frank T. (Frank Theodore), 1926–
II. Title.
E357.3.T83   1996
973.5′21—dc20   95-46458

Printed in the United States of America on acid-free paper ⊗

03 02 01 00 99 98 97 96   9 8 7 6 5 4 3 2

First printing

Title-page illustration: detail from a painting by William Gilkerson

Contents

Preface

This book is the first comprehensive treatment of the June 22, 1807, *Chesapeake-Leopard* Affair, the most important confrontation between the United States and Great Britain in the period between the American Revolution and the War of 1812. We believe it to be an important contribution to the naval and diplomatic history of the period.

The Napoleonic wars and the resultant need for sailors on Royal Navy ships was the background to this event and one of the principal causes of the War of 1812. Neither Britain nor the United States was in a position to court conflict. Exhausted from her long struggle against France, Britain could ill afford the hostility of the world's leading neutral trading nation. The United States not only was woefully unprepared militarily on land and sea but risked the loss of profitable markets, an economic recession, and a potential split in the Union itself. Yet reactions in both countries to the attack of the British warship *Leopard* on the U.S. Navy frigate *Chesapeake* forced their governments into untenable positions and so narrowed the area for negotiation of long-standing differences that by April 1812 President Madison had little choice but to ask Congress for a declaration of war.

This "Second War of American Independence" was not inevitable. But since the end of the Revolutionary War in 1783 relations between Britain and America had been so strained that every negotiation between the two countries was clouded with mistrust and misunderstanding. The British looked upon the United States as an upstart nation with an ineffective, experimental form of government, while the Americans regarded Britain as the bastion of economic conservatism and political corruption. Public opinion on both sides of the Atlantic shared the mutual mistrust and too often ignored obvious and important cultural similarities that could have drawn the two countries closer together.

Developing domestic politics underscored the differences rather than the similarities. In Britain successive ministries considered the United States as on the fringe of world affairs and worth little consideration, even though opposition leaders called for more lenient policies. In America simplistic thinking blamed Britain for most of the problems confronting the fledgling nation. After the Anglo-French War began in 1793, British policies—especially Royal Navy practices—spurred in the United States a strong, vocal political opposition to the seemingly pro-British attitude of Washington's second administration. Under the intellectual leadership of James Madison and Thomas Jefferson, the Republican Party coalesced around a series of controversial issues concerning federal policies, the most significant of which was the conduct of relations with Great Britain. By the time Jefferson became president and Madison secretary of state in 1801 distrust of Britain had become enshrined as a cornerstone of Republican philosophy.

Even before the *Chesapeake-Leopard* incident in 1807 an increasing number of confrontations between the Royal Navy and American merchant ships gradually hardened attitudes in both London and Washington. The principal issue in all of this was "impressment." The British insisted that the United States was doing little, if anything, to stop the practice of enticing Royal Navy sailors into service in the American merchant marine or navy. The Americans argued that Britain's searches of American vessels for so-called deserters violated their nation's rights and insulted their flag, particularly when hundreds of men taken from American ships claimed to be U.S. citizens. Both governments could easily trap themselves in unreconcilable definitions of the legalities of impressment and recruitment.

The *Chesapeake-Leopard* Affair sprang the trap. As historian Henry Adams noted, "That the accident which then happened should not have happened long before was matter for wonder, considering the arbitrary character of British naval officers and their small regard for neutral rights."[1] American public opinion was inflamed over a number of recent impressment incidents when an order from Vice Adm. Sir George Cranfield Berkeley, commander in chief of the British North American Station, triggered the event of June 22, 1807. When the *Leopard* fired into the unprepared *Chesapeake* to force her to accept a search party for deserters, Britain actually had attacked the United States.

The affair had important repercussions for Anglo-American relations. Indignation in the United States produced an immediate clamor for war. State governments called up militia and the Jefferson administration ordered gunboats into service. For weeks Norfolk, Va., lay under threat of imminent British naval attack. Anger was so strong in the United States that Jefferson unwisely demanded Britain renounce publicly the whole concept of impressment. This non-negotiable demand backed the London ministry into a corner. The British adamantly refused to abandon their centuries-old practice; even Britain's domestic critics of impressment—and there were many—considered Jefferson's demand blatantly high-handed. The United States, attempting to avoid the war Jefferson's demand implied, tried coercing Britain into acceptance through a series of trade embargoes. When these failed, the inflexibility in each country's policy toward the other was obvious. Only war could result. Perhaps the only surprise was that the stalemate lasted almost five years.

In addition to its important repercussions on diplomatic relations between Britain and the United States, the *Chesapeake-Leopard* Affair also profoundly affected the U.S. Navy. Although it did not lead to additional naval construction (Jefferson in fact saw the affair as vindication of his opposition to a large sea-going force), the subsequent board of inquiry into the encounter and courts-martial of Commodore James Barron and other officers bitterly divided the officer corps. It undoubtedly influenced Commodore John Rodgers, who, in the *President–Little Belt* Affair, avenged U.S. Navy honor.

The *Chesapeake-Leopard* Affair focused more clearly than any other event the real differences between Great Britain and the United States. It is an excellent example of how a single incident can hinder the pursuit of rational choices in foreign policy, in particular when such an incident engenders an emotional public response. The fact that the British had fired on an unprepared U.S. warship fostered a desire for revenge that helped prepare the American navy for the war that would soon come.

Despite its great importance and the fact that the *Chesapeake-Leopard* Affair is mentioned in virtually all naval and diplomatic studies of this period in U.S. history, the only book on it since the appearance of several short contemporary accounts is John Cloyd Emmerson's 1954 privately printed work, *The* Chesapeake *Affair of 1807* (Portsmouth, Va.). While useful, it is little more than a collection of source materials and does not treat the diplomatic aspects of the affair. An unpublished dissertation by Edwin Metcalf Gaines, "Outrageous Encounter: The *Chesapeake-Leopard* Affair of 1807" (University of Virginia, 1975), deals principally with the military reaction in Virginia. The incident also receives several chapters in Leonard Guttridge and Jay Smith's *The Commodores,* but their account contains a number of errors, including misquotations.

Our book is intended to be a comprehensive examination of this most important of confrontations between Britain and the United States before the War of 1812. It begins with a brief recounting of the event itself and then traces the long history of mistrust between the United States and Britain between the end of the American Revolution and June 1807. We discuss naval issues and antagonism between the two countries over the issue of impressment; the immediate political, diplomatic, and military reaction; the divisive nature of the event for the U.S. Navy; and attitudes expressed by U.S. Navy officers at the time. We also discuss in detail the preliminary naval inquiry into the affair. No record of this proceeding was thought to exist, but a copy has been found in Record Group 45 of the National Archives and has been used here. We also treat Barron's court-martial. We have a chapter on the political and diplomatic repercussions for the United States and Great Britain, and a final chapter examines subsequent naval events, including the *President–Little Belt* encounter, the post-1807 history of the *Chesapeake,* and the subsequent careers of Barron and other participants, including the duel between Stephen Decatur and Barron.

Frank Reuter's expertise is diplomatic history, and that of Spencer Tucker is naval affairs. It is appropriate to inform the reader that Reuter wrote chapters 3, 4, and 7, and Tucker chapters 1, 2, 5, 6, 8, 9, and 10. We each take full responsibility for the entire manuscript, however.

Our sources include various collections of papers of Thomas Jefferson, Albert Gallatin, and other key U.S. leaders, the *American State Papers,* state department correspondence, foreign office and admiralty papers in the Public Records Office in London, the Grey family papers in Durham, letters to and from the Secretary of the Navy, private collections of letters of American naval officers (especially the James Barron papers at William and Mary University), contemporary American and English press accounts and books, proceedings of the preliminary inquiry and Barron's court-martial, memoirs, and numerous secondary accounts.

We very much appreciate the kind assistance of Dr. William M. P. Dunn. Informed of his work on Stephen Decatur, we thought he might be able to help. He immediately sent more than a hundred pages of material he had gathered on the *Chesapeake-Leopard* Affair. Some of this, especially information on Dr. John Bullus, was unknown to us and has been of great assistance. We would also like to thank Comdr. Tyrone Martin, William Gilkerson, and Professors Donald Worcester and Gene Smith for their generosity in reading the manuscript. Don Worcester is an excellent editor and Gene Smith, who specializes in the Jeffersonian period, had many helpful suggestions. Bill Gilkerson and Ty Martin are acknowledged experts on naval warfare in the age of sail and provided much assistance on technical details. Also very helpful have been Barbara Pierce, office manager of the History Department at Texas Christian University; Margaret Cook, Curator of Manuscripts and Rare Books at Earl Gregg Swem Library, College of William and Mary; Patti I. Houghton, rare book specialist at Dartmouth College Library; and the staffs at the National Archives, Library of Congress, and Naval Historical Center, and at the "Prior's Kitchen," University of Durham Archives, Durham, England. Acclaimed marine artist William Gilkerson did the wonderful cover illustration. We are also grateful to Joseph Helmick, dean of the Graduate School at Texas Christian University, and the Faculty Research Committee of TCU for providing financial assistance that made research travel possible and aided in the purchase of research materials.

INJURED HONOR

ONE

The Encounter

From a distance the two-decker HMS *Leopard* and the frigate USS *Chesapeake* seemed the picture of serenity as they rode the gentle swells off Cape Henry on the afternoon of June 22, 1807. On the decks of the two warships it was a different story. Aboard the *Chesapeake* men rushed to find their battle stations and clear obstructions from the gun deck, while on the *Leopard* sailors stood tense and ready by their cannon. The United States and Great Britain had been at peace for two decades, but it had been an uneasy peace. Suddenly years of bitterness and mistrust found expression in a broadside from the *Leopard*. It crashed into the American ship some fifty yards away, tearing away her rigging and sending lethal wooden splinters in all directions.

This is the story of how these two ships came together and their two nations came to the brink of war.

In January 1807 Secretary of the Navy Robert Smith had ordered the *Chesapeake* (40 guns) prepared for service. She and the ship sloop *Wasp* (18) were to form a squadron under Commodore James Barron to relieve the frigate *Constitution*, brig *Hornet*, and schooner *Enterprize* on Mediterranean station.[1]

Readied at Washington, the *Chesapeake* proceeded down the Potomac to Hampton Roads, where she completed her outfitting. Bad weather delayed her sailing, but Monday, June 22, was clear and began with light breezes from the southwest. At 6:00 A.M. the weather became favorable for sailing. An hour later the *Chesapeake*'s crew hoisted out her jolly boat, ran it up at the stern, and took aboard the second cutter. At 7:15 they weighed anchor and made sail; the frigate stood down the Roads bound for the Atlantic and Gibraltar.[2]

The *Chesapeake* sailed with a crew of 329 and 52 Marines.[3] There were also civilians aboard: the wife of Marine Capt. John Hall; and Dr. John Bullus, his wife Charlotte, their three children, maidservant, and a young black servant. President Thomas Jefferson had appointed Bullus consul to the Balearic Islands and navy agent to the Mediterranean squadron.[4] The frigate also carried as many as ten Italian members of the Marine band, who were returning home at their request.[5]

The American frigate was hardly prepared for fighting. The gun deck was piled high with civilian baggage belonging to Mrs. Hall and the Bulluses. It was also littered with "the range of the starboard bower cable," empty gang casks which had been taken out to enable the crew to get at provisions, the armorer's forge, sick men in hammocks (thirty-two men were on the frigate's sick list that day),[6] the steward's cupboard, a wooden secretary on each side of the cabin between the two after guns, and cases of claret abaft the after guns. More sick men lay in the sun on the spar deck.[7] The frigate's guns were lashed up for heavy weather, and some implements for serving them were stowed below. Articles filled the passageways leading to the magazines. Barron later said the frigate seemed "intended then rather as a store ship, than one which was supposed to meet and engage an enemy."[8]

Replacement of the *Constitution* was long overdue, and Secretary Smith was anxious that the *Chesapeake* reach her Mediterranean station as soon as possible. One historian has contended that "a peremptory order" from Smith led to the frigate's sailing before she was ready;[9] no evidence to support his assertion has been found, however.

Barron knew there were at least three deserters from the British frigate *Melampus* aboard his ship.[10] Should he have made ready for the possibility of action? He anticipated no difficulty; the *Chesapeake* was a powerful and recognized U.S. warship, and Barron was convinced of the peaceful intent of the British.

At 9:00 in Lynnhaven Bay, a few miles from the Capes, the *Chesapeake* sailed past two British vessels: the *Melampus* (40) and the ship of the line *Bellona* (74). Barron recalled that "their Colors [were] flying and their appearance friendly."[11] Three hours before the *Chesapeake* had sailed, however, the two-decked British ship *Leopard* (50, Capt. Salusbury Pryce

Humphreys) departed Lynnhaven Bay and proceeded into the Atlantic. At six o'clock she reanchored about three miles north of Cape Henry lighthouse with the ship of the liner *Triumph* (74). After the *Chesapeake* passed the *Bellona* the latter ran up the signal, "weigh and reconnoitre S.E. by E."[12] In response at 9:15 the *Leopard* weighed and made sail.

The signaling from the *Bellona* was visible from the *Chesapeake*. Her captain, Master Commandant Charles Gordon, reported it to Barron in his cabin. Barron went on deck and observed it through a spyglass,[13] but he was unable to read the signals and found nothing untoward in the *Leopard*'s movements.

The wind was out of the south-southwest, "therefore fair for her [the *Leopard*] to proceed to sea." Instead of taking advantage of this to clear land, the British ship "hauled by the wind, close around Cape Henry, and stood to the Southward, under easy sail, thereby showing that it was not her intention to get off the land speedily." At about noon the wind became "light and baffling and likely to shift, and was out from the Eastward." The *Leopard* then "shortened sail and stood to the eastward." At about 1:00 the wind shifted to the south-southeast.[14]

Meanwhile the *Chesapeake*'s crew stowed her larboard anchor and secured her boats. The frigate then bore off, forced by the wind change to tack several times to clear the land as her crew continued preparations for sea.[15] The frigate cleared Cape Henry around 2:00. Her crew hauled in her courses, took in her topgallant sails, and at about 2:15 tacked inshore to await the boat to debark pilot Charles Nuttrel. The *Leopard,* about five to six miles to the west, also "tacked and stood in."[16]

Dinner was served in the captain's cabin aboard the *Chesapeake* about 2:30. Barron was joined there by Gordon, Captain Hall, and the Bulluses. Mrs. Hall was sick and remained in the frigate's after cabin. Through the open ports those at dinner could see the *Leopard,* several miles to the south. The British ship had "three times got the weather gauge" (position upwind) and preserved it by "tacking in shore when the *Chesapeak* [*sic*] did so . . . ."[17]

At 3:00 P.M. the *Chesapeake* again stood to eastward. She was then "laying off and on under easy sail" about three leagues (approximately nine miles) east-southeast of Cape Henry waiting for the pilot boat. At this point the *Leopard*, three to four miles away, wore and stood for the *Chesapeake*. The wind was light, so it took nearly a half hour for the British warship to close to about sixty yards of the *Chesapeake* on her windward, weather, quarter. Meanwhile, many of the *Chesapeake*'s crew were occupied in stowing anchors, unbending the sheet cable, and stowing below ranges of lower cable. Gordon gave no orders to clear lumber from the gun deck.[18]

At 3:27 Captain Humphreys hailed the Chesapeake, saying that he had a dispatch for her captain.[19] Perhaps Barron assumed he would be asked to carry mail to Europe, a normal courtesy extended at sea to vessels of other nations. Only a few days before the *Bellona* had put dispatches for Europe aboard the *Wasp*.[20] There was, however, some cause for alarm. The *Leopard* had her lower-deck ports open, and the tompions—the plugs that protected the guns when not in use—has been removed from the muzzles. The pilot, Nuttrel, assumed from the *Leopard*'s tacking that "she wanted something from us" but found nothing untoward in her lower ports being open; there was a good breeze, but the sea was smooth and the ship was not careening.[21]

On receiving the hail from the *Leopard*, Barron, who was standing in the starboard gangway with speaking trumpet in hand, replied that he would "heave to" and that the British captain had permission to send his man on board. He instructed Gordon to throw the main-top sail to the mast, which was done. The *Leopard* also hove to.[22]

Barron did not call his crew to quarters. Regulations called for this on the approach of a warship of another power, but historian Henry Adams noted that Barron later said the idea of an attack "was so extravagant that he might as well have expected one when at anchor at Hampton Roads." The practice "of going to quarters in such cases was seldom strictly observed," Adams noted.[23]

At 3:32 Humphreys sent Lt. John Meade in a boat; Meade went aboard the *Chesapeake* at 3:39.[24] He asked to speak privately with Barron, and Gordon escorted him to the commodore's cabin. There Meade handed Barron a note from Captain Humphreys introducing a circular letter of June 1 signed by Vice Admiral of the White, Sir George Cranfield Berkeley, commander-in-chief of the British North American Station. The circular read:

> Whereas many Seamen, subjects of His Britannic Majesty, and serving in His Ships and Vessels as per margin, while at Anchor in the Chesapeak deserted and entered On Board the United States frigate called the *Chesapeak,* and openly paraded the Streets of Norfolk in sight of their Officers under the American flag, protected by the Magistrates of the Town, and the Recruiting Officer belonging to the above mentioned American Frigate, which Magistrates and

Naval Officers refused giving them up, although demanded by His Britannick Majesty's Consul as well as the Captains of the Ships from which the said Men had deserted, the Captains & Commander of His Majestys Ships and Vessels under my Command are therefore hereby required and directed in case of meeting with the American frigate the *Chesapeak* at Sea, and without the limits of the United States to shew to the Captain of her this Order; and to require to search his Ship for the deserters from the before mentioned Ships, and to proceed and search for the same, and if a similar demand should be made by the American, he is to be permitted to search for any Deserters from their Service, according to the Customs and usuage of Civilized Nations in terms of peace and Amity with each other.

The British ships specifically mentioned in the left margin were *Bellisle, Bellona, Triumph, Chichester, Halifax,* and the cutter *Zenobia.*[25]

Humphreys later wrote: "No person could regret more than myself that the Admiral should have issued such a circular to the different ships under his command; but my duty was to obey, as a subordinate officer, and as a gentleman, to soften and ameliorate the apparent severity and harshness of the order."[26] Indeed, Meade bore a note from Humphreys expressing the hope that matters might be settled amicably:

The Captain of the *Leopard* will not presume to say anything in addition to what the Commander in Chief has stated, more than to express an hope, that every circumstance respecting them may be adjusted, in such a manner that the harmony subsisting between the two countries, may remain undisturbed.[27]

Barron must have been shocked by what he read. He politely but firmly refused to recognize Royal Navy authority over his ship and pointed out that the U.S. government did not permit such searches. The only men he said he knew to be British "deserters" on the *Chesapeake* were those from the *Melampus,* a ship not mentioned in Berkeley's dispatch. He was thus correct in telling Meade that he did not know of any men fitting the description in Berkeley's order. Barron discussed the matter of the *Melampus*'s deserters with Meade and told him that David Erskine, the British envoy to the United States, had been "perfectly satisfied in the subject, in as much as they were native American citizens." Barron then called Dr. Bullus to his cabin and told Meade that the doctor was "particularly acquainted with all the facts and circumstances relative to the transaction" and had received his information from the secretary of the navy. Barron said he was prepared to go to the *Leopard* and give Captain Humphreys "all the information he possessed." Meade apparently made little comment but did tell Barron he had no idea who Erskine was.[28]

Barron then called Captain Gordon to the cabin, handed him the paper listing names of British deserters, and asked if any of them were on the ship. Gordon told Barron that "our men were all new recruits, and I did not know them by name or description." He did not read the paper, but laid it on the table and left the cabin. After more discussion Barron again called Gordon from the quarterdeck to entertain Lieutenant Meade while the commodore wrote a reply to Humphreys. While Gordon and Meade carried on a "sociable conversation" on the port side of the cabin, Barron and Bullus were in "close conversation" on the starboard side.[29]

Barron then drafted this reply:

> I know of no such men as you describe; the officers that were on the recruiting service for this ship, were particularly instructed by the government, through me, not to enter any deserters from his Britannic Majesty's ships; nor do I know of any being here.
>
> I am also instructed never to permit the crew of any ship that I command to be mustered by any other but her own officers; it is my disposition to preserve harmony and I hope this answer to your dispatch will prove satisfactory.[30]

As James Fenimore Cooper later pointed out, "It would have been illegal for Commodore Barron to give up a man regularly entered among his crew, as a deserter. He might have returned a deserter that came on board his ship, but nothing more."[31]

Although Barron's discussion with Meade lasted thirty-five to forty-five minutes, neither he nor Gordon made any effort to ready the *Chesapeake* for action. At 4:15 the frigate's officer of the deck came to the cabin to report a signal flying from the *Leopard,* and Meade said it was for him to return. Gordon then went up on deck while Barron and Meade talked for several more minutes. Meade then left the *Chesapeake* and within ten minutes was back aboard the *Leopard* with Barron's written response.[32]

Barron apparently anticipated nothing other than an angry verbal exchange with the British captain. After Meade had left, Barron sent for Gordon and showed him Humphreys's letter (he no longer had Berkeley's order) and his answer. He asked Gordon for his opinion, and Gordon said he thought the answer was "plain and decisive." Barron then said, "you had better get your gun deck clear, as their intentions appear serious."[33]

Gordon left the cabin. He later testified that he considered Barron's remarks not "a decisive order, but rather a request" in order "to prepare the gun deck prior to going to quarters." He passed along Barron's instructions to 1st Lt. Benjamin Smith on the gun deck and shortly afterward sent 2nd Lt. William Crane to assist him. A few minutes later Barron came up on deck and went to the gangway, where he called Gordon and asked if the guns of the *Leopard* had tompions out and were trained on the *Chesapeake*. Gordon replied in the affirmative. Barron ordered Gordon to call the crew to general quarters, but as quietly as possible and without the traditional drum roll and without the men showing themselves through the gun ports (which would preclude them from removing tompions or taking out half ports). As Barron put it, "If we are seen going to quarters, they will charge us with making the first hostile show." Gordon later said that Barron told him that "the ship would sink before he would give up a man; and asked me what I thought of it.—I replied certainly." Gordon said "the order was given in such a way too, that all the officers then on the gun and spar decks, I think must have heard it."[34] Captain Hall asked Gordon whether he should order his marines to take up their arms. Gordon replied in the affirmative, and the marines drew their weapons from the arms' chest and loaded them. Bullus told Hall that they had better get their wives below, and they escorted them and the children from the cabin to the less exposed cockpit.[35]

While Barron was trying to determine Humphreys's intentions, he was startled by the sound of the *Chesapeake*'s drummer beating to quarters. Gordon halted this by hitting the drummer with the side of his sword.[36] All gun deck lieutenants and Gordon subsequently testified that halting the drumming delayed the process of readying the guns to fire because it threw the crew "into confusion."[37] It is indeed doubtful Barron gained any advantage by the silent call to quarters; the vessels were so close that the British could easily see the Americans belatedly clearing for action.

Lieutenant Crane went to the wardroom and said: "officers to your quarters."[38] Although the lieutenants quickly reached their battle stations, all was confusion. The frigate's guns had all been loaded with round shot before sailing, as per normal naval procedure, but none was ready to fire. A number were insecurely fitted on their carriages, so that there was about a half an inch difference in seating the trunnion properly against the wood of the carriage; at least one had a carriage cap square that would not fit over the trunnion. Sufficient round shot, grape, and canister were on the gun deck and quarterdeck, but the guns were not primed, and only five powder horns of the fifty-four aboard the frigate were filled. All the powder horns were in the magazine. Matches and loggerheads were not available, and some of the rammers were not in their proper places. Some guns did not have handspikes or sponges.[39]

Lieutenant Crane, who commanded the First Division battery, found a cluttered scene. Hammocks with sick men were slung over the guns. The gun deck was covered with cable. The armorer's forge and anvil, the fore hatch ladder, cooper's horse, a large grindstone, a pile of boards on two of the guns, and several casks hindered preparations. Crane ordered the deck cleared and guns cast loose. He also sent to the magazine his powder boys, and later two midshipmen, for cartridges and powder horns.[40]

Told by Crane that the frigate was going to quarters, Lt. William Henry Allen took his side arms and went to his station as commander of the Second Division on the gun deck. His division was littered with three pork barrels (one filled), a grog tub, and cable. Midshipman John T. Shubrick assisted some of the men of the division in carrying nine sick men to the cockpit. Their belongings were thrown down the hatch after them.[41]

Fourth Lt. John Creighton commanded the Third Division, the after battery. He went to quarters on his own without being ordered, but his guns were obstructed by a large canvas screen for the cabin servants. This concealed trunks, a table, a cask, and a locker for cabin furniture. The cabin bulkhead which could be dismantled during a battle, was still standing, a large sideboard was near the mizzen mast, and a table and chairs were within the cabin. Creighton later claimed that these did not cause any delay in firing: "That was occasioned by the want of powder horns and matches."[42]

Clearing the guns took all hands, and Allen ordered this to be done first. Midshipman Jesse D. Elliott later said it would have taken twenty minutes just to clear all the guns of the Third Division.[43]

A few minutes after Meade had returned to the *Leopard* she edged closer and Humphreys hailed. Several witnesses reported him as saying: "Commodore Barron, you must be aware of the necessity I am under of complying with the orders of my commander-in-chief."[44] Another account had him saying, "I have been ordered to remove British deserters from your ship, sir!" Barron, who had stepped into the gangway, said he answered Humphreys, "I do not understand what you say." (One witness on the *Leopard* reported him as saying, "You may do as you please.")[45]

Humphreys later said that he was prompted by "motives of humanity, and an ardent desire to prevent bloodshed . . . by repeatedly hailing and remonstrating, but without effect." He believed Barron understood his words: the water was calm, the British warship was to windward, and those on the *Leopard* were able to hear what Barron said.[46]

Immediately after this exchange Barron told Gordon to "hurry" the men to their quarters.[47] Humphreys was convinced Barron was merely stalling; the British captain was not going to allow the *Chesapeake*'s crew time to get ready for action. The *Leopard* had more sail set and was slowly pulling ahead of the American frigate when Captain Humphreys ordered a shot fired "athwart her bows" as a signal to heave to. Barron chose to disregard this. Humphreys said that he then hailed the *Chesapeake* again, but found "the answers were equally evasive."[48] He claimed it was only after this, at about 4:30, that he gave the order to open fire, beginning with the foremost gun on the lower deck.[49]

There is a dispute about the time between the warning shot and the broadside. Lieutenants Sidney Smith and Crane said the interval was only a few seconds. Gordon, however, stated there was a warning shot, followed by Humphreys's hails and a delay of several minutes before the broadside. The *Leopard*'s log gives the length of time as two minutes.[50] The two ships were within range of a pistol shot ("about one-third cable length").[51]

That Humphreys had serious misgivings about opening fire on the *Chesapeake* is shown in the report of the action he wrote later that day: "Conceiving . . . that my Orders would not admit of deviation, I lament to state, that, I felt under the necessity of enforcing them, by firing in the United States Ship."[52] Years later he wrote that after having received Barron's reply, "I had only a plain straightforward course to pursue—viz., to execute the order of my superior—a painful duty; but I had no alternative."[53]

The ships lay nearly abeam as the *Leopard*'s side erupted in smoke and flame. Shot crashed into the *Chesapeake*, principally amidships.[54] Wooden splinters flew in all directions. Among the wounded was Barron, hit in the right leg and thigh by splinters. He was standing in the gangway, known as "the slaughterhouse" because it was the most exposed part of the frigate; he remained there, save for several trips aft, during the entire engagement. Certainly Barron "made no attempt to shelter himself. His situation was generally much exposed."[55] Midshipman James M. Broom, his aide, was also wounded. Barron ordered Gordon to hurry the men to their stations.[56]

Either before the *Leopard*'s first shot or at the beginning of her firing, Captain Gordon discovered ship's Gunner William Hook on the quarterdeck. The captain always kept the key to the magazine, and Gordon passed it to Hook and ordered him there.[57]

Hook unlocked and entered the magazine as the *Leopard*'s first broadsides crashed into the frigate.[58] Conditions in the magazine that day were such that it would have been impossible for the *Chesapeake* to have carried on a sustained action. The "magazine appeared in great confusion, and the gunner could not find anything he wanted."[59]

Hook and Gunner's Mate (serving as Gunner's Yeoman) Thomas Garnet (or Garnett) found only eight filled cartridges: four of full charge and four of reduced. They had been filled by Garnet before the frigate sailed. Hook and Garnet passed to the boys who would carry them to the batteries the five filled powder horns to prime the guns, and Garnet filled two more before going to the fore storeroom to secure matches. He found three bundles of about twelve matches each already cut into lengths, but they were neither primed nor in their linstocks, the holders used when handling them in action. He handed out two of the bundles before returning to the magazine, where powder horns were still being filled.[60]

Captain Gordon was on the quarterdeck along with the two Lieutenants Smith, ten or eleven midshipmen, the marine officers, and Sailing Master Samuel B. Brooke.[61] Although the guns there were unencumbered, few were cleared and there were no matches, loggerheads, or powder horns for priming. Several were without sponges, and there were no cartridges. Midshipman Peter Muhlenburg later said: "The side tackles of some of them (I believe two) were cast loose but not of all. I did not perceive the breechings of any cast off. Besides we had no powder on hand to fire."[62] Gordon dispatched Lt. Sidney Smith below to end the delay.

Barron meanwhile hailed the *Leopard* twice; once from the gangway and once from abaft atop the signal locker. He said he would send a boat, but just then a second broadside thundered from the British warship. Seeing preparations for battle aboard the *Chesapeake,* Humphreys interpreted Barron's offer to be what Barron subsequently admitted it was: a *ruse de guerre* to gain time. With British firing continuing, Barron ordered a boat lowered, and Lt. Benjamin Smith got down the gig.[63]

Barron seemed unable to comprehend why his guns were not firing. Three or four times he went from the gangway to the main hatch to hail the gun deck, asking whether the men there were ready to return fire.[64] He said later that he could not understand why his subordinates had failed to return fire; he believed them guilty of disloyalty and dereliction. As British shot struck, he saw only chaos. He later charged that no officer on the quarterdeck made any effort to try to secure the rigging and that both Lieutenants Smith were within earshot but did nothing. Barron later wrote of them: "they would have been as usefull to me if they had been in the infernal Regions where they will go if an abominable design of cowardice will send a man there neither of these men I am confident ever had the use of their Reason after the first gun was fired from the *Leopard* until the fire was over."[65]

His lieutenants later charged Barron was confused and indecisive. The court of inquiry later found that in the midst of the action he "drew his men from their guns to lowering down boats to send on board of the attacking ship and that he ordered his first lieutenant from his quarters during the attack, to carry a message on board of the *Leopard* at that time firing upon him." The court also held that Barron used "language in the presence of his men calculated to dispirit his crew." This referred to a call from Barron to men who were standing on the guns, carronade carriages, and signal locker in order to look out over the hammocks at the *Leopard*. The commodore told them to keep down or they would be cut to pieces. The men, who were unnecessarily exposed and in any case not at their proper stations, immediately got down. Barron's order was undoubtedly motivated by common sense rather than cowardice, although Lieutenants Crane and Allen later drew a different conclusion.[66]

Seamen, many of them wounded, huddled in the debris falling from aloft. Surgeon Joseph Hunt, himself wounded, was below. Barron, who had climbed down from where he had hailed the *Leopard* to observe some of the damage to the rigging, cried out, "For God's sake, gentlemen, will nobody do their duty?" He asked Sailing Master Brooke, "is it possible we can't get any guns to fire?" Brooke, whose duties involved maneuvering the vessel, replied that he "knew nothing of guns" and then noticed that Barron was bleeding in the leg and offered to bandage the wound. Although Barron said it was "of no consequence," he did get up on the signal locker to allow Brooke to tie a handkerchief around his leg.[67]

Even the marines aboard the *Chesapeake* failed to return fire. Captain Hall refused permission to fire their muskets unless Barron ordered it. When he reported the men ready to Gordon the latter did not reply. When he told Barron, the commodore said, "it is well," but gave no order to fire.[68] The marines remained huddled around the arms chest throughout the encounter.

Barron ordered Gordon to the gun deck "to get the guns to work." Gordon went to Lieutenant Creighton's Third Division. Creighton said they were not firing because they had no powder horns. One man sent for matches returned wounded but with a loggerhead; it was, however, too cold to fire the guns.

Another problem for the Americans was that not all the crewmen went to their battle stations. Eight to ten men were the normal complement per long gun; fewer could service one, but sustained fire would have been difficult. Midshipman Elliott said that only about two-thirds of the men in the Third Division were at their stations during the attack. One fled during the encounter and two others asked to leave, saying that "they could not stay and be shot at like so many sheep." Elliott refused them permission. Midshipman Charles Norton of the First Division had to roust out two of his men who had sought safety under the heel of the bowsprit. They obeyed his order to go to quarters.[69]

In the Second Division Captain Gordon found three men wounded and a fourth dead. Hall arrived with a desperate message from Barron: "for God's sake to fire one gun for the honour of the flag, I mean to strike."[70] Gordon demanded of Allen what was holding up the return fire. The lieutenant said he needed powder horns and matches. Gordon went to the steerage, where he met a boy returning from the magazine with two filled powder horns. Gordon took these, ran the length of the gun deck, and tossed them across the hatch to Allen, who primed three guns. Gordon then returned to the quarterdeck; he expected that other powder horns and matches would soon follow and that with these "we should at that instant return a warm fire." Allen tried to fire the forward gun with a loggerhead, but it was not hot enough. He finally fired off one of the primed 18-pounders by means of a burning coal from the galley stove at the other end of the deck. There is no proof of the story that Allen juggled the coal in his bare hands all the way to the gun.[71]

Allen was about to fire a second gun when Barron hailed down the hatchway, "Stop firing, stop firing. We have struck, we have struck." According to Allen, Barron called down, "How many guns have you fired?" "One sir," Allen answered. Barron replied, "You have fired two, you have fired two." "No sir," said Allen, "but one."[72]

Returning to the quarterdeck, Gordon "hailed the forecastle" and was about to give an order regarding the ship's sails when Barron, "stretching out his hand stopped me, observing, 'stand fast Sir we have struck.'"[73]

Before the flag could be hauled down, another British broadside hit the frigate. Both the flag and commodore's broad pendant came down. British fire then stopped. Gordon asserted that the *Leopard* had fired four or five broadsides. Humphreys and the British maintained that the *Leopard* fired only three, over a span of ten to fifteen minutes. The American officers later estimated British firing at between seven and fifteen minutes. The *Leopard*'s log reports the British firing three broadsides, "which were returned by a few guns." In his report, Humphreys said only "a few American shot" were fired; none struck the *Leopard*. In his subsequent report to Secretary Smith, Barron certainly exaggerated when he said British fire went on for approximately thirty minutes, but he did admit that "our resistance was but feeble."[74]

This is how the encounter is described in the *Chesapeake*'s log:

> We being unprepared and Ship much lumbered, it was impossible to clear Ship for action in proper time, though every possible exertion was made, & we not suspecting an enemy so near, had not begun to clear the decks until after the Enemy had commenced firing, in about thirty minutes, after receiving much damage in our hull, rigging & spars, & having 3 men killed & 16 wounded, & having one gun ready, fired it, and hauled down our Colours, the *Leopard* ceased firing, and sent her Boat on board.[75]

The *Chesapeake*'s colors were hauled down at 4:45. There is controversy over whether the gun was actually fired before the colors came down. Lt. Sidney Smith testified, "The Colours were struck before any gun was fired by us during the attack," and the court of inquiry concluded that Barron ordered the colors struck before any gun had fired.[76] Several others, including Sailing Master Brooke, also testified that they believed no gun was fired before the colors were struck.[77] Midshipman James Wilson said:

> The orders were given to strike the colours I know before a gun was fired. After Commodore Barron had sent Captain Hall below, he waited some time, long enough for the gun to be fired and as it was not fired, he then ordered the colours to be struck. The order was repeated by two or three officers aft. I heard one of them say, "God damn you haul down the colours."[78]

Midshipmen Glen Drayton and Peter Muhlenburg stated that one of the Second Division guns was fired, but only as the colors were coming down. (As Drayton put it, "The gun was fired just as the colours struck the taffrail.") Drayton also said that the *Leopard* fired a broadside into the

Chesapeake "after our colours were down." Gordon supported this when he said the frigate's ensign and pendant were both down before the final shots were fired.[79]

After the colors were down Barron instructed that the yards be braced back to stop the ship's forward motion. This was not easily accomplished because of damage aloft. Contemporary British naval historian William James, noting that one writer chided the British for having done so little damage to the *Chesapeake*, asserted that three more broadsides would have sunk her.[80] This conclusion seems valid. On August 19, 1812, in a heavy sea, the *Constitution*, with fifty-five guns (about the same as the *Leopard*), totally disabled the *Guerrière*, a frigate of forty-nine guns, in less than thirty minutes to the point that she sank within twenty-four hours. And the *Constitution*'s gunners had to contend with the return fire of the *Guerrière*'s entire broadside of twenty-four guns.[81]

The *Chesapeake* had three seamen killed: John Lawrence (or Laurence), James Arnold, and John Sheckly (or Shakely or Shukly). Eight men were seriously wounded and ten less seriously, including Barron and Midshipman Broom. One of the wounded, Robert McDonald, died later at Norfolk.[82]

It is difficult to imagine any other outcome from the encounter, given the untrained state of the *Chesapeake*'s crew. The only possibility of an American victory would have been effective fire from the frigate's 32-pounder carronades. Likely only honor would have been salvaged. As Lieutenant Allen put it:

> Altho the *Leopard* was certainly very superior to us in guns She mounting 54, we might still have gained . . . it, to our flag by a brave defense, they expected a hard fight I know; and she had a number of volunteers, officers and men from the squadron, she had been at quarters for us all the morning and the *Triumph* 74 was lying with a block under her cable and an axe ready to cut in case we should conquer.[83]

After the Americans struck, Barron ordered the gig down. A seaman's finger got caught in the block, however, and Barron ordered the jolly boat lowered. Finally the gig was got down and Barron sent Sidney Smith to the *Leopard* with a message for Captain Humphreys: "Sir, I consider the frigate *Chesapeake* your prize, and am ready to deliver her to an officer authorized to receive her." Barron, no longer able to stand, retired to his cabin.

At about 5:00 Smith returned, followed by two boats from the *Leopard* with Royal Navy Lieutenants Gordon Thomas Falcon, George Martin Guise, and Meade and several petty officers and men. The British officers demanded that Captain Gordon produce the books of the American frigate and muster his crew. Gordon announced that he was no longer an officer of the ship and withdrew to his cabin, and Sailing Master Brooke mustered the crew. Gordon remained in his cabin about half an hour until Barron summoned him. In Barron's cabin Gordon found Lieutenant Creighton, who had come to ask Barron's permission to secure his guns. Barron replied, "I have nothing more to do with this ship. She is surrendered." Gordon replied, "I regret we had not gone to quarters and returned the *Leopard*'s fire." Barron said that he was the victim; he alone was responsible and no other officer was accountable.

Barron then summoned the remaining lieutenants and Brooke, ordered the servant outside, shut the doors, and asked for their comments relative to what had transpired. At first there was hesitation, but Gordon finally spoke: "In my opinion Sir you have spared the effusion of blood, but it would have been better had we given her a few broadsides first." Lieutenant Crane said, "It had been better if the *Chesapeake* were blown from under us than to be thus dishonored." Lieutenant Allen had difficulty concealing his disgust. He felt the surrender was an unforgivable act of cowardice. "We have disgraced our flag," he told Barron. Crane then said: "the *Leopard* mounted but ten guns more than we did, we were able to contend with her, and you had better Sir have suffered your Ship to have been blown from under you than thus shamely dishonored us." To this Barron replied, "Gentlemen I am sorry you differ in opinion with me, I acted for the best. I have heard enough." He dismissed them.[84]

After the meeting Gordon went to the quarterdeck, where he saw four sailors, alleged by the British to be deserters, standing apart from the rest of the crew. Of the five men who had deserted from the ship-sloop *Halifax* the British found only Jenkin Ratford; Master's Mate George Tincombe of the frigate *Melampus* discovered him hiding in the coal hole. Ratford protested that he was an American named John Wilson (he is identified as such in the *Chesapeake*'s log) and had never been on the *Halifax*. Abraham Preston, the *Leopard*'s purser, knew and identified him, however.[85] The other three men, who were not specified in Berkeley's order, were deserters from the *Melampus*: William Ware, Daniel Martin, and John Strachan. A British officer told Gordon that there were between twelve and fifteen others among the crew who were British subjects, but that they would not be taken.[86] Humphreys reported that these men "did not claim the protection of the British flag, and [were] not within the limits of my orders from the Commander in Chief, I therefore allowed them to remain."[87]

Barron himself admitted that three of the four men taken were deserters: "They [the *Leopard*'s officers] called on the purser, who delivered his book, when the men were examined, and the three men demanded at Washington, and one man more, were taken away." While these men had not been mentioned in Admiral Berkeley's circular, Humphreys may have had verbal instructions to search for them. In any case, Humphreys had done only the minimum required by Berkeley's instructions; Berkeley later declared that the *Leopard*'s captain had conducted himself properly throughout.[88]

At about 7:30 the *Leopard*'s boat returned to the British frigate with the boarding party and the four prisoners. Immediately after they departed Barron sent a boat of his own with Lieutenant Allen and this letter to Captain Humphreys: "Sir, I consider the frigate *Chesapeake* as your prize, and am ready to deliver her to any officer authorized to receive her. By the return of the boat I shall expect your answer; and have the honour to be, Sir, Your most obedient, Humble servant, James Barron."[89]

At 8:00 Allen returned to the *Chesapeake* with word that Humphreys refused the surrender of the *Chesapeake*. His message to Barron was: "Having, to the utmost of my power, fulfilled the instructions of my Commander in Chief, I have nothing more to desire; and must, in consequence, proceed to join the remainder of the squadron. . . ." He did, however, offer to render "every assistance in my power" and also said that he "most sincerely deplore[d], that any lives should have been lost in the execution of a service, which might have been adjusted more amicably, not only with respect to ourselves, but to the nations to which we respectively belong."[90]

At about 8:00 the *Leopard* made sail and stood back to Lynnhaven Bay. At the same time Barron called a council of his officers to determine the next course of action. He showed them the letter to Humphreys and the latter's reply and said he felt it best that the ship return to Hampton Roads "and report the affair to the government." After a considerable pause, Barron again spoke and said "our poor men have done nothing that we should endanger their lives by keeping the sea in our then crippled situation." The officers unanimously concurred. Barron then said "on our meeting with the *Melampus*, he should submit another question to us." The nature of the question was not revealed, although the frigate did pass the *Melampus* without incident the next day before reaching port.[91]

The *Chesapeake* made sail and stood in toward shore as her crew spliced, patched, and pumped 3.5 feet of water from her hold. On June 23 she limped back to land, passing Cape Henry at 8:00 A.M. and anchoring in Hampton Roads at 12:30 P.M.[92]

The Lion and the Eaglet

It was not inevitable that a British man-of-war would attack a ship of the United States Navy. But thoughtful observers of Anglo-American affairs during the thirty years following the Revolution should not have been surprised that it happened.

Great Britain's recognition of the independence of the United States in 1783 did not assure good relations between the two countries. Mistrust and misunderstanding characterized sentiment in both countries and their governments. Many prominent Englishmen held an arrogant disdain—almost contempt—for the former colonies. On their part, Americans were oversensitive and often overzealous in defending their newly created institutions. And when tempers flared, distance exacerbated problems of communication. The fastest ships took five to six weeks to sail from London to New York. And so by the time of Jefferson's presidency mutual respect was a rare commodity. By then each country had adopted attitudes toward the other that made successful negotiation of differences almost impossible.

It all began when the British took a good look at the generous terms their government had granted the United States in 1783. Lord Shelburne, who dominated the ministry that ended the war, hoped to lay the basis for long-lasting cooperation with the new country. He seemingly took literally a warning from an American acquaintance: "Do not act as though America was your enemy and France your friend." Shelburne seemed almost to be buying America's friendship by granting more territory than the United

States had actually conquered; he also held out the promise of a profitable commercial treaty.[1] Many in England believed that Americans deserved much less.

In the United States, however, a euphoric public celebrated independence during the winter of 1783–84 with bonfires and church bells. Citizens in every town offered thirteen toasts to honor the thirteen-state union. Indeed, there was much to celebrate. The territorial settlement extended eastward from the Mississippi River and south from the Great Lakes to Spanish Florida. An area half the size of Europe, it was full of valuable resources awaiting exploitation by three million Americans: timber in Maine, furs in the northwest, rich bottom land along the Mississippi. New Englanders could still work the lucrative cod and whale fisheries off the coasts of Newfoundland and Labrador, while Southerners were promised compensation for slaves carried off and damage done to plantations by invading British armies.

In their excitement, unfortunately, most Americans had not read the fine print in the peace treaty. Their negotiators in Paris had agreed to permit Loyalist supporters of King George III to return home and be reimbursed for property confiscated during the war. Another stipulation promised no "impediment" to the collection of debts owed to British creditors. These debts, amounting to millions of pounds sterling, had been accumulated by the high living of two generations of influential Southern tobacco planters. And for those New England fishermen the vital ability to land at convenient bays on the shores of Newfoundland and Labrador was a "liberty," not a "right." There was a vagueness, too, in the British pledge to withdraw "at all convenient speed" from seven fortified trading posts south of the Great Lakes.[2] No American in 1783 realized how these broadly stated commitments made by each side in the treaty would haunt Anglo-American affairs for decades.

While Americans celebrated, there was much soul-searching in England. The war "jolted the national pride, and the national system. It underlined and revealed defects in administration. It pointed the weakness of Government finance, and the uncertain assumptions for trade."[3] Pessimists felt concessions to the United States, Holland, and traditional enemies France and Spain had reduced Britain to the status of a second-rate power. They feared that the former colonists would soon rival the English in the carrying trade of the West Indies and Europe, and they worried that in times of war the Royal Navy would not have adequate manpower without the old colonial merchant marine as a training ground for seamen.

Other Englishmen insisted England need only return to traditional mercantilism, with its tighter controls over intercolonial trade, and she would be as prosperous as ever. They vehemently opposed any agreement reopening American trade with the British West Indies. To promote these ideas they found Lord Sheffield their most effective spokesman. One of the new industrial leaders and a member of the Board of Trade, he published in late 1783 "Observations on the Commerce of the American States." In this widely read pamphlet he predicted continued American consumer preference for British-made goods and ultimately the breakup of the American union.

Many other dissatisfied Britons considered the peace treaty an unnecessary giveaway. These men were influential enough to force Shelburne from office. Agreeing that a more dynamic leader was needed to restore the empire to preeminence, George III entrusted leadership of his kingdom to twenty-four-year-old William Pitt.[4]

Brilliant, loyal, dedicated, son of the Great Commoner, Pitt the Younger shared his father's grand vision of empire that had propelled Britain to her glorious victories in the Seven Years War. The father recognized in the teen-aged son unusual leadership abilities and encouraged him into an early political career. The young man did not disappoint father or king; he served George III well for more than twenty years. He was shrewd enough to bring to his ministry men like William Grenville and Charles Jenkinson who were equally dedicated to rebuilding the empire. He listened to Sheffield and his friends and heard the pleas and complaints of sugar planters, fur merchants, bankers, manufacturers, ship owners. He learned enough about markets and finances to devise with his cabinet policies that did restore the empire's prestige and prosperity. He asserted later that it was the sole object of his political life "to unite and connect what yet remains of our shattered empire."[5]

All of this meant that Great Britain would neither forgive nor forget the American Revolution. Lord Shelburne's vision of Anglo-American cooperation was replaced by aggressive policies meant to exploit weaknesses in the American political and economic systems. British West Indies ports were closed to American vessels, thereby destroying the basis of New England's prosperity, the prewar triangular trade between North America, the Indies, and England. American cod fishers soon encountered resistance when attempting to land at convenient "unsettled" bays to pack their catch. And new import duties excluded American whale oil from the highly profitable English market. Most significant of all, British garrisons remained in the seven forts scattered across the northern United States from Oswego to Detroit.

Americans suffered their first great depression by mid-1785. Merchant ships and whalers rotted at their docks, while shipbuilders, sailmakers, chandlers, coopers, coppersmiths, sailors, and fishermen were out of work. Farmers producing wheat, flour, rice, smoked meats, even livestock for the West Indies market watched helplessly as commodity prices fell and their debts rose. In the West, settlers seeking to tap the rich fertility of the Ohio country often encountered bloody resistance from the region's Indians. The settlers accused British garrisons still in the frontier posts of abetting the Indian depredations. Fur traders from Albany and Pittsburgh complained bitterly that Indians trapped furs in U.S. territory but sold their pelts to British factors at those same forts, diverting through Montreal what should have been a profitable American catch destined for the European market. Although England was not entirely to blame for the depth of this economic malaise, the destitute farmer who watched his land auctioned for back taxes or the unemployed sailor jailed as a vagrant had much reason for anti-British sentiments.[6]

Deliberately anti-American or not, Britain's actions harassed the United States all through the 1780s. Canada's governor general, Lord Dorchester, secretly entertained Levi and Ethan Allen, who were in Quebec seeking support for an independent Vermont.[7] And Dorchester was ordered "for the Protection of the Fur Trade and perhaps the general security of the Province of Quebec" to continue giving supplies to the Indians so they would not "be discontented or dissatisfied at this moment." He was also to put the posts "into a temporary state of defense, to resist any attack which the citizens of the States may meditate."[8] This directive obviously was meant to protect the interests of London fur merchants, who admitted that two-thirds of all pelts coming from Montreal had been trapped within the United States.

Other London merchants had dreamed of exploiting the rich potential of the Mississippi valley ever since the end of the Seven Years War in 1763. After years of studying the movement of settlers into Kentucky and Tennessee a committee of the Lords of Trade recommended to Lord Grenville that the government take steps "for the benefit of this Country to prevent Vermont and Kentucke [sic], and all the other settlements now forming in the Interior part of the great Continent of North America becoming dependent on the Government of the United States."[9] As early as 1784 British agents promoted among the settlers along the Tennessee River ideas of separatism and independence.[10] Of course, success for a commercial empire on the Mississippi depended on British occupation of the frontier posts. All that was needed was a rationale, and that conveniently came from London: "America has not, on her part complied even with one article of the Treaty, I think we may reconcile it in the present instance to delay evacuation of those Posts."[11]

Here was America's problem. It was too weak, too divided, too decentralized to enforce its own treaty commitments. If it could not abide by the agreement, neither would England, and Congress was powerless to do anything about it.

Congress was the victim of the Articles of Confederation. Adopted in 1781, the Articles formalized the union of thirteen sovereign states and made Congress the creature of those states. When the war with Britain ended, the need for cooperation ended too. Individual states soon began to pursue separate policies, and American nationalism degenerated into regionalism at best and localism at worst. Decisions made by Congress were enforced by each state at its own discretion. There was no national judiciary, and worse still no executive leadership.

From London's perspective the United States barely had a government. It was quickly apparent Loyalists could not return home, nor would they receive the promised compensation. Britain found itself responsible for the care of 100,000 refugees. Ultimately most of these hapless families were settled on the king's lands in Nova Scotia, New Brunswick, and Ontario, much to His Majesty's anger. Meanwhile, frustrated creditors complained they were unsuccessful in state courts when they attempted to recover legitimate prewar debts. These and other aggravations prompted Pitt's ministry to insist the United States must reciprocate if England were to make good on its own treaty promises.

Congress tried to minimize the growing hostility by sending John Adams as the first U.S. minister to the Court of St. James. Adams was expected to overcome misunderstandings, negotiate differences, and in particular revive discussions on Shelburne's idea of a commercial treaty to reopen American trade in the West Indies. But Adams was frustrated almost from the beginning. No one in London took him seriously. Although he was treated politely enough, his efforts to improve relations between the two countries were ignored. Disgusted after three years, he returned to Boston in 1788.[12]

To alarmed American nationalists, the inability of the United States to fulfill its treaty obligations or even be taken seriously by Europeans made obvious the need for a new form of government. Gathering support from along the Atlantic seaboard, they forced the call for a constituent convention to meet at Philadelphia in 1787. Most intended initially to revise the Articles of Confederation, but zealous nationalists among them led the convention into drafting an entirely new Constitution. The result of their efforts was a plan for a federal government with centralized authority, a national judiciary, and a strong executive. The pervasive distrust of Great Britain was one of the themes the nationalists exploited in the long, acrimonious debate over ratification.[13] They succeeded finally in getting a government that could promote national unity, protect American self-interests, and perhaps avenge years of British disdain.

George Washington was a near-unanimous choice to lead the new system during its critical first years. He was a nationalist—though not ardent enough for some—and many hoped that his enormous personal prestige would adhere to the Constitution, thus assuring its acceptance by the public. Even the English, calling him "that illustrious character," were hopeful that these new developments in America might end long-simmering aggravations between the two peoples.[14] All concerned watched eagerly to see what the first months of the new administration would do to improve Anglo-American relations.

But President Washington did not help the situation. Insulted by the treatment Adams had received in London, he refused to send another minister to England until the English first sent theirs to the United States. This meant there still would be no formal diplomatic contact between the two governments, an uncomfortable situation that did not change until 1791. Yet Washington shrewdly recognized that something must be done to minimize the mutual distrust, and he was willing to take the initiative. In October 1789 he requested Gouverneur Morris, a New York merchant traveling in Europe on business, to go to London as his personal representative and hold informal discussions with members of Pitt's cabinet.[15] However, the English were no more cooperative with Morris than they had been with Adams.

In the meantime James Madison emerged as leader of an anti-British contingent in the House of Representatives as Congress considered the first national revenue act. Madison proposed a tariff and tonnage bill that provided low preferential rates for American shippers, higher rates to ships from countries—such as France—having commercial treaties with the United States, and much higher rates for those from all other nations. This was obvious tariff discrimination against the British. Privately Washington favored the idea, and ardent nationalists in the House passed the measure. But there were many in the Senate who feared such legislation would invite British retaliation. A majority of senators, mostly representing the shipping interests of New England and New York, forced a compromise bill that maintained the preferences for Americans but treated all foreign shippers equally. Washington reluctantly signed the bill.

Now the alarm shifted to London. By 1789 British merchants supplied 80 percent of all imports to the United States and had extended extensive credit that supported the trade. Pitt's ministry wasted no time in protecting such a valuable market from the apparent hostility of the new U.S. government. It quickly dispatched to New York its own unofficial spokesman, Maj. George Beckwith, to threaten influential members of Congress privately with a tariff war "you could never win."[16] Some congressmen took the threat seriously, but in sending Beckwith Pitt's government had once again insulted the United States.

Beckwith had no diplomatic status. He was merely Lord Dorchester's military aide who was returning to Quebec from leave in England. But during the Revolution Beckwith had served as an intelligence officer in New York City, and he still maintained contacts with some local citizens. Pitt's cabinet half-heartedly hoped that he would know the right people to receive its intimidating message. To its surprise, he did. In fact Beckwith was so successful in finding sympathetic congressmen and members of the administration—especially Treasury Secretary Alexander Hamilton—that he returned twice to the American capital. His reappearances, however, undermined his effectiveness because other locals considered him a spy, not a diplomat.[17]

In late 1789 Beckwith stumbled on several significant trends in domestic politics that would influence Anglo-American relations for the next twenty years. Anti-British sentiment was growing in the House of Representatives, and Madison would reintroduce his tariff discrimination bill in almost every subsequent session of Congress. Yet Hamilton feared British trade reprisals would be disastrous for his delicately balanced fiscal program, which depended heavily on import duties. By necessity he sought support for greater cooperation with Britain from seaboard mercantile interests in and out of Congress. Although it would be several years before discernable political parties appeared in the United States, it was apparent that the conduct of U.S. relations with Great Britain was already a major political issue.

Complicating these relations was Washington's long delay in finding someone to be the first secretary of state. It was not until March 1790 that he convinced Thomas Jefferson to organize the new department. In the meantime, through Beckwith, the British found in the sympathetic Hamilton a contact with the American administration worth cultivating. They knew little about the new secretary of state and had no idea whether or not he would also be friendly toward Britain.

Jefferson had been America's minister to France and an excited, enthusiastic witness of the opening months of the French Revolution. When he came home to Virginia in late 1789 he planned to return to Paris the following spring and so was reluctant to accept the secretary's post. His attitude toward Britain at the time is unclear. It is certain, however, that during his years in France he developed a great admiration for French culture, especially its architecture, and an equally strong appreciation of the ideals of the French Revolution.[18] It is also certain that early on he was chagrined at an apparent pro-British drift in Washington's administration. Although Madison, his friend and fellow Virginian, could influence him, Jefferson approached his responsibilities with freshness and objectivity. Soon, however, two situations challenged his objectivity toward Britain: the "Nootka Crisis" and the arrival of the first British minister to the United States.

Nootka was an Anglo-Spanish war scare that President Washington feared could threaten the sovereignty of the United States. It started in early 1790 when a Spanish man-of-war captured four British merchantmen trading with Indians at Nootka Sound on the west coast of Vancouver Island, which was claimed by Spain.[19] A minor incident perhaps, but Pitt saw it as a challenge to England's commercial expansion in the Pacific, and that prompted him to threaten war. Washington worried the British might attack Spanish New Orleans by marching troops south from Canada, and in the process seize the entire Mississippi valley. He asked his cabinet how the government should respond if the English asked permission to cross American territory. For him the answer was the key to maintaining the dignity of the United States in all future relations with Great Britain. Jefferson and Hamilton split over how much, if any, cooperation should be granted. Nor could they agree to have Morris in London take advantage of the crisis and press Pitt to withdraw the garrisons from the frontier posts.

While Washington worried, London was awash with rumors about what the United States might do. Morris had arrived just as the crisis broke and had no instructions concerning Nootka. Pitt's government half-expected overzealous American nationalists to take matters in their own hands and seize the posts. Fortunately for all concerned, there was no war; Spain backed down and reluctantly accepted the British wedge into its old Pacific commercial empire. Although Pitt had dealt successfully with the Spanish, his ministers were forced to recognize the potential threats to their policies coming from an aggravated United States too long ignored and too little understood. The Nootka affair showed the importance of having a formally accredited representative in the American capital.

George Hammond was the first in a succession of unhappy British ministers to sample the cultural poverty of primitive America. The nation's capital had been moved in 1791 to Philadelphia. Although it was the country's most sophisticated city, Philadelphia was nonetheless an unwelcome sight to this young-man-on-the-rise in the king's service when he arrived in October. He considered the unwanted assignment fraught with danger for his country and for his own career. And his flexibility was limited by "instructions" from Lords Grenville and Hawkesbury, the foreign minister and the president of the Board of Trade. Both warned that a solution to the question of the frontier posts still depended on U.S. compliance regarding Loyalists and prewar debts. Grenville insisted that "on these grounds His Majesty would be fully justified in . . . refusing to enter into any Negotiation on the Subject." Hawkesbury repeated the long-held notion that the posts were "certainly of great importance to the Security of Canada, and to the Interest of this Country, both in a commercial and political view." Hammond was, moreover, "on no account to conclude anything without previous and express directions" from London.[20]

Hammond's instructions frustrated Jefferson and Washington. The young minister could protest American noncompliance with treaty terms but not discuss solutions to specific problems. The secretary of state was so disgusted that he communicated with Hammond only in writing, never taking an opportunity to develop a relationship through informal conversation. And the president seemed to blame him personally for the embarrassing American military reverses against the Indians in the Ohio country. Just a month before Hammond's arrival, Maj. Gen. Arthur St. Clair had been routed by a strong Indian force near the Wabash River, the second such disaster in a little more than a year. These defeats nullified federal efforts to force the Indians to negotiate a withdrawal from a region long coveted by white settlers. Despite Hammond's denials, Washington remained convinced the English had supplied the Indians with guns and ammunition from the frontier posts.[21]

Washington was, nonetheless, also a practical man. Despite his chronic distrust of the British, he too had learned from the Nootka experience. He had to acknowledge that Grenville and Pitt's ignoring of Morris was not much different than his treatment of Beckwith. When he learned of Hammond's appointment, Washington decided to send Thomas Pinckney of South Carolina as U.S. minister to Britain. By mid-1792, then, common sense finally appeared in both Philadelphia and London. With the formal exchange of ministers, perhaps both countries might find ways to understand each other's significant national interests. The future course of Anglo-American affairs would now depend on how each country defined those national interests.

For Jefferson the two greatest threats to America's interests were British troops in the frontier posts and British impressment of American seamen. He dramatically made his point in a long extraordinary document drafted as an answer to Hammond's instructions. It blasted the British by tracing in detail the impact of England's own violations of the peace treaty since 1783. Jefferson accused them of fomenting instability in the West and insisted "instead of evacuating the *Upper posts with all convenient speed . . .* I conclude [no order to evacuate] had ever been *intended."*[22] Equally adamant about impressment, in June 1792 he ordered Pinckney to protest the practice and sent him a long explanation that cited legal precedents for the U.S. position. In October he forwarded a stack of new complaints from American ship captains and directed Pinckney to argue the case with Grenville. This time he described a specific incident of a merchant captain watching helplessly while a British boarding party forcibly took most of his crew, leaving barely enough men for the ship safely to make port. Jefferson insisted that "so many instances of this kind have happened that it is quite necessary that their government should explain themselves on the subject, and be led to disavow & punish such conduct."[23]

Impressment was already a disturbing issue straining relations between the two countries, and each government clung tenaciously to its view of the legality of the practice. But unless England was at war it remained chiefly a concern between the shipping interests in both countries, annoying yet relatively minor compared to more immediate problems.

Tragically, however, England did go to war again, a war no one in March 1793 foresaw would last almost continuously for twenty-two years. Radicals in Paris had carried their revolution to its logical extreme: they proclaimed a republic, found Louis XVI guilty of treason, and executed

him. They also declared war on the surrounding monarchies that threatened their survival. With Great Britain now in a war it really did not want,
Pitt's government strove to bring France's enemies into a coalition to
punish the regicides and restore the French monarchy.

While Europe began to tear itself apart, Americans swarmed the
wharves of their port towns, eager to meet ships bringing news of these
startling events. Every scrap of information about victories of French
Republican forces inspired public celebration. Accurate news or rumor, it
made little difference to the enthusiasts of what they proclaimed a French
version of the "Spirit of '76." Some, declaring that the "Torch of Liberty"
had crossed the Atlantic, wondered openly how the United States might
help the French defeat the forces of conservatism and monarchy.

Washington was justifiably anxious. Such excited Francophiles could
easily commit acts violating the rights of one or other of the belligerents
and drag the still-fragile federal government into a European war. He
badly needed advice and hastily called on his cabinet to help him devise a
policy for the conduct of the government and its citizens. This was a new
situation for the United States, and rules had to be established. All the
cabinet members favored neutrality, but they debated what the nature of
that neutrality ought to be. They did agree that a presidential "Declaration" should set forth guidelines for the conduct of Americans regardless
of personal sentiments. And Washington accepted Jefferson's warning to
avoid offending the French by omitting the words "neutral" or "neutrality" from his statement. Yet despite this slight victory the secretary of
state was worried, as he wrote Madison, for "if anything prevents it's being
a mere English neutrality, it will be that the penchant of the P[resident] is
not that way."[24]

Events so quickly distorted the neutrality policy that Washington hardly
knew how to defend it even before he could define it legally. Both major
belligerents began a long process of undermining what the American
government was trying to preserve.

In May 1793 Edmund Genêt arrived in Charleston as the first minister
from the Republic of France. Instead of going directly to Philadelphia, he
dallied in the South for a month organizing opposition to U.S. neutrality.
He issued letters of marque to American ship captains as French privateers
and ordered the French consul at Charleston to establish a prize court
there. He even dispatched a commission in the French army to George
Rogers Clark in Kentucky that authorized him to lead any army against
Spanish New Orleans. By the time he reached Philadelphia Genêt had so

inspired Francophilia in the United States that he was treated as a conquering hero. And pro-French sentiment from the press and the platform attacked the neutrality policy and its supporters. For the first time the noble Washington felt barbs from a growing and virulent opposition press.

The president's problems worsened after he publicly (but coldly) received Genêt and thereby formally recognized the Republic of France, making the United States the first government to do so. The British minister immediately protested French privateers bringing captured British ships as prizes into U.S. ports; one of these was even fitted out as a privateer in Philadelphia. But Genêt became even more popular after he bought up surplus grain for shipment aboard American merchantmen bound for France as "provisioning ships." And he announced that traditional French restrictions on intercolonial trade had been waived, opening all French West Indies ports to neutrals. It did not take long for American farmers and shipowners to scent potential profits made from someone else's war.

But Britain had different ideas. In no way would she let American entrepreneurs enter markets they had never known before, nor would she permit even indirect aid going to her enemies. Britain was willing to risk American anger to win her wars and preserve her domination of world trade.

As early as March Foreign Minister Grenville instructed Hammond to counter French manipulation of U.S. neutrality. If Hammond could not prevent Genêt's purchases of provisions he was to remind Washington's administration that even though shipped on American vessels such purchases were still French property and "as such, liable to Capture." Hammond was also to emphasize that "the Principle of free ships making free goods, is one which has never been recognized by this Country."[25] In this one directive Grenville bluntly set the stage for twenty years of animosity between Great Britain and her former colonies.

Clearly Grenville was countering something that had started between France and the United States back in 1778. Benjamin Franklin had negotiated both an alliance and a commercial treaty that brought the French into the War for Independence. Each country agreed to follow what were called "small navy principles": a very narrow definition of contraband of war and an assertion that goods, regardless of origin, carried on neutral ships were the property of the neutral—thus, "free ships make free goods." The British obviously opposed such ideas. Historically their chances of victory in war depended heavily on the ability of their "big" navy to control the seas and to prevent neutrals from supplying their enemies.

By early autumn of 1793 Americans nonetheless took their chances. Hundreds of ships flying the Stars and Stripes swarmed the West Indies, bringing supplies to the French islands and carrying island produce to France. They easily replaced the French merchant marine that the Royal Navy had already swept from the seas. This was, of course, an intolerable situation for the British, but they had abetted it by causing confusion among American shipowners. The War Office had dispatched Sir Charles Grey to the Caribbean with enough troops to seize the French islands. After he took an island he was to prevent "undo hardship" for the local population by importing foodstuffs "provisionally permitted from the United States, in American vessels of one Deck."[26] Grey's orders actually augmented the opportunities for Americans that had been created by Genêt's announcement of the opening of the French island ports.

Yet in November the West Indies squadron of the Royal Navy was ordered to enforce "The Rule of 1756," a tactic used during the Seven Years War to prevent neutrals from nullifying Britain's control of the seas. Traditionally an eighteenth-century empire prohibited foreign ships from the carrying trade between the mother country and its colonies. During war, however, when they could not protect their own merchant marine from a powerful enemy, countries such as France opened to neutrals this intra-empire trade so vital to their own economies. Britain could not tolerate neutral ships replacing enemy ships. Her policy was simply, "what is prohibited in peacetime is prohibited in war."

Inevitably, then, Britain's "big" navy power would clash with America's "small navy principles." It happened soon enough: during the winter of 1793–94, 262 American merchantmen were swept from the Caribbean Sea. The ships were condemned or left to rot, their cargoes confiscated by British prize courts, and their crews interned, impressed into the Royal Navy, or dumped on the beach to fend for themselves. Dozens of protests poured into London and Philadelphia from captains who insisted they carried only legitimate cargoes. Even Grey admitted some of the seizures were illegal.[27]

The blatant use of British power incited a war hysteria not seen in the United States since Lexington and Concord. Mobs assaulted Royal Navy officers visiting American ports and broke all the windows of the British minister's house in Philadelphia. Snarling editors denounced anything British and demanded strong action from the government. One, more moderate than most, asserted, "in short, the insults, murders, and depredations committed against our general government by & through the influence of the British nation, is too great for a republic like ours, or any other nation under heaven, tamely to bear."[28] Meanwhile, the Canadian governor general, Lord Dorchester, had advised a group of Indian chiefs to prepare for imminent war between England and the United States and to demand the Ohio River as the southern boundary of Indian territory. This new threat added to the public outcry. In March, an outraged Congress embargoed all trade with Britain and authorized the president to prepare military defenses. And Washington, who had so long suppressed his anger toward Britain, carefully supervised the details of defense preparations.

But the president was anxious, for common sense told him his country could never survive a war against Great Britain. And so he waited, hoping for a signal from London that might avoid a war neither nation really wanted. Fortunately, Pitt's cabinet quickly realized it had blundered and took the first steps toward maintaining peace. Dorchester was reprimanded, and Grenville ordered Hammond to head off any possible "clamour" resulting from the seizures and to explain that the noxious Orders of November had been modified.[29] When these instructions finally reached the hapless Hammond the "clamour" was almost out of control. Washington did, however, recognize Grenville's invitation for accommodation. After consulting his cabinet and members of Congress, he concluded that a special emissary to London might be able to negotiate away most of the aggravations between the two countries. After much soul-searching and too much unwanted advice he selected Chief Justice John Jay as the best available diplomat to deal with Pitt's ministers.

Jay's mission is one of the most controversial in the annals of American diplomatic history. Jay accomplished much and did bring a brief era of stability in Anglo-American affairs. However, many of his contemporaries felt he had accomplished too little. Under the treaty he signed in November 1794, Britain agreed to evacuate the frontier posts; arbitration commissions would be established to determine compensation for prewar debts and damages to Southern planters; and surveying commissions would determine the boundaries of Maine and modern Minnesota. The pact also opened trade for Americans in the East Indies and permitted a limited trade in the British West Indies. The treaty, however, was silent on definitions of contraband and the whole issue of impressment. In essence Jay's Treaty yielded to Britain's "big" navy on the very issues that had brought on the war crisis.

When news of the treaty's terms leaked to the press, many Americans were convinced Jay had betrayed the interests of the United States. In towns all along the seaboard Jay was hanged in effigy and copies of the treaty were burned in public bonfires. A mob in New York City stoned Alexander Hamilton as he attempted to defend the treaty in a public speech. Newspaper editors attacked the characters of both Jay and Washington; some accused the president of wanting to be king, and one demanded his impeachment. What should have been the climax of Washington's painstaking efforts to improve relations with London became instead an object of public outcry and a rallying point for the Republican opposition.

Washington admitted that he too was dissatisfied with Jay's Treaty. Yet he knew it was the best settlement he could get and called for the Senate to convene in June 1794 to consider it. While the senators debated, the Royal Navy renewed its meddling with American shipping. Yet the Senate did approve the treaty (with no votes to spare) and the president, though again irate at Britain, ratified it. But in doing so he faced the greatest leadership challenge of his career. He had to stare down the Republican-controlled House of Representatives to obtain funds for the several arbitration commissions. When Republican leaders tried to nullify the treaty by refusing the appropriations, Washington insisted that Jay's Treaty, now ratified, was the law of the land and the House had no choice. This dissention over the treaty focused attention on other controversial issues and helped lay the basis for American two-party politics. Virulent Anglophobia became the catalyst for the creation of the Republican Party.[30]

In Europe the treaty created new and potentially dangerous situations for the United States. Madrid mistakenly saw it as an Anglo-American alliance directed at Spanish Louisiana. Secretly Spain planned to withdraw from the war against France anyway, and so the Spanish government offered Washington an unexpected opportunity to renew moribund negotiations concerning American rights in the Mississippi valley. Thomas Pinckney hurried from London to Madrid and by the end of 1795 had an agreement that minimized Spanish influence in the Southwestern United States and opened the region to American settlers. For the president Pinckney's popular settlement was a happy counterbalance to Jay's negotiations.[31]

Like the Spaniards, the French misinterpreted Jay's Treaty. Fervent nationalists insisted it betrayed the principles of the Franco-American Alliance of 1778 and harshly criticized the United States for capitulating to British power to the detriment of France.

Anglo-American relations did improve after the treaty was ratified. British garrisons finally withdrew from the frontier posts, and both governments appointed amiable men to the arbitration commissions. There was, moreover, a new exchange of ministers, with the more amenable Rufus King replacing Pinckney in London and the more experienced Robert Liston going to Philadelphia. And the British—for a time at least—did attempt to minimize the worst abuses of their navy captains in searching American merchant ships.[32]

Yet it was these same American merchantmen that gradually undermined the new cordiality. The United States could not escape the implications of its role as a neutral carrier trading with both sides in an extensive war. Total tonnage of American vessels involved in foreign trade almost doubled between 1790 and 1796, with 80 percent of the increase coming after the European war started in 1793.[33] It was the beginning of a long boom spurred by demand for U.S. products and the decline of other countries' carrying trade threatened by the Royal Navy. Exports from the United States went from an average of $20 million a year during 1790–92 to $94 million in 1801 and $108 million in 1807. Imports also rose dramatically, from $23 million in 1790 to $110 million in 1801 and $138.5 million in 1807. Yankee traders were making profitable inroads into what once had been exclusive markets for the British or the French or the Dutch or the Spanish. These Americans not only supplied each belligerent's enemies but also threatened to achieve a permanent penetration into the global market.

To make matters worse, the United States was not a maritime nation with a long tradition of producing well-trained sailors. Most Americans were farmers, and it took months to turn a Pennsylvania farm boy into an able-bodied seaman acceptable to a Massachusetts merchant captain. And so this maritime boom created a manpower problem for American shipowners. The number of sailors required for their merchant vessels increased from about 22,000 in 1793 to nearly 36,000 in 1797 and more than 50,000 by 1807. With a critical shortage of experienced sailors, the boom came to depend on the employment of foreign sailors. Each captain signed on crews wherever he could find them, thus bringing about an international crisis for the U.S. government.

Seamen's wages in the American merchant marine skyrocketed. Peacetime wages had been from $5 to $8 per month, but by 1800 they had risen to at least $15. In 1800, seamen in New York earned at least $18 a month, and in Philadelphia the merchant Stephen Girard offered $20 to $30 a month from 1797 to 1801.[34] Such pay inspired many farm boys "to go down to the sea in ships." But the preferred sailors who earned the higher rates more often than not were from the ships of other countries. And because the English merchant fleet paid barely half the American $15 minimum, the temptation to jump ship was great. American merchant crews quickly became tiny international communities. Even U.S. Navy officers, competing with the high pay offered by American merchants, had difficulties enlisting crews for their warships.[35]

Great Britain had a manpower problem too, but for different reasons. By 1796 the Royal Navy had stripped the British merchant fleet of as many experienced sailors as it dared, and press gangs had exhausted the supply of available recruits. Life for seamen in the Navy itself was terrible and wages, set by Cromwell in 1653, had been raised slightly only after 1797.[36] Yet the Navy was vital for England's defense, particularly after France invaded Holland and Spain jumped to the French side. In peacetime the Royal Navy had required 40,000 men, but by 1805 this number had grown to 100,000.[37] It was essential that Pitt's government maintain adequate manpower throughout the fleet, even if this meant searching neutral vessels for suspected deserters.

After Jay's Treaty the United States government tacitly acquiesced in the stopping of its merchant ships, but it protested strongly when overzealous British search parties seized as deserters bona fide American citizens. The problem was two-fold: physical identification and proof of citizenship. In general Britons and Americans—especially New Englanders—looked alike; after all, most Americans were of English, Scots, or Irish descent. And the Atlantic separation had not yet developed a distinctively American accent. Moreover, the countries disagreed about the nature of citizenship. The English government did not accept "naturalization"; instead it held "once an Englishman, always an Englishman." In 1796, London modified its definition, recognizing as an American any citizen of any one of the individual states as of the end of the Revolutionary War. But, it maintained, any English emigrant to the United States after 1783 could never be an American and thus was liable for service to the British crown.

Over the years Congress had empowered government officials, usually U.S. consuls, to give proofs of citizenship. Then in 1796, in "An Act for the Relief and Protection of American Seamen," it authorized agents in England and the West Indies to issue "protections" for American citizens and to secure the release of those already impressed into the Royal Navy. British authorities cooperated for a time but soon cried fraud and accused the agents of selling protections to English deserters. In the West Indies Admiral Sir Hyde Parker adamantly refused to allow any American agent to board his ships to look for impressed Americans. Parker was later transferred as a gesture of goodwill, but only a few American seamen actually gained release. Despite efforts at cordiality, impressment smoldered as a continuing irritant between the two countries well into John Adams's presidency.

Changing events could have enhanced that cordiality, for the French, overestimating the improvement in Anglo-American affairs, nearly drove the Americans into the arms of the British. In quick succession Paris broke off formal diplomatic relations with the United States, attempted to influence the presidential election of 1796, and rejected C. C. Pinckney as the new American minister. The French believed that Thomas Jefferson was their true friend and would bring changes in U.S. policies. But when Adams, the Federalist, was elected, their anger turned venomous. Their government ordered French merchantmen to arm as privateers and prey on American commerce. France began an undeclared naval war against the United States that would last almost four years. And French treatment of American ships, cargoes, and men was actually worse than anything the British had done.[38]

Tempers within the United States did a complete about-face. France became the new public enemy. But like Washington before him, President Adams worried that the country was not yet capable of surviving a war. He dispatched a special mission to Paris in hopes the French leadership would negotiate differences. He soon found out otherwise. The three Americans were met by French agents who demanded bribes before any negotiations could begin. This stupid outrage, the infamous "XYZ Affair," moved the United States even closer to war. American anger was so pervasive that Congress quickly appropriated funds for a new navy and for expanding the army. Pro-French Republicans fell into an embarrassed silence, while High Federalists publicly called for a formal alliance with Britain.

Pitt's government took advantage of the situation. Grenville anticipated a Franco-American war and directed Liston on how to proceed.[39] The British never did propose an alliance, but they did offer to convoy and protect American merchant ships from French privateers. They minimized interferences with American shipping and tried to rein in the most abusive navy officers making impressment searches. During 1798 and 1799 there appeared to be a closeness in Anglo-American relations not seen since before the American Revolution.

In those same years John Adams rode the crest of war-borne popularity. An unlikely war-hero president, he clearly saw a Franco-American war as a Pandora's Box that once opened would unleash events and personalities he could not control. Happily for Adams, the latest leader of the French government, Napoleon Bonaparte, had much the same thoughts. In an all but formal apology for the XYZ insult he let Adams know he would treat a new mission with the respect and dignity the United States deserved.

To the chagrin of the High Federalists, Adams accepted Bonaparte's offer and dispatched a new three-man commission to Paris. Adams recognized that in doing this he had undermined his unusually high popularity and in all probablilty ruined his chances for reelection in 1800. But peace was far more important to him.[40] And peace he got. The commission signed the Convention of 1800 that ended the Quasi-War and, perhaps of greater importance, abrogated the Franco-American Alliance of 1778. The United States was now free of its only "entangling alliance." (It would not make another until 1949.) The United States had eliminated any vague commitment that could suck it into the current or a future European war. In the long run this agreement of 1800 was the greatest achievement of Adams's presidency, but it did cost him reelection.

The Convention of 1800 also meant the British had lost the opportunity to build something permanent on the momentary spirit of cooperation with the United States. They had not attempted to find accommodation on the friction points dividing the two countries: the rights of American citizens and their ability to trade where they wished. Lord Grenville could only express disappointment that war had not come; he had offered no opportunity for negotiations on the volatile questions of impressment and American maritime rights. Only if the wars of the French Revolution came to an end would these noxious issues die.

Bonaparte, however, *was* talking peace in 1801. The future of Anglo-American relations depended on how seriously Bonaparte wanted peace and whether Thomas Jefferson, Adams's successor as president, could overcome his well-known disdain of the British and try, as his predecessors had done, to find an accommodation with them.

THREE

Thomas Jefferson and a Changing World

No one knew what kind of president Thomas Jefferson would be, least of all die-hard Federalists. After all, the election of 1800 was the first time in history that a democratic process replaced a country's founding leadership with its political opposition. Die-hard Federalists from the Washington and Adams administrations considered Jefferson and his fellow Republicans to be radicals who would destroy what the Federalist leaders had labored so hard to create. To them, all Republicans were opposed to religion, emerging sources of wealth, and strong central government. Jefferson was forced to calm their fears and dedicate his entire administration to proving the success of a democratic republic of five million souls. In his first Inaugural Address he told the cynics at home that "we are all Federalists, we are all Republicans." And to the cynics abroad who might distrust this change of leadership in the United States he promised "peace, commerce, and honest friendship with all nations—entangling alliances with none."[1]

In England a few of those cynics remembered how Jefferson had lambasted their government and blamed Britain for America's problems in his final report to Congress as secretary of state in December 1793. But most Englishmen could have cared less about affairs in the United States. The few curious page-turners of English journals found little if anything about events on the other side of the Atlantic. Even the London *Times*, already England's most prestigious newspaper, reported only the Electoral College vote (which it did not understand) and later the president's Inaugural Address, but offered no editorial comment or evaluation of the new American leadership. The *Times* reflected the widespread English public disinterest in affairs in the United States.[2] And in France only a few remained of the philosophers of the French Revolution who still admired Jefferson's ideas and ideals. Most Frenchmen were as indifferent to America as the English and far more interested in what the young Corsican general, Napoleon Bonaparte, could do for the glory of their republic.[3] Thus, in London, in Paris, even in Madrid, Jefferson's promise of "peace, commerce, and friendship" was considered totally irrelevant to a Europe still in the throes of a great war.

Fortunately for Jefferson, he had some help making good on his promise. Several significant events in the months prior to his inauguration encouraged his administration. John Adams's negotiators in Paris had ended the undeclared naval war with France as well as the entangling Franco-American Alliance of 1778 that entailed dangerous commitments to defend French possession in the West Indies. And then a British Admiralty court in the *Polly* case modified the infamous "Rule of 1756." The Royal Navy was to follow a new "broken voyage" rule permitting neutral vessels to carry enemy colonial produce to a neutral port if duties were paid and cargoes unloaded to be sold in the domestic market. This was a boon for American merchants who resold these products overseas and claimed them to be "neutral" goods. But perhaps most significant was the end of William Pitt's bellicose ministry in February 1801. War-weary, economically exhausted England welcomed a change in leadership when a new cabinet headed by Henry Addington took over the government and dedicated itself to finding an honorable path to a general peace in Europe. All of this boded well for the new president's foreign policy.[4]

Jefferson wasted little time in pressing his advantages. He promised the British chargé that his administration would be as friendly as those of Adams and Washington. He asked Rufus King, the American minister in London, to let Addington know that with the "sincerest pleasure I have observed on the part of the British government various manifestations of just and friendly disposition toward us. The interesting relations between Great Britain and the United States, are certainly of the first order . . . and will be faithfully cultivated by us."[5] Even James Madison, the new secretary of state, overcoming his chronic distrust of the English, shared this enthusiasm. He directed King to express on behalf of the American people and government his official satisfaction with the improving relationship.[6] Addington was honestly doing his part. Within weeks of assuming office his cabinet ordered naval squadron commanders to be more circumspect in dealing with neutral merchantmen. At the cabinet's urging, Parliament passed new regulations for prize courts in the British West Indies that minimized the worst abuses from arbitrary decisions based on greed rather than law. As a sop to angry American ship captains the Admiralty removed Sir Hyde Parker from command of the West Indies squadron for flagrantly violating the *Polly* decision. It also recalled a Captain Pellew who was notorious among American sailors for the capriciousness and cruelty of his press gangs. And when the English learned that the bashaw of Tripoli had declared war on the United States, King George opened the ports of Gibraltar, Minorca, and Malta to the American Mediterranean squadron and directed that the Americans "should moreover be supplied from His Majesty's magazines in these Ports with whatever necessities from time to time [they] require."[7]

This last was a most unusual gesture and forced the still-dubious Madison to admit the appearance of "a juster policy toward the United States."[8] But he saw all too clearly that at best these were cosmetic changes in British policy. There were still deeper, more meaningful issues aggravating relations between the two countries. The worst and most obvious, of course, was impressment. Madison reminded Rufus King of this, citing a July 1801 report that listed 130 *new* appeals for release by Americans forcibly detained in the Royal Navy; old cases, he said, numbered "near two thousand, more than four fifths of whom are native of the United States."[9] From the American viewpoint, British sincerity would be demonstrated by their willingness to dig away at this divisive issue.

But could they? Far greater challenges to Addington's ministry than those seemingly minuscule ones across the Atlantic loomed across the English Channel. Bonaparte, described by the *Times* as "a slippery negotiator," constantly changed his mind about peace and upped his demands at each bargaining session.[10] Any concessions made to the French brought howls of protest from the Opposition in Parliament and the press. The English had too much national pride to beg for peace even though their economy was fragile, their tax burden crushing, and their food prices so high that they triggered workers' demonstrations. And while all of this was going on the Russian czar was assassinated, throwing into total confusion Britain's already fragile treaty system in northern Europe. The *Times*, normally a strong supporter of the ministry, considered "the state of the North of Europe" as "anxious and critical" and apprehensively listed the sizes and firepower of the navies of Russia, Sweden, and Denmark. It worried whether Alexander, the new czar, would cooperate in a general peace or would combine the fleets of the northern states to create a threat to the Royal Navy.[11] Addington had the same concern and recognized that peace would be difficult, if not impossible, to achieve. While his country was still at war, any accommodation with the Americans regarding impressment would weaken the navy and therefore be political suicide for Addington.[12]

Through some miracle, however, peace of sorts did come to Europe when the Treaty of Amiens went into effect in March 1802. It was not much of a peace, and public opinion in Britain was divided over its effectiveness. Many thoughtful Englishmen—correctly, as future events proved—considered it a mere truce. And the Opposition so thoroughly castigated the government for being unnecessarily generous to France that it weakened support for Addington's leadership. The *Times* rushed to the defense of the ministry in a rare (and sickening) adulatory editorial, describing the cabinet as "the *Men Unknown* to the *Country*" and reminding its readers that "in Athens they erected altars to the *unknown* Gods!"[13] Despite such divided public opinion, the Peace of Amiens provided both a much-needed breathing spell after eight years of war and the opportunity for groups or individuals to push their own agendas for change.

Reformists in England had feared prolonged war would destroy "the traditional balanced English constitutional system." They now brought forward long-suppressed proposals for major political and religious change.[14] Americans hurried new instructions to speed up dragged-out negotiations with the British. President Adams had sent William Pinkney, a Federalist lawyer from Baltimore, to England to finish the work of the several arbitration commissions established by the Jay Treaty in 1794.[15] David Lennox, the "agent for protection of American seamen," was urged to secure the release of all impressed American sailors. Madison took advantage of the opportunity to remind Rufus King that impressment "ought to be considered as taking place thro' distress [and] is contrary to our laws, if not the law of nations." And King again pressed the English for a formal diplomatic settlement on the twin issues of interference with American commerce and impressment of American citizens. King almost succeeded.[16]

But Bonaparte was the most successful of all in exploiting the military lull of Amiens. He freely moved troops around Europe, intimidated smaller countries, and forced shifts in diplomatic alliances. He deliberately ignored most of the pledges he had made at Amiens, while accusing the British of not honoring theirs. With the French so obviously jockeying for a stronger position if war started again, there was fear in London that Addington's ministry would not be prepared. Of more concern for the United States, Bonaparte's ambition also stretched across the Atlantic, where he planned to reestablish the old French empire in North America.

Panic spread in Washington when a rumor surfaced that Spain had ceded Louisiana and the Floridas to France.[17] The panic worsened after Rufus King reported the English were also aware of the rumor and preferred to see themselves in possession of both territories.[18] If these rumors were true the administration confronted its first major foreign challenge. Jefferson expressed American belief that "whatever power, other than ourselves, holds the country east of the Mississippi becomes our natural enemy."[19] To get the French to understand this point he wrote Robert Livingston, America's minister in Paris, that "the day that France takes possession of New Orleans, fixes the sentence which is to restrain her forever within her low-water mark. . . . From that moment, we must marry ourselves to the British fleet and nation."[20]

Given his long-held distrust of the British, Jefferson could not have meant to reverse completely his traditional sentiments. Like most Americans he had tolerated weak Spanish control at New Orleans and believed that in time Spain's hold would wither and the United States would take ownership by default. France or Britain in control of the mouth of the Mississippi was an entirely different matter: either country was strong enough to threaten American security. If Bonaparte were as ambitious as it appeared, the United States would have no qualms at seeking common interests with England. Yet the British themselves were a threat. At one time or other groups of English merchants had promoted their own exploitation of the great interior of the continent. Also, there had been rumors that they too had offered to trade Spain some other territory for the Floridas. Thus a scenario involving either the French or British on the Mississippi River challenged the peaceful expansion of the United States the president envisioned. He had little choice but to enter the unfamiliar and dangerous game of playing one great power against the other.[21]

Bonaparte's schemes became clear to Jefferson in January 1802. Fifty thousand French troops landed in Santo Domingo to subdue the independent republic established by slaves who had revolted against the French planter aristocracy. The island would then be a base for a rejuvenated French West Indian empire that must include Louisiana as a source of food and timber to support its sugar economy. If successful, these troops would greatly increase the French presence in the Caribbean and give France control of the sea lanes to the American West. The French could easily choke off the vital waterborne commerce from American settlements along the Ohio and Tennessee river valleys.

This frightening prospect forced Jefferson to realize that the United States must acquire at least New Orleans before the French troops met initial success in Santo Domingo. New Orleans was the gateway to the entire Mississippi valley and the only port of consequence for the export of cotton, corn, wheat, flour, furs, and hides produced on the American side of the valley. If this port were closed to western Americans their agricultural economy would probably die. Obviously, time was running out for the U.S. government if it wanted to purchase the Crescent City. With check in hand, James Monroe, fellow Republican and neighbor of the president, rushed to join Livingston in Paris and make the offer to Bonaparte.

Events worked in Jefferson's favor again. Stiff native resistance and a malaria epidemic decimated the French force by the end of the summer. Bonaparte realized his American empire was a will-o'-the-wisp now buried in the coffins of tens of thousands of French soldiers. With little remorse for the vast numbers of the dead and even less for the sentiments of the Spanish, the mercurial Bonaparte decided to cut his losses and abandon his American project. He shocked Monroe and Livingston when he offered to sell to the United States the entire province of Louisiana, including New Orleans. Jefferson and Madison, equally surprised, quickly overcame their scruples that the Constitution said nothing about buying territory and authorized the purchase. Congress moved just as quickly to appropriate the necessary funds. Even the British, daily more suspicious of France, saw their own advantage in the collapse of the French Caribbean venture. Addington, in yet another friendly gesture toward the cash-starved American government, permitted London's banking firm of Baring Brothers to loan the United States the funds necessary to meet Bonaparte's terms.[22]

But a problem lurked behind the smiles of the satisfied participants of the Louisiana Purchase. What exactly had the United States bought? "Louisiana" was really a geographic expression rather than a specific entity. The French and, after 1763, the Spanish each had organized the territory differently, and both at one time or other had claimed that it included lands east of the Mississippi. Spain now complicated the problem by refusing to transfer Louisiana to France, insisting that the French had not fulfilled promises made to Spain and therefore that the sale to the Americans was illegal. Bonaparte, always in need of cash, ran roughshod over Spanish opposition and forced Madrid to accept the change in ownership. Jefferson was astounded by this strong French influence over Spain and sought to capitalize on it. Expecting France to back him, he put forward his own claim that what the United States purchased also included West Florida— east from the Mississippi to the Perdido River. France refused to support such an obvious land-grab, and Jefferson's crass maneuver further weakened Spanish-American relations. Jefferson unfortunately misread the reasons for the French refusal of support. He wanted the Floridas, and so he developed a fixation on having France help the United States acquire them from Spain. His expansionist aims were so strong that they clouded his judgment when changing circumstances threatened war again in Europe and compelled him to develop new policies for the protection of American neutrality.[23]

Jefferson's misjudgment was understandable given the three thousand miles that hid details of European events in perpetual fog. Americans always had to wait weeks for news about Europe. And in 1803 they strained to confirm the rumors of renewed war that floated across the Atlantic. In New England eager merchants and shipowners who had suffered a nearly 50 percent decline in their export business during the interlude of peace were poised to profit from renewed hostilities. The president no less than his fellow citizens needed answers; he plaintively wrote to a friend in England, Sir John Sinclair, asking, "what is going on in Europe; if they are back at war?"

When reliable news arrived, it was startling: Bonaparte had been proclaimed "First Consul for Life," making him virtual military dictator of the French Republic. And Europe indeed was back at war after Britain had had enough of blatant French violations of the Amiens treaty. A very disillusioned Jefferson wrote Sinclair that "the events which have taken place in France have lessened in the American mind the motives of interest which it felt in that revolution." Even more startling was his revelation: "we see, at the same time, with great concern, the position in which Great Britain is placed, and should be sincerely affected were any disaster to deprive mankind of the benefit of such a bulwark against the torrent which has for some time been bearing down all before it."[24] This from the man who wanted France to help him acquire the Floridas.

How well Jefferson foresaw the extent of the war that broke out in May of 1803 is open to conjecture. Perhaps no one could at the time. But this conflict would develop tremendous proportions with worldwide repercussions, dramatically threatening British power and influence. It quickly became a struggle for the survival of systems: Bonaparte's continental unity versus Britain's tradition of European balance-of-power. England became the heart of a series of military coalitions organized to destroy the French empire, while Bonaparte determined to reduce "the nation of shopkeepers" to second-rate status. To survive "the torrent" Jefferson described, the English girded themselves for the greatest challenge they had faced in centuries, a threat of a magnitude they would not confront again until 1940.

Such a war trapped neutrals, for the old gentlemen's rules for conduct of warfare and diplomacy were thrown out. Each side harnessed its national resources and tolerated no interference with the national effort. More often than not the rights of individuals and of neutrals were ignored. Neutrality appeared to both sides as aiding the enemy. Whatever claims to previous international law a neutral might make merely bounced off the hard commitments to victory of the belligerents.

Neither Jefferson nor Madison was equipped to develop proper policies to confront the dynamics of this changing world. Perhaps no American was. They certainly did not understand the plight of other neutrals, such as Sweden, Denmark, or Turkey, nor did they attempt to make common cause with them. Instead they recognized only that renewed war meant the return of the old vexations in Anglo-American affairs.[25] Rufus King, considering Addington's cabinet "the most favorable that has existed or can exist for the interests of the United States," had come close to getting the British government to moderate its policies regarding neutral commerce and impressment.[26] But he failed. Warning that public confidence in the ministry was eroding, he asked to come home. An Adams appointee, King had effectively improved communications between both governments, and his absence from London would be sorely felt at this critical juncture in European affairs.[27] Jefferson, hoping to get something accomplished before a change of ministry, hurried James Monroe from Paris. Flush with success in the purchase of Louisiana, Monroe was probably a poor replacement for the amenable King; the English of long memory would not forget that Monroe's public admiration of the French Republic had been so unrestrained that the embarrassed Washington administration had been forced to recall him as its minister to France in 1796.

Addington's ministry was willing to aid Monroe—if it could stay in office long enough. It certainly tried, despite a few growls from the Opposition. To improve contact between the governments on both sides of the Atlantic it sent Anthony Merry as its representative to fill the vacancy in Washington. This appointment proved a mistake; Merry was an obnoxious snob who became increasingly ineffectual at explaining his government's positions on various issues.[28] On the other hand, Lord Hawkesbury, the foreign minister, expressed such sympathy for the many American complaints that Monroe was encouraged to propose a draft treaty to replace the expiring Jay Treaty of 1794. But Monroe was frustrated by Hawkesbury's chronic procrastination; it took months of vague meetings before he could present some semblance of a treaty in April 1804. His draft pushed for expanded trading privileges with the British Empire and the American position on neutral trade. Still stymied by cabinet inaction, Monroe came to agree with Rufus King's evaluation that Addington's ministers were well meaning and cooperative but not overly competent. And he agreed that the ministry could not last long. His apprehension was realized when Addington resigned in May and William Pitt returned to power with a whole new government committed to destroy at whatever costs the France of Bonaparte.

Discussion of American neutral rights was clearly not on Pitt's agenda. Lord Harrowby, the new foreign secretary, made certain Monroe understood at their first interview that he would not even read the proposed treaty. From then on the American knew exactly where he stood in "arranging with the existing ministry any of the important points of his country that were depending with the British government."[29]

Anglo-American relations deteriorated. The Royal Navy increased its searches of U.S. merchantmen, and more American seamen were impressed from their decks. Following new instructions, British squadrons renewed the old practice of diverting to England American trade destined for Europe or European colonies. By August the situation was bad enough that Monroe protested to the Foreign Office that over 1,500 Americans had been pressed involuntarily into navy service since March of 1803.[30] Worse still, British men-of-war were bolder—and closer—in their hovering surveillance of major U.S. ports. Sooner or later an incident would occur to inflame the American anger that Addington had tried so hard to dampen.

Despite these rapid changes in the conduct of Europe's war Jefferson continued to insist on getting international recognition of an American definition of neutral rights. He reasoned that "the place occupied by an individual in a highway, a church, a theatre, or other public assembly, cannot be intruded on, while its occupant holds it for the purposes of the institution. . . . No nation ever pretended a right to govern by their laws the ship of another nation navigating the ocean. By what law then can it enter that ship while in peaceable and orderly use of the common element [the sea]?"[31] Jefferson ignored or forgot that Russia, then a neutral, had signed a treaty with Britain in 1801 that gave up the idea that free ships make free goods and agreed "that Enemy Goods and contraband of war, on board of Neutral Ships, shall be liable to capture."[32]

Jefferson's stubborn convictions—certainly correct from an American viewpoint—trapped him in an unwillingness to see the British side and offer compromise on impressment. The renewed and more extensive war in Europe not only increased the economic opportunities for American shipowners but also increased the economic incentives for British seamen, naval or commercial, to seek the higher-paying berths aboard American merchantmen. Within a year of the failure of the Peace of Amiens America's export trade almost doubled, and the need for experienced sailors increased correspondingly. Even though Congress had clarified the terms for the "protections of American seamen" the British still complained of fraud. They insisted that U.S. consuls in various world ports readily sold certificates of American citizenship to British-born subjects. Sometimes only a dollar turned one of His Majesty's sailors into a native-born American.[33]

From England's perspective, much of America's war-bred prosperity depended as much on British sailors as it did on American seamen. Secretary of the Treasury Albert Gallatin inadvertently supported this contention by warning the president that almost one-quarter of the total manpower in the American merchant fleet was foreign, some French but mostly British.[34] If the government prohibited employment of such sailors and ordered the release of those not bona fide U.S. citizens (even by U.S. definitions of naturalization) America's international trade would suffer a dramatic contraction. This in turn could easily stop the growth in the country's economy that began with renewal of Europe's war. Jefferson's administration was therefore unwilling to bargain for limits on impressment by agreeing to end recruitment of British-born seamen. Instead, Jefferson and Madison took out their frustrations by badgering the hapless Anthony Merry with such strong protests of British depredations that they doomed his mission in Washington.[35]

Probably this was as much the fault of Jefferson as of the policy-makers in London. By the start of his second term in 1805 the president's specific goals for his country began to conflict with each other, causing confusion at home and abroad and pushing his administration toward untenable positions. He continued his requests for French aid in getting Spain to cede the Floridas. When these proved fruitless he blamed Bonaparte's indifference on America's inability to defend its national rights against the British, bitterly complaining that "we cannot be respected by France as a neutral nation."[36] Yet his own domestic policy had called for debt reduction and lower taxes, and this meant minimizing expenses, including the high cost of the army and navy. Jefferson pared the navy, replacing most larger vessels with a flotilla of gunboats to patrol the coast. Held to be cheaper, the gunboats were hardly a check on British cruisers stopping American merchantmen.[37]

At the same time, Jefferson wanted the government to promote overseas markets for surplus farm produce as a way to guarantee prosperity for the agrarian society he believed essential to the survival of the republic.[38] And he recognized the importance of the reexport trade in foreign products as stimulation for the growth of New England's shipping industries.

But warring England and France had entirely different views of where Americans would sell their produce. Certainly British merchants wanted no rivals in markets that traditionally had been their own, especially in Europe. Wartime inroads had to be curtailed immediately lest they become permanent when the war ended. The French, on the other hand, worried less about the future than the present. They welcomed whatever supplies they could get from the Americans as a temporary wartime expedient. After Nelson's victory at Trafalgar in 1805 Britain tightened its rule of the seas and France reacted by consolidating its hegemony over the continent. Both countries regarded the United States as a nervy little neutral, too weak to promote its foreign policy or defend its national claims.

Yet with their insatiable, war-bred appetites for goods, neither country could afford to ignore the efficient traders who made America the largest of the neutral carriers. U.S. foreign trade increased by a factor of six during the period from the pre-war early 1790s to 1807. Almost half of this came from the reexport trade. Intrepid Yankees pushed into new regions to market exotic products from the Far East, the Caribbean, the Mediterranean, and South America. Europe and its overseas colonies still took from the Americans not only their home-produced wheat, flour, rice, fish, timber, hides, cotton, and finished goods but also great quantities of sugar, tea, coffee, cocoa, and spices.[39] As the conflict expanded to become a people-to-people war, many of these items became essential to each nation's war effort. It was obvious to each side that denial of food and fiber to its enemy was an effective and legitimate, if tragic, tactic. By 1806 Britain declared a blockade of most of Europe's Atlantic coast; France retaliated by closing the continent to English ships or to any ship that had first called at an English port. The machinations of war held American prosperity hostage: each belligerent considered "neutral trade" with the other side as aid to its enemy.

Now British squadrons hovered even nearer to U.S. ports. Based as far away as Halifax in Nova Scotia and the West Indies, individual warships often called at American ports for revictualing or repair, and at dockside their officers easily recognized sailors from other ships whom they considered to be British deserters. Once at sea again, they lay close, ready to pounce on the unfortunate vessel and take off the offenders as the ship cleared the port. The often arrogant British captains frequently stopped suspected vessels within sight of the shore, offending American sensibilities.

With such deliberate carelessness, sooner or later some captain would make a stupid mistake. And in June 1804 one did. HMS *Cambrian* stopped the *Pitt*, an English privateer, and took off fourteen of her crew *within* New York harbor. This was such a glaring violation of American sovereignty that even the normally anti-American British consul-general at New York protested to the Admiralty. Madison demanded an apology from Capt. William Bradley of the *Cambrian,* delivery of the lieutenant who had violated U.S. revenue laws, and return of the impressed men. The men were returned, Bradley was relieved of command, and officers were ordered to be more circumspect in searching ships and certainly not to search them within American territorial waters.[40]

This was not much of a concession, particularly since British ship captains paid little attention to the new orders. From 1793 to 1802 the Royal Navy impressed some 2,400 men from American vessels; 6,000 were taken between 1803 and 1812.[41] Lord Castlereagh admitted in Parliament just prior to the War of 1812 that there were 3,300 seamen claiming to be Americans serving in the Royal Navy against their will, and one-fourth of these had proven their citizenship. Another source has put the figure in 1807 as high as 6,000.[42] Jefferson complained that the Royal Navy committed "aggressions within the common law."[43] And on his desk the pile of protests from merchant groups grew. One association from New York probably stated the American case more clearly than did Jefferson himself: "We deny, however, that the rights of commerce, as claimed by us, are to be deemed favors . . . *that the goods of a neutral consisting of articles not contraband of war, in a neutral vessel, employed in a direct trade between neutral countries and ports of belligerent country, not invested or blockaded, are protected.*" They protested that "we ought not to be exposed to humiliating inquisitions, in the verge of our port."[44]

Regardless of Americans' sentiments British policy continued the aggravations. In early 1805 two prize court cases heightened the tension. In the *Aurora* case of March and the more significant *Essex* decision of May Admiralty courts reversed the moderate *Polly* rules followed since 1801. England restated its traditional belief that free ships did *not* make free goods, thus again making subject to capture neutral ships carrying produce from enemy colonies. With no warning of this new policy, hundreds of neutral captains saw their cargoes seized. Adding to the tension was the publication in October of *War in Disguise: Or the Fraud of Neutral Flags*. The book, written by James Stephen, a strongly anti-American lawyer for the West Indian interests, supported the new *Essex* rules, arguing that neutrals were aiding the enemy as well as stealing British markets by hiding illicit cargoes as "free goods." Although he denied it, Stephen wrote the book at the request of Pitt's ministry; its success in quieting opponents of the new restrictive trade policies earned him a seat in the House of Commons.[45]

These new policies of the British government added to the anger and frustration of Jefferson's administration. Secretary of State Madison submitted a detailed protest that his representative in London was to present to the ministry. Smarting from continuous complaints by American ship captains, he insisted that impressment "deprives the dearest rights of persons of a regular trial and leaves their destiny to the will of an officer, sometimes cruel, often ignorant, and generally interested, by his want of manners in his own decision."[46] To him the arbitrary authority of these officers was the most damnable aspect of impressment. And Monroe was even more frustrated because Foreign Minister Harrowby refused to discuss these latest seizures of American ships, cargoes, and men. His formal protest challenged that worthy: "it requires but a slight view of the subject to be satisfied that these condemnations are incompatible with the law of nations. . . . None of the cases have involved a question of contraband, of blockade, or any other kind, that was ever contested till of late in favor of a belligerent against a neutral power."[47]

Madison turned in his anger to Congress. In January 1806, after months of research and writing, he gave each member of both houses his detailed,

200-page *An Examination of British Doctrine.* In this he focused on British violations of American neutral commercial rights, ransacking international law for precedents to brand Britain an aggressor. By this time congressmen's tempers had reached a level that demanded retaliation. Prompted by Madison's pamphlet they finally passed a "nonimportation act" that prohibited importing most British products into the United States.

This legislation was a confusing form of economic coercion, however, more insult than effective diplomatic weapon. It contained too many exceptions that protected from loss too many special interest groups, and it put off the actual embargo until the following November, deliberately allowing more than enough time for American ships to bring home their cargoes of British goods. Making the bill even weaker, Congress gave the president discretion to grant additional delays. And Jefferson's own role—or lack of it—added to the confusion. His apparent disinterest offered his followers in Congress no indication of just how strong a legislative reprisal he really wanted to support his British policy.[48] On the contrary, in the midst of all this heated reaction to *Essex,* he was still harping about his Florida ambitions. Should Spain continue to deny that West Florida fell within the "rightful boundaries of Louisiana," Jefferson suggested, Madison should consider negotiating a provisional treaty with England that would go into effect if the United States went to war with Spain or France. Rather naively the president assumed "the first wish of every Englishman's heart is to see us once more fighting by their sides against France."[49]

Events in Europe again saved Jefferson's policies from potential failure. William Pitt had died in January 1806 with no obvious successor among his followers. After an embarrassing hesitation at both Buckingham Palace and Parliament, George III was forced to accept a considerably different kind of leadership to head his government. Called "the Ministry of All the Talents" and headed by the same Lord Grenville who had negotiated the treaty with John Jay in 1794, this new cabinet brought into high office personalities who had for years been shrill critics of Pitt's "win at all costs" war policies. Most notable of these were Charles James Fox as foreign minister and his protegé Charles Grey (Lord Howick) as first lord of the Admiralty. A remarkable and influential orator in the House of Commons, Fox as far back as the American Revolution consistently had attacked what he considered England's unnecessary, unfair treatment of the United States. He and his "Foxites" in both houses of Parliament also had been irritants to successive English ministries by calling for electoral and parliamentary reform, some degree of civil rights for Catholics, and serious efforts to find general peace in Europe.[50]

All this prompted Jefferson to assure Monroe that "no two countries upon earth have so many points of common interest and friendship . . . the change in ministry I consider as insuring us a just settlement of our differences, and we ask no more. In Mr. Fox, personally, I have more confidence than in any man in England. . . . While he shall be in the administration, my reliance on that government will be solid."[51] Fox also wanted to improve relations; he urged Merry to apologize in Washington for Lord Harrowby's unwillingness to negotiate a new treaty with Monroe and to promise that Fox "will not suffer the Business to be delayed one Day beyond what is absolutely necessary."[52]

Jefferson and Madison capitalized on the friendliness of the new ministry by sending William Pinkney back to London to assist Monroe in negotiating a replacement for the Jay Treaty. Monroe may very well have considered this appointment a slight on his own capabilities, but Pinkney was a shrewd choice. Having already spent years in England working out implementation of the original treaty, he personally knew many of England's commercial and political leaders. And coming directly from the United States, he was privy to Jefferson's latest thoughts. Even more important, as a Federalist he could help garner bipartisan support in Congress if a treaty was actually concluded.[53] But Congress had almost undermined the Monroe-Pinkney mission even before it could present its credentials by passing the poorly timed nonimportation bill, which seemed an insult to a friendly British ministry. The *Times* considered it such; the paper attacked "the violent party in Congress" and insisted "all this heat is less to be imputed to the violence offered to liberty by the impress of a few seamen, than, as we have said before, to the disappointment consequent upon the detection and prevention of the neutral contraband trade."[54]

Fortunately for the United States, Grenville's ministry ignored "the violent party in Congress" and moved in several directions to change British policies. It initiated talks with Napoleon for a general peace in Europe. And it pushed through Parliament an "American Intercourse Bill" that again liberalized British policy regarding neutral trade. Lord Auckland, the new president of the Board of Trade, had promoted the bill and saw it as enhancing British commercial opportunities in the growing U.S. economy. But George Canning, the most strident of the Tory Opposition, argued that it was an unnecessary concession to American leaders whose "sentiments toward this country are avowedly of hostile nature."[55]

Once again a moderating policy shift by the English government was not reflected in the behavior of Royal Navy commanders on patrol off the coast of the United States. Their surveillance of America's ports became tighter, and their ships continued searching vessels within U.S. territorial waters. Unless the civilian leadership of Grenville's ministry was more successful reining in the navy than its predecessors, an incident was likely to occur to inflame anew American opinion and erode Fox's honest cultivation of improved relations.

The predictable episode came in late April 1806. Three British warships— *Leander, Cambrian,* and *Driver*—were off New York harbor stopping and searching maritime traffic. The British usually brought merchantmen to by firing a shot across their bows. On April 24 a misplaced shot from the *Leander* (Capt. Henry Whitby) killed John Pierce, helmsman on the little Delaware sloop *Richard.* Egged on by the *Richard's* captain (Pierce's brother), an irate mob paraded the dead man's body in New York City that night and terrorized the British consul by hurling stones through the windows of his house. While local newspapers called for war, the mob so frightened British naval officers on shore leave in the city that civic authorities had to arrest them and, in the dead of night, secretly return them to their ships.[56]

As the tension spread to Washington, a furious Jefferson took a staccato series of retaliatory actions. Militarily, there was little he could do; of three U.S. frigates then in service, two were in the Mediterranean and the other was undergoing repair, and none of the new Jeffersonian gunboats was yet in New York. Instead, Jefferson demanded an apology from Britain, ordered the three British ships permanently from U.S. territorial waters, and directed port authorities to deny the offending cruisers all supplies, including water. Then, through Monroe, he insisted the British government try Capt. Whitby of the *Leander* for murder. Fox's embarrassed reaction was just as quick. He apologized for his government and promised a full investigation of the incident. The Admiralty relieved Whitby of command and returned him to England to face a court-martial. (He was acquitted the following March.) The haste to recall Whitby, six weeks before Monroe had an opportunity to lodge a formal protest, indicated how much the ministry wanted to make amends.[57] Secretary of State Madison was mollified, even though Merry complained to him that denying supplies to the offending ships was a bit severe.[58]

American anger over the *Leander* affair made little impression on the Royal Navy's captains. William Bradley, Whitby's successor in command of that infamous frigate, continued to impress men from ships in U.S. territorial waters. After Thomas Barclay, the British consul at New York, warned London of growing American resentment at this blatant disregard of Jefferson's orders, the Admiralty recalled Bradley.[59] Midsummer brought new tensions. Fox had failed to find peace for Europe and naval activity between the Royal Navy and the fleets of the French alliance increased markedly and spilled over onto American territory. During September portions of a French squadron from the West Indies, battered by an Atlantic gale and chased by a British squadron, limped into the shelter of Norfolk, Baltimore, and Charleston. Only one of the pursuers needed refuge in an American port; the others hung off the mouth of Chesapeake Bay ready to pounce whenever the French attempted an escape. One unfortunate French vessel ran aground in its dash toward the safety of the Virginia Capes and was burned by the British, who captured its crew and marched them to Norfolk.[60]

Continued insults to American sovereignty belied the sincerity of the Grenville ministry's professed desire to treat the United States with fairness and dignity in its negotiations with Monroe and Pinkney. And Fox's untimely illness made matters worse by postponing the talks, much to the dissatisfaction of the Americans. In August Grenville finally realized that further delays were unacceptable and gave full responsibility for the British side to Lord Auckland and Lord Holland, Fox's thirty-three-year-old nephew.[61] Fox's death in September changed the focus of the negotiations and again put them on hiatus. In October Monroe, in desperation, prodded Charles Grey, Fox's successor as foreign secretary, to restart them.

Grey, however, had inherited a deteriorating situation in Europe and had little time for the lesser concerns of America. Bonaparte, now the self-proclaimed Emperor Napoleon, so successfully managed European affairs that Britain seemingly was on the defensive everywhere. He drove out pro-British governments in Italy, forced Prussia to annex Hanover (George III's ancestral holding), challenged the neutrality of Denmark, and got the Turks to declare war on Russia. The reaction of Grenville's government was a series of unmitigated disasters.[62] An Anglo-Russian force abandoned all of Italy except Sicily to French influence. A poorly coordinated attempt to force the Turkish Straits worsened the situation in the Middle East. And a costly conquest of Buenos Aires was short-lived.

Grey did, nevertheless, move to appease Jefferson's government. He replaced the irritating Merry in Washington with young, affable, but inexperienced David Erskine, who immediately informed Madison of new and more generous Orders-in-Council. This opened for neutrals a limited trade in the British West Indies, particularly for barrel staves, lumber, and livestock, items always in short supply in the islands. Obviously benefitting British planters as much as American merchants, the new policy at least legitimatized the Yankee presence in the region.[63] And Erskine apologized for the actions of Hudson's Bay Company traders who had incited Indians along the Canadian border to attack the United States.[64] Grey himself requested Monroe to get evidence "which cannot be obtainable here" for Captain Whitby's court-martial. And unknown to the Americans, the Grenville ministry rejected at least two projects within their own government to restrict American trade, most interestingly with South America.[65]

Auckland and Holland did the most to help the situation. Both were friendly, cooperative, and genuinely respectful of Monroe and Pinkney. They did reemphasize that American nonimportation legislation was an unnecessary threat overshadowing the talks. Yet they were willing to offer compromises. Monroe and Pinkney wanted compromise as well, and after several weeks of profitable meetings a reasonable treaty draft emerged. The four negotiators agreed on commercial terms similar to those of the original Jay Treaty, adding a few new concessions for the Yankees in the East India trade. But they could not finalize the treaty because the Americans insisted it had to include some modification of British policy regarding impressment.

It was obvious to Auckland and Holland that Pinkney had brought fresh instructions from Jefferson to make this demand. So they countered with their own argument that the United States government do something to limit employment of British subjects aboard American vessels and stop the fraudulent sale of "protections" verifying U.S. citizenship. They based their argument on an earlier report from Merry, who asserted that although most congressmen believed only a small number of English deserters were in American service, U.S. naval officers had told him "that above two thirds of the non-commissioned officers and men on board the Squadron in the Mediterranean were Foreigners, and almost altogether were English."[66] In response Monroe and Pinkney could only promise that Jefferson's administration would use federal regulation to stop recruitment of foreign sailors, but neither Auckland nor Holland believed such regulation enforceable. They explained to the American diplomats "the impossibility of our allowing seamen to withdraw themselves from our service during war."[67] And they cited the ruling of the King's Advocate, Sir John Nicole, that "individuals owe an Allegiance and Duty to that State of which they are natural born Subjects . . . they cannot, without the consent of the State, release themselves."[68] Simply put, British constitutional practice did not accept the idea that anyone could become a U.S. citizen who had not been a resident of the United States at the end of the Revolutionary War.

The British were adamant, and time was running out. If Monroe and Pinkney wanted to get any sort of treaty, they would have to bow to reality and ignore their official instructions. They finally agreed to a treaty that did not mention impressment. Auckland was actually surprised, and in return offered to commit the English to moderate the *Essex* decision regarding the reexport trade. The return, at least in part, to the more amenable practices of the *Polly* case would certainly be a benefit for American merchants.[69] But Auckland and Holland were not empowered to include in the treaty a formal statement that permanently reopened trade between the United States and the British West Indies, something every American administration had tried to get since 1783. Monroe and Pinkney had to accept the terms they could get and hope that people at home would recognize they had done the best possible under most difficult circumstances.

Just as the talks were concluding, Napoleon almost destroyed the entire effort. In November 1806 he issued his "Berlin Decree," placing the British Isles under blockade. Any neutral vessel going to or from a British port risked French seizure of ship, cargo, and crew. In retaliation Grenville's government announced new Orders-in-Council that drastically restricted neutral commerce with the continent. Of more specific concern for Monroe and Pinkney, the ministry added a rider to the treaty that permitted the British to ignore its terms when necessary as protection against any "unfair" commercial tactics of the French or of neutrals. In a practical sense Napoleon had forced the British to nullify most of the treaty's terms at the moment they signed it. Nonetheless, Grey was satisfied that the treaty provided "all proper means of conciliation" with the United States, even though he admitted he believed "we certainly have much to complain in the conduct of America." And in seeking the king's formal approval he asserted the agreement was "consistent with your Majesty's honour and with the Interests of the Kingdom."[70] Other Englishmen disagreed. The *Times* was far more moderate in reaction to the treaty than most English newspapers, yet even it claimed: "Our Government, we are persuaded, felt a disposition to concede everything that they could have claimed with justice, or that they could have allowed with honour."[71]

Opinion in the United States was also divided. Most Federalists were satisfied that the treaty stablized relations between the two countries. Rufus King, the former minister to London, expressed their sentiments the clearest in a letter to Sir Francis Baring. He apologized for the threat implied in the Non-Importation Bill and asserted that "we are each deeply interested in the prosperity of the other, and there must be a want of prudence somewhere, if we do not continue to be good friends."[72] On the other hand, Republicans complained that the treaty had drawn few major concessions from the British. Some even grumbled that Monroe had betrayed the principles of his own party.

President Jefferson was probably the most dissatisfied Republican. Even though Congress was still in session when he received a copy of the treaty, he disliked it and refused to send it to the Senate for confirmation. Instead, he explained to Monroe and Pinkney his reasons for rejecting their efforts, stressing the point that any treaty not providing "satisfactorily against the impressment of our seamen . . . could not be ratified."[73] Trying to ease the disappointment, perhaps anger, of his negotiators in London, Madison sent them his detailed analysis of the treaty's shortcomings, article by article. Even more adamant on impressment than the president, Madison was convinced Congress held the issue "as the primary rank." And he felt that acceptance of the practice "on our part would violate both a moral and political duty of the government to our citizens." He also considered specious the British counter-argument that the number of their subjects employed in the U.S. merchant marine more than equalled the number of impressed Americans; by forcible impressment, he asserted, "more of a wrong is done to the United States than of right to Great Britain."[74]

Jefferson and Madison wanted Monroe and Pinkney to reopen negotiations and try again for a minimum concession on impressment. Madison even wanted to offer a counterproposal that the United States would discharge all the British sailors on American ships who had been employed within two years prior to the ratification of a renegotiated treaty. But Treasury Secretary Gallatin reminded Jefferson's cabinet of the importance to American prosperity of those same British sailors. In his frank assessment, "our tonnage employed in foreign trade has increased since 1803 at the rate of 70,000 tons a year, equal to an increase of 8,400 sailors for two years, and I would estimate that the British sailors have supplied from one-half to two-thirds of that increase." Madison's proposal "would materially injure our navigation, much more indeed than any restrictions which, supposing no treaty to take place, they should lay upon our commerce . . . the fact as to numbers and consequences being very different from what we apprehended, I think the sacrifice too great for the object."[75]

And there the matter stood. Facing the friendliest English administration since recognition of its independence, the United States still could not find the basis for an effective compromise on the overriding issue of impressment. Instead, Erskine felt the brunt of Madison's temperament. The secretary of state angrily insisted the new Orders-in-Council were "a ground for serious complaint and remonstrance" and refused Erskine's requests to surrender the deserters British officers claimed were aboard American ships.[76] Frustrated himself, Erskine meekly protested again the denial of port facilities for the three ships involved in the *Leander* incident and, hoping to ease tensions, voluntarily denied any British complicity in Aaron Burr's plot to detach the West from the rest of the country.[77] But the hardest challenge for him was to explain to his superiors in London just why Jefferson remained so adamant about impressment and would reject a treaty the English honestly believed was so generous to the United States.[78]

If Erskine in Washington or Monroe and Pinkney in London hoped they might somehow find a way to improve relations between Great Britain and the United States, they lost their opportunity in March 1807. The entire Grenville cabinet resigned when King George refused to discuss their proposal of limited reform for Catholics in Ireland. A more forceful, more bellicose group of ministers took over the government from the reform-minded but unfortunately ineffective "Ministry of All the Talents." This meant dramatic shifts in English policies, both in the conduct of the war against Napoleon and in Britain's relationship to the United States. Nominally headed by the Duke of Portland, the new cabinet was dominated by Spencer Perceval at the Exchequer, Robert Castlereagh at the War Office, and George Canning as foreign minister. These three had been the loudest critics of Grenville's policies, and Canning in particular considered the concessions made to the Americans almost treasonous.

Monroe clearly understood the impact of this change in British leadership. In closing his official correspondence with Grey he went beyond normal diplomatic practice to thank the outgoing foreign minister for the "high respect, with which your sincere disposition to cultivate harmony and mutual confidence between our respective countries, has inspired me."[79] He knew he would not receive such respect from Canning—nor would his country. David Erskine's father, a confidant of the Grenville cabinet, was even more pessimistic when he warned "with regard to America . . . we are only *just at peace with her* and we know that from what our opponents avow publicly the system they would instantly pursue would lead to an instant exclusion of all our manufactures most probably & a war under the wing of France, which might distress us in the West Indies & retard all the views we may have hereafter in the Western World."[80]

Jefferson might soon conclude that Erskine senior could very well be correct. By rejecting the treaty Monroe and Pinkney had made with the Grenville ministry the president probably lost his last opportunity to put Anglo-American relations on some permanent, mutually satisfactory level. But for him and for the vast majority of Americans impressment was a moral issue that eclipsed all others, and any agreement that did not settle the matter was hardly an agreement worth considering.

Two constants bedeviled Jefferson's foreign policy. Regardless of who headed Britain's government during his presidency—Addington, Pitt, Grenville, or Portland—each ministry was committed to the Royal Navy's right to impress suspected deserters found on American ships. Even the friendly cabinets of Addington and Grenville were unwilling to modify a traditional practice so vital to the integrity of their nation's first line of defense. And the navy itself, particularly after Trafalgar, became increasingly independent of the civilian leadership in London, ignoring orders to be more circumspect toward Americans. As a result it was clear by mid-1807 that the future of Jefferson's policies regarding Great Britain, France, and Spain depended too heavily on the whims of a few very resolute men who were well beyond his ability to influence or control.

FOUR

The *Leopard* and the Royal Navy

In 1807, as the *Chesapeake* was fitting for sea, relations between Britain and the United States had sharply deteriorated. The wars of the French Revolution and Napoleon were the cause, and the key issues were naval: the Orders-in-Council of January 7, 1807, and the impressment of seamen.

The Orders-in-Council were a form of economic warfare against France and French-dominated continental states. After Britain went to war against France in January 1793 the British saw their nation as "the only barrier between France and Universal Empire."[1]

Except for the brief respite during the Peace of Amiens of 1802–3, fighting did not end until 1814. Britain contributed little in land forces to coalitions against France; her chief weapon was the Royal Navy, which blockaded France and the countries she had occupied or with which she was allied. The Orders-in-Council were retaliation for Napoleon's Continental System, which prohibited British trade with the continent, a policy designed to force that nation into economic exigency. London claimed that Napoleon's actions absolved Britain from traditional limits in war and retaliated by closing the ports of Europe to neutral shipping. This immediately affected the United States, then second only to Britain in the world's carrying trade.

During the 1798–1800 Quasi-War between the United States and France naval relations between Britain and the United States had been quite friendly, even to the point of exchanging signals.[2] But even before the 1807

Orders-in-Council London had adopted a tougher position vis-a-vis the United States. British mercantile interests could not tolerate American incursions into trade normally carried in British ships, especially the reexport trade. This included goods from France and Spain shipped to the United States and there off-loaded. American shippers paid taxes on the goods, which were reloaded and shipped to British colonies, sometimes in company with other goods. Such arrangements were known as separate or "broken" voyages.

Guided by the *Polly* case, Royal Navy captains had permitted off-loading, payment of duties, and reloading of ships. But as U.S. merchants claimed a growing share of the carrying trade, such men as Lord Sheffield and the essayist James Stephens urged a return to the "Rule of 1756" and its stricture that neutral countries should not trade in wartime with countries with which they were not allowed to trade in peacetime. To an influential segment of British opinion, it seemed that American prosperity was nothing more than a reflection of London's relaxed navigation laws. In response, the Admiralty now instructed its captains to seize vessels whose papers indicated they were on "broken" voyages. Between 1803 and the Orders-in-Council of 1807, the British seized 528 American flag vessels; France seized another 206 U.S. flag merchant ships between 1803 and the Berlin Decree of 1806.[3]

The tougher British position was codified in the *Essex* decision of May 1805. The *Essex* was an American merchant brig. She was wholly loaded with Spanish goods and bound for Spanish America when the British privateer *Favourite* captured her. Her goods had been landed at Salem, Massachusetts, and almost immediately reshipped for Havana. Her master, Joseph Orne, claimed that landing the cargo had rendered the law of 1756 null and void. The Vice-Admiralty Court of Nassau, New Providence, held, however, that the goods "were landed for the sole purpose of obviating or avoiding the danger to which, in a direct voyage, they would necessarily be exposed." There had been no transfer of the goods in America; the cargo was precisely as it had been when it left Spain. The court held there was no question that the intention was, from the start, to send the cargo to a Spanish colony and that it was essentially traffic between Spain and Cuba. The court condemned the *Essex* and her cargo, a decision subsequently upheld by Whitehall.[4] After the *Essex* decision the Royal Navy stepped up its seizures of American vessels for infringement of the "continuous voyage" rule. This in turn heightened resentment in the United States toward Great Britain.

Equally vexing to Americans was the issue of impressment, the Royal Navy's practice of stopping American merchantmen and taking off sailors presumed to be British subjects. From the 1793 start of the war with France to 1807 it was the most constant source of friction between the two nations.[5] In 1797 Robert Liston observed that "the greatest obstacle to a perfect understanding is impressment."[6]

Even in peacetime the Royal Navy's appetite for manpower forced the British to resort to various expedients at home and abroad to secure men. These included press gangs and impressment of British subjects on foreign vessels. Royal Navy captains routinely stopped British and foreign merchant vessels, mustered their crews, and pressed men from them. The British practice of pressing men for naval service did not begin with the Napoleonic Wars; in fact, it dated back to at least the fourteenth century and perhaps as far as the tenth.

Impressment rested on "the doctrine of indefeasible allegiance and the recognized prerogative of the crown to require the services of all seamen for defense of the realm." This doctrine held that an individual owed primary allegiance to the sovereign of his birth and that bonds between sovereign and subject were perpetual unless the sovereign chose to dissolve them.

Naturalization was no protection; the British government did not recognize the principle that its citizens could renounce their nationality and become citizens of another country. In time of need the crown could call any sailors of British birth to naval service. Individual seamen not heeding this call might be seized wherever they could be located, on land or on British and foreign vessels on the seas.[7] While search of foreign warships was rare, the British government claimed that right as well. When the Dutch government complained, King George III called on the Admiralty to review the practice but recommended its continuation.[8] Brutal and unfair, impressment was also inefficient; even the Lords Commissioners of the Admiralty expressed hope that "some better method" would be found "to man his Majesty's Ships."[9] But none was discovered and, under the strain of the naval wars of the period, demands for seamen increased aboard "his Majesty's Ships."

U.S. independence posed problems. The crown at first refused to recognize that independence had dissolved the obligation to the British crown of seamen of British birth who lived or served in the colonies before 1783. London consistently refused to release seamen of British ancestry who were not natives of the United States, although it never claimed this right for those born in the newly independent colonies.

Poor food, bad medical care, and brutal punishments by an occasional sadistic commanding officer all caused desertions.[10] But the principal cause of desertion in the Royal Navy, if seamen themselves are to be believed, was low pay and the fact that it was often in arrears. Wages in the Royal Navy remained unchanged from the time of Oliver Cromwell in the mid-seventeenth century until 1797. Able seamen received 24s per month, or about $5; ordinary seamen and landsmen received 19s and 18s respectively. By 1806 pay had risen to 33s 6d, 25s 6d, and 23s 6d respectively; but these rates were still not competitive with private British or foreign shippers. American service provided British seamen "a combination of comparably high wartime wages with the natural protection that nationality and language offered from the impress and the ease with which a British sailor could acquire at least the trappings of American citizenship." It was relatively easy for a British sailor to acquire a certificate declaring him to be a native American. U.S. officials routinely sold these instruments, known to sailors as *protections,* to anyone who could pay a fee of $1 to $5, and the Admiralty routinely sent repeated evidence of such activity to the foreign office.[11]

Although seamen deserting from Royal Navy warships faced the death penalty, it was rarely imposed, usually only to set an example. Even sentences of 100 to 300 lashes were often reduced. Those who ran the navy saw little advantage in executing or maiming the individuals it so desperately needed as sailors.

While no definitive figures of the number of British deserters are available, Lord Admiral Horatio Nelson estimated that 40,000 men fled the service between 1793 and 1801, and this figure may be low. There were frequent reports of U.S. merchant ships with a majority of British crews, and at any one time there were probably between 10,000 and 20,000 British seamen serving under the U.S. flag, mostly aboard merchant vessels. Not all, of course, were deserters from the Royal Navy, but in the eyes of the British government nearly all were liable for British service. In March 1807 Vice Admiral Sir George Cranfield Berkeley, commander in chief of the British North American station since the summer of 1806, reported to the Admiralty that "high wages given both in their Men of War and trading Ships cannot be withstood by the Men," and that there were "according to the best intelligence I can procure above 10,000 English Seamen under these protections are at present employed in the Service of the Americans." U.S. Secretary of the Treasury Albert Gallatin concluded early in 1807 that in 1805 and 1806 approximately 9,000 men, or one-half of the able seamen aboard U.S. merchantmen employed in foreign commerce, were British subjects.[12] It is impossible to establish the accuracy of these figures; indeed, one search of day-to-day reports of British commanders in American waters for the year preceding the *Chesapeake-Leopard* encounter led to the conclusion that desertions were relatively few in number and that the Admiralty in fact refused to give the British cabinet any approximation of total desertions, other than saying that most took place in American ports.[13] The fact remains, however, that it was an irritant, and there was a persistent belief that large numbers of refugee British seamen manned American merchant and naval vessels.

There were simply not sufficient numbers of British seamen available to man Royal Navy warships and maintain the statutory requirement that merchantmen carry crews of three-quarters British seamen. Even Parliament's modification of the requirement to one-fourth British seamen on British merchantmen proved insufficient. Although London offered bounties for seamen who would join, these were never more than a minority.[14] Seamen had to be found somewhere, and one means was to secure the British sailors on American vessels. At no time did London claim the right to impress foreign seamen; in fact, this was expressly forbidden by statute.[15]

With few warships, the United States was hardly in a position to resist. British naval officers were quick to take advantage and routinely bent the law when they felt it necessary. It was a common complaint by American shippers that the British routinely selected those seamen presumed to be the best and claimed they were British subjects. One historian has concluded that

> the severe manning problem of the Royal Navy after 1795, the general instructions from the Admiralty, and ambiguous orders from individual commanders-in-chief gave officers wide latitude for abuse. . . . Despite British denials, it is clear that naval officers who abused their powers usually went unpunished, and that American charges were completely justified.[16]

One British captain on North American station wrote in 1797: "It is my duty to keep my ship manned, & I will do so wherever I find men, that speak the same language with me, & not a small part of them British Subjects, & that too producing Certificates of being American Citizens."[17] The British knew they were in a life-and-death struggle with Napoleon, and necessity knows no law.

Even the contemporary English naval historian William James, who always took a pro-British stance in his writing, was forced to admit that "Between England and the United States of America, a spirit of animosity, caused chiefly by the impressment of British seamen, or of seamen asserted to be such, from on board of American merchant-vessels, had long unhappily subsisted." He noted that crews of U.S. merchantmen and warships consisted of one or more of four classes: "native American citizens; American citizens, wherever born, who were such at the time of the Treaty of Paris of 1783, ending the Revolutionary War; foreigners, who might or might not have become citizens subsequent to the treaty of Paris; and deserters from the British army or navy, whether citizens of Britain or any other country." He held that Britain had no right to the first classification and had barred herself even from those of the second group who were British-born by having signed the Treaty of Paris. In the third classification, James maintained, she had a right to the subjects of powers with whom she was at war and her own citizens. And she had every right to the fourth classification.[18]

The expanding U.S. merchant marine, increasingly relying on British seamen, thus

> clashed sharply with the requirements of British security, making conflict inevitable. At the same time, the American government's attempt to protect British as well as American seamen from impressment at sea, its unwillingness to renounce the use of British sailors, and its inability (or unwillingness) to regulate the issue of certificates of American citizenship in order to prevent fraudulent use by British mariners made any settlement unlikely.[19]

The failure of the American government to curb fraudulent practices, for which both Congress and the Executive were responsible, encouraged unscrupulous British naval commanders to justify the impressment of native Americans.[20]

Royal Navy deserters presented a particularly vexing problem to the British. After late 1806 Madison refused to cooperate with British requests for assistance in recovering deserters. The American government held that there was no treaty requiring mutual restitution of deserters from each other's national service. Madison hoped to link British demands on this issue to a comprehensive agreement ending impressments at sea. Until there was such an agreement he would not aid British authorities even in cases where known British deserters had joined the U.S. Navy. As one historian has noted, "Madison's effort failed to impress upon Britain the importance of accommodation with the United States. Instead, the persistent refusals to aid in the recovery of deserters created a tense and volatile atmosphere, resulting in the attack on the *Chesapeake* . . . and very nearly led to war in 1807."[21]

There is no doubt that a great many British deserters were aboard U.S. warships. What is more important is perception, and the British thought the numbers were substantial. Months after the *Chesapeake-Leopard* affair British envoy George Rose reported to Canning that the *Chesapeake* was "now lying at Anchor at Norfolk; I am informed, that two-thirds of her Crew, are British Subjects."[22]

While the British had no qualms about removing their nationals from neutral merchant ships, foreigners on U.S. warships usually were immune from seizure. But there were precedents for the *Chesapeake-Leopard* incident.

On November 16, 1798, the U.S. Navy sloop-of-war *Baltimore* (24 guns), a converted merchantman commanded by Capt. Isaac Phillips, was escorting merchant vessels off the coast of Cuba. The sloop fell in with Capt. John Loring's British squadron, which included two ships of the line. When the British demanded to search his ship, Phillips protested that the *Baltimore* was a U.S. Navy vessel, but he could not produce papers to prove it; the sloop had been rushed to sea before they were ready. While Phillips was discussing the matter aboard the British flagship, the 74-gun *Carnatic*, British officers mustered his crew and took five of its fifty men.[23]

Although the Adams administration considered the incident a great insult to the American flag—there being no legal basis for the impressment of men from warships of another nation—Secretary of State Timothy Pickering lodged only a lukewarm protest with British Minister Liston, and President Adams directed most of his anger at the unfortunate Captain Phillips, who was immediately dismissed from the navy without benefit of court-martial.[24] Samuel Barron, brother of James, took over from Phillips. Secretary of the Navy Benjamin Stoddert informed all commanders: "It is the positive command of the President . . . to resist to the utmost of your power" in such a situation and, specifically, to "surrender your ship before you surrender your people."[25] Still, after Liston presented evidence in Loring's behalf, Pickering and Stoddert let the matter drop, and it had little effect outside the administration.[26] James Fenimore Cooper summed up the affair's impact: "while the British government did not appear disposed to defend the principle involved in the act of its officer, the American so far forgot what was done to its real interests, as not to insist on an open and signal reparation of the wrong."[27]

Another incident occurred early the next year. On January 8, 1799, in the Windward Passage a converted merchantman, the 24-gun ship *Ganges* (Capt. Thomas Tingey), was stopped by a British sixth-rate, the *Surprise* (24 guns, Capt. Edward Hamilton). Having experienced on his cruise only goodwill from the British, Tingey hove to when Hamilton hailed. The British captain sent a boat, and when a lieutenant from the *Surprise* was on board he demanded of an astonished Tingey "whether any Englishmen were in my crew, observing that my assurance would be sufficient to prevent an officer being sent to examine their protections. . . ." Tingey told the lieutenant that "I considered all my crew Americans by birth or adoption—but I also observed to the officer, that there were no protections on board to my knowledge—the only one we carried in our public ships being our flag." While the lieutenant returned to his ship, Tingey met with his officers to consider the situation. At this point another British boat was seen pulling for the *Ganges*. Tingey was resolute with his officers: "I declared to them my determination to fall sooner there than suffer an investigation or permit any man's name to be called over." The second British emissary turned out to be the ship's surgeon with a request for medical supplies. Perhaps he was sent to ascertain Tingey's resolve or to rattle him. Tingey provided the supplies, and the *Surprise* sailed away.[28]

There was another, little known incident that did result in sailors being taken from a U.S. Navy vessel. James Zimmerman was incorrect when he wrote that the *Chesapeake-Leopard* Affair, "being the only instance of impressment from an American public vessel, occupies for that reason alone a unique position in the history of impressment."[29] On June 12, 1805, U.S. Navy Gunboat No. 6 had just crossed the Atlantic when she was brought to off Cádiz by vessels of the British blockading squadron; her armament, two 32-pounders, was still stowed in her hold. After British officers boarded her, three crewmen—all former British sailors who were perhaps unnerved from crossing the Atlantic in such a small craft—claimed British protection. Her captain, Lt. James Lawrence, was aboard the British flagship when the three seamen were removed and was subsequently cleared of responsibility. Commodore Rodgers, commander of the U.S. Mediterranean squadron, did suspend Lawrence's second-in-command, Midshipman John Roach, and sent him home, ending his naval career. The incident prompted Rodgers to issue a general order to captains not to allow, "under any pretence whatever," their vessels to be detained or men taken off them, unless compelled by superior force. Captains were to resist "to the utmost of your power" and then "surrender your Vessel as you would to any other Common Enemy, but on no account to leave her until after you have struck your Colours."[30]

The incident involving No. 6 was soon forgotten, except perhaps by Lawrence, who, while commanding the *Chesapeake* during the War of 1812, unwisely accepted a challenge to engage the HMS *Shannon*. The incident with No. 6 may also have reinforced British captains in their belief that Americans could be treated cavalierly, as occurred later with the *Chesapeake*. There is a difference between the two, however; in the former incident the officers had not come on board looking for deserters, whereas that was the express intent of the commander of the *Leopard*.[31]

In August 1806 a Royal Navy fleet commanded by Adm. Sir Richard Strachan (seven ships of the line and two frigates) chased a sizable French squadron (seven ships of the line and three frigates, commanded by Adm. Jean Baptiste-Philibert Willaumez). On the eleventh a hurricane blew up; it lasted two days and scattered warships of both squadrons to the northwest. Three of the French ships took refuge in American waters: the *Patriote* (74), her topmasts gone and several guns thrown overboard, put into Annapolis, the frigate *Cybelle* (40) made it to Norfolk, and the frigate *Valereuse* (40) took refuge in the Delaware. From Halifax, Nova Scotia, Vice-Admiral Berkeley sent a sizable British squadron to take position off the Virginia Capes to prevent the French warships undergoing repairs at Norfolk and Annapolis from regaining the Atlantic. This squadron, which was to remain over the winter, consisted of two 74s, *Bellona* (Capt. John Erskine Douglas, squadron commander) and *Triumph*, the frigate *Melampus* (Captain Hawker), and a number of smaller vessels. The British established anchorages in Hampton Roads and Lynnhaven Bay, four miles west of Cape Henry, just inside the Chesapeake Bay. Among the smaller British vessels was the store-ship *Chichester* (a reduced 44, Capt. Edward Stopford). She arrived in Hampton Roads in mid-August, but a fortnight later, while outbound, she ran aground. In danger of sinking, the *Chichester* limped to a Gosport wharf, where she was unloaded and careened to be repaired. In early September the *Melampus* anchored in Hampton Roads to watch the *Cybelle* at Norfolk. The presence of significant French and British naval units brought this reaction from the *Norfolk Gazette and Publick Ledger*: "Our coast it is probable will be the scene of a great Naval enterprise."[32]

On September 14 the *Bellisle* (74) and *Bellona,* along with the *Melampus,* were about ten leagues south of Cape Henry when they discovered to leeward, dismasted, *L'Impétueux* (74), another of the French warships damaged in the hurricane. The British ships gave chase, and the French captain ran his ship ashore with colors flying. After the *Melampus* fired a few shots into *L'Impétueux,* the French struck. Some of the crew had gotten ashore, but the British captured the remainder and set fire to the ship.[33] President Jefferson "deemed it expedient to make particular enquiry into the circumstances of this case." With Secretary Smith away from Washington, Jefferson directed Charles Goldsborough to ask Capt. Samuel Barron to arrange an investigation. Goldsborough ordered Barron to go to where *L'Impétueux* was destroyed "and ascertain precisely the distance of that spot from the margin of the nearest shore" to determine whether it was within U.S. territorial waters.[34]

The French did make efforts to get their repaired vessels to sea in April 1807,[35] but no good opportunity presented itself. The *Cybelle* and *Patriote* were not able to escape until October 1807.

Meanwhile, British officers made occasional calls at Norfolk and Hampton seeking water and supplies. Crews and junior officers were kept on board ship, and the officers who did go ashore gave no offense. Still, the proximity of British ships to land brought the possibility of desertions, which indeed led to the *Chesapeake-Leopard* Affair.

By the end of 1806 hostilities were building between the British and American governments. In December Minister Erskine approached Madison unofficially about several British seamen who had been part of a British prize crew charged with mutiny and desertion. The men were known to be at Boston, and Admiral Berkeley had already petitioned the collector of customs there for assistance. He had referred Berkeley to the civil authorities and, after a further rebuff, Berkeley had appealed to Erskine. Madison refused to intervene, informing the British minister that "as no existing article of the Treaty between G. Britain & the United States [Jay's Treaty] gave any authority to the Government of the U.S. to exercise such a power, they did not dare to interfere." Erskine renewed his request in writing. When Madison again declined to intervene Erskine sent copies of the correspondence to Captain Douglas and Admiral Berkeley; several weeks later he also sent copies to the foreign office.[36]

Meanwhile, the Royal Navy contributed to the tension. On December 13, 1806, the British consul at Norfolk, Col. John Hamilton, transmitted an American request to Captain Douglas for the release of three seamen aboard his Chesapeake squadron. In replying to Hamilton, Douglas said that two of the men had not been impressed and were simply being held pending possible release of their seized vessel. The third individual had been impressed only because he had lied about his birthplace and appeared to be an Englishman. Claiming that the man had subsequently volunteered and been given a bounty, Douglas refused to release him. In obvious reference to the failed British attempts to secure release of their seamen at Boston, Douglas informed Hamilton that in the future all American requests for return of their seamen should be made from the U.S. government through Admiral Berkeley, his commander-in-chief.[37]

Dissatisfied, Secretary of State Madison escalated the controversy between the two nations. Although in the past the U.S. government had refused to challenge the British refusal to surrender deserters who had taken a bounty, Madison now did just that. He demanded the return of the seaman Douglas had refused to release and accused the British of violating American neutrality. Madison said that the ship on which the seaman served was in U.S. territorial waters in the Chesapeake and that the British had an obligation to surrender him. Madison threatened reprisal if redress was not forthcoming.[38]

Admiral Berkeley was under strict instructions from the British government to be "cautious" in his dealings with the Americans "so as not to give the slightest cause of dissatisfaction by the detention of American seamen." He subsequently claimed he had done all he could to release any seaman "who could bring the smallest proof of being an American," and neither Jefferson nor Madison made complaint about Berkeley's conduct in his first five months on American station. Berkeley professed puzzlement over Madison's new position: "I am at a loss in what Manner to act. If the position of the American Secretary of State be allowed, 'that Men having entered and received the Bounty in his Majesty's Service, are liable to be demanded and discharged directly' there will be no end to the impositions which it will occasion." Rather than act on his own, on February 2 Berkeley requested Admiralty instructions.[39]

In his conversations with Erskine, Madison stressed that Britain would benefit from accepting the American position on impressment and return of deserters; after all, the U.S. government did not object to impressment of Englishmen from U.S. merchant vessels in British ports, and most American vessels touched at British ports at some point in their voyage.[40]

The brief respite in the war of words between the British and American governments was ended by desertions from British warships of the Chesapeake squadron. The problem was the refusal of the U.S. government to consider British entreaties for deserters' return without formal agreement with London.

The presence of their ship at Gosport proved too great a temptation for some of the *Chichester*'s men. Five marines and soldiers, all British-born, deserted. Three or four of them enlisted in the U.S. Army and were seen by their former comrades wearing American uniforms. Repeated requests by Captain Douglas for their return were met with the response that the men could not be found and had probably been sent to the interior.

In early February 1807 U.S. Army Capt. John Saunders, commander of Fort Nelson, went with a sergeant, corporal, and four privates, all armed, to Captain Stopford's quarters near the wharf and demanded the return of deserters whom it was claimed had left the fort and gone aboard the *Chichester*. Captain Stopford admitted he had three American deserters and went with the Americans to the store-ship. After a protracted search they were located, still in U.S. Army uniforms, and returned. Stopford later ordered one of his midshipman confined for telling Saunders "that he thought it was not right to give up their deserters, when they would not give up ours." The three U.S. soldiers given up were natives of Great Britain; Stopford had returned them only because the *Chichester* "had no means of opposing force with force." English naval historian William James asserted this was the "prevalence of power over right."[41]

The men from the *Chichester* were not the only deserters. Seamen also left the three 74s, *Bellona, Bellisle,* and *Triumph.* In early March 1807 the *Melampus* and the ship-sloop *Halifax* (16, Capt. Lord James Townshend) arrived in Hampton Roads, the former from Bermuda and the latter from Halifax.[42] Soon five seamen from the *Melampus* seized the captain's gig and, in a hail of gunfire, escaped the frigate while she was lying at anchor off Hampton. Consul Hamilton wrote the U.S. Navy commander of the area, Capt. Stephen Decatur, identifying William Ware, Daniel Martin, John Strachan, and John Little as deserters from the *Melampus.* Hamilton said that "the first three are stated to have entered at the [recruitment] rendezvous now open here [for the *Chesapeake*]."[43]

Seamen also deserted from the *Halifax.* On the evening of March 7 the ship-sloop was in Hampton Roads when Captain Townshend sent a Midshipman Turner and five men in her jolly boat to weigh a kedge anchor dropped to swing the ship. Taking advantage of the dark and heavy rain, the men seized control of the boat and rowed toward shore. Turner repeatedly hailed the *Halifax* until silenced by William Hill, a native of

Philadelphia, who threatened to kill him if he did not stop. Lt. Thomas Carter of the *Halifax* ordered small arms fire opened on the boat and even dispatched one shot from a long gun, but by then the boat was almost out of sight. When it reached Sewell's Point the five men jumped out and left Turner to get back to the ship as best he could.[44]

Hill was the only native-born American of the five. Born in Philadelphia, he had voluntarily enlisted in the Royal Navy in Antigua. The others were all born in Great Britain: Richard Hubert in Liverpool, Henry Saunders in Grenock "and brought up to the sea," George North in Kinsale, and Jenkin Ratford in London. Ratford, who became the best known of the *Halifax* deserters, was thirty-four years old, short (5 feet, 4½ inches) and slight of build, of "dark swarthy complexion," and a "breeches maker" (tailor) by profession.[45]

The day after the five deserted from the *Halifax* they signed up with Lt. Arthur Sinclair for the *Chesapeake*.[46] The Navy Department had ordered its officers not to enlist deserters, but this had been largely ignored. Indicating that Sinclair knew where the men came from, he asked each of the five if they didn't have "a second name." Ratford, for example, was entered in the books of the *Chesapeake* as "John Wilson."[47]

Consul Hamilton also was pursuing deserters from the British merchantman *Herald*. John Murphy, her master, reported that an apprentice, his son John Murphy, and a seaman, John Wilson, "both subjects of His Majesty," had deserted his ship and enlisted in the U.S. Navy at the *Chesapeake*'s rendezvous. After Hamilton complained to Captain Decatur, young Murphy was "delivered up to the Civil Authority."[48]

On the morning of March 8 Captain Townshend sent Lieutenant Masters of the *Halifax* to Norfolk to inform Hamilton of the desertions from his ship. Upon his return, Masters reported that he had seen some of the men, including Hubert, at the rendezvous for the *Chesapeake*. Townshend went to the rendezvous and asked Sinclair for the return of the five, pledging his word that they were British deserters and could be enrolled only in violation of U.S. Navy orders. Sinclair replied evasively that none had entered "by those names" and referred Townshend to the civil authorities. Townshend then went to the mayor and "Civil Powers," as well as to Captain Decatur (who referred him back to Lieutenant Sinclair), all in vain.

On March 10 Captain Townshend encountered Saunders on the street in Norfolk. He persuaded the seaman to return to the ship and the two had gone about twenty yards when Ratford came up, "laid hold of his

[Saunders's] arm, and said he would be damned if he should return to the ship; that he was in the Land of Liberty; and that he would do as he liked, and that I had no business with him." Ratford also used abusive language to Townshend. The British captain went to Hamilton's house and told him what had happened. He also went a second time to Sinclair and asked for permission to go to the rendezvous and point out the deserters, but Sinclair refused. Townshend said he later saw some of the men at the rendezvous, although not Ratford.[49]

Hamilton appealed to Decatur regarding the deserters, but the latter refused to interfere. He claimed he had no jurisdiction and referred Hamilton to Sinclair, who still refused to help without orders from the civil authority. No local officials were willing to assist. Mayor Thomas Parker of Norfolk, on the advice of Littleton Tazewell, an eminent lawyer and Virginia politician, declined to order the men up on the grounds that the case was not covered by either federal treaty or state law.[50]

Consul Hamilton appealed to Erskine in Washington, who in turn demanded of Madison that the deserters be returned. Again Madison claimed that without a formal treaty concerning delivery of deserters the federal government had no jurisdiction. Later he told Erskine he believed the men in question were Americans.[51]

Madison referred the matter of the *Halifax* deserters to Secretary of the Navy Smith, who on April 6 wrote Commodore James Barron and asked him to look into the matter:

> It is represented to me that William Ware, Daniel Martin, John
> Strachan, John Little and others, deserters from a British Ship of War
> at Norfolk have been entered by the recruiting officer of that place
> for our service. You will be pleased to make full inquiry relative to
> these men (especially if they are American Citizens) and inform me
> of the result. You will immediately direct the recruiting officers in no
> case to enter Deserters from British Ships of War.[52]

Barron responded the next day. He concluded that three of the men enrolled on the *Chesapeake* were indeed from the *Melampus* but that they were American citizens who had been forcibly impressed by the British. William Ware had been pressed by the *Melampus* fifteen months earlier while in the Bay of Biscay on board the American brig *Neptune*. Barron said Ware, described as "an Indian looking man," was born on Pipe Creek, Frederick County, Maryland. He said Daniel Martin, a "Coloured Man" pressed at the same time as Ware, was a native of West Port, Massachusetts. John Strachan claimed to have been born on the Eastern Shore in Maryland. He had been pressed by the *Melampus* out of an English Guineaman off Cape Finisterre but, "to better his situation," had consented to enter almost immediately afterwards. He served on the frigate two years. Ware and Strachan had protections. Martin claimed to have lost his after leaving the frigate.[53]

After the *Chesapeake-Leopard* Affair there was some debate over whether the men in question had indeed been pressed aboard the *Melampus*. British authorities established that the three had entered British service willingly while U.S. citizens, indeed at their own request. According to Lt. J. S. Creighton of the *Melampus*, Strachan had volunteered for the frigate on March 15, 1805, from a Liverpool Guineaman, and it was only "with some difficulty that I prevented the principal part of her Crew, from leaving her. . . ." The British acknowledged that Martin and Ware had initially been pressed, but the official position was that both men had been returned to the *Neptune* when the *Melampus* reached Plymouth a few weeks later. Capt. Steven Poyntz of the frigate had an aversion to colored men and only reluctantly accepted the men because they seemed such ardent volunteers.[54]

Captain Crofts, American master of the *Neptune*, corroborated much of the British account in August 1807. Responding to a request from Secretary Gallatin, Crofts stated that on October 13, 1805, his brig was in the Bay of Biscay bound for Bordeaux when she was stopped by the *Melampus*. All aboard, save him, one boy, and two children among the passengers, were taken aboard the British frigate. An officer and nine men from the *Melampus* then boarded the brig and sailed her to Plymouth. She was still there on January 1, 1806, in need of repairs and a crew, when the *Melampus* arrived. The pressed men were returned. A day later, Ware, Martin, and two others went ashore without leave. A bag of coffee was reported missing; when the men returned and were confronted about the theft, Ware "swore he would do no more duty on board, he being intoxicated I did not take much notice of him." Both Ware and Martin deserted on January 3 when sent ashore to fill some water casks. Crofts confronted Ware ashore; the seaman said he had no intention of returning to the brig. The next day Crofts saw Poyntz and asked if he had pressed any men from the *Neptune*; Poyntz replied that both men had volunteered but that he did not want to enter them "for he had his complement of men and they were coloured People and he believed them to be great scoundrels." That was the last Crofts heard of the two men until the *Chesapeake-Leopard* Affair.[55]

There is no question that Barron knew the men were deserters from British warships, but he always maintained that he thought the British had accepted his explanation—that they were pressed Americans—or at least would not act further. In any case, he refused to give the men up. When the three were forcibly removed from the *Chesapeake* on June 22, 1807, Stracham, Ware, and Ratford all testified that Commodore Barron had promised them protection even though he knew they were deserters from British warships. The British position was that Barron had conducted only a perfunctory investigation that rested solely on the testimony of the deserters.[56]

When he received Barron's report, Madison told Erskine that U.S. law prohibited the enlistment of Americans in the service of a belligerent power; Britain had no claim to them merely because they had accepted the bounty. Erskine communicated this information to Admiral Berkeley, who was then preparing to sail from his winter station at Bermuda to Halifax.[57]

Blame for the *Chesapeake-Leopard* Affair rests with Berkeley. He was a man of rather mediocre ability, who owed his North American command to family connections. Prime Minister Grenville had misgivings about the appointment and attributed it to political influence. George Berkeley was the second surviving son of the fourth Earl of Berkeley. His grandfather had been First Lord of the Admiralty (1717–27) and his father a general. Young George began his navy career at thirteen under his cousin, Adm. Augustus Keppel. In 1774, while a navy lieutenant, he ignored Admiralty wishes and indulged his interest in politics by standing for Parliament. He was defeated and was placed on the navy's inactive list. But in 1783 he was elected to Parliament (he represented Gloucestershire there until 1810), where he soon became a supporter of the Young Pitt. In 1783 he also gained powerful in-laws when he married the daughter of Lord George Lennox. Berkeley also was related to Grenville's family (Grenville's eldest brother, the Marquis of Buckingham, married Berkeley's half-sister); and he was related to Earl Bathurst, president of the Board of Trade, and to the Duke of Richmond, the Lord Lieutenant for Ireland. Berkeley had returned to sea as a lieutenant during the Revolutionary War in 1778 and captured nine American privateers off Newfoundland. During the wars with the French he commanded the 74-gun *Marlborough* in the 1794 battle of the "Glorious First of June," in which he was wounded and was one of the few rewarded with a gold medal.[58]

Berkeley was promoted to rear admiral in 1799 and, after Pitt returned to power in 1805, to vice admiral. Pitt died in January 1806; that same year Berkeley secured command of the North American Station. He arrived at Halifax in July 1806 to assume command of three ships-of-the-line, a 50-gun ship, four frigates, and twelve smaller vessels. These would soon be augmented by fifteen schooners built at Bermuda, the North American Squadron's winter station.[59]

Grenville noted Berkeley's "unsubtle mind" and his belief that, if Britain refused compromise, the United States would always back down.[60] It may be that Berkeley thought he was sufficiently well-connected politically that his career would be safe no matter the result of his aggressive policy. He was, moreover, chafing under the banning of three of his ships from American ports because of the *Leander* affair. Berkeley also needed seamen for the new schooners arriving from Bermuda.[61]

Captain Townshend informed Berkeley of the desertions from the *Halifax* and that "the whole of the above Men have entered on board" the *Chesapeake* "& were seen by me & several of the Officers" of the *Halifax* "patrolling the Streets of Norfolk in triumph." Townshend told Berkeley that he had learned there were thirty-five British sailors on the *Chesapeake*. On March 21 Hamilton wrote the admiral to tell him that he had been unsuccessful in his efforts to obtain the British seamen. The consul warned that "the Encouragement held out in this Country to promote the Desertion of Seamen from His Majesty's Ships is an Evil which has been, and may be seriously felt by the Commanders in Chief on the North American Station."[62]

Berkeley was angered by what he read. To the Admiralty he repeated Townshend's report that "Deserters from His Majesty's Ships openly parade the streets of Norfolk bearing the American flag under which they have enlisted for the Frigate *Chesapeak* now fitting at Norfolk for the Mediterranean" and the report of at least thirty-five British deserters aboard the *Chesapeake*. He said it was virtually impossible for any British warship to enter a U.S. port without desertions. He also informed Whitehall: "according to the best intelligence I can procure above 10,000 English Seamen under . . . protections are at present employed in the Service of the Americans." Such remarks were bound to stiffen London's resolve in the negotiations with Pinkney and Monroe.[63]

Berkeley did not act precipitously. He had been informed that the *Chesapeake* would probably sail for the Mediterranean around the beginning of May. He merely asked the Admiralty for "instructions how to act," and then on May 4 sailed in the *Leopard* for Halifax, where he arrived ten days later. He did, however, inform Captain Douglas that "the conduct of the Americans on the subject of Deserters must come to a crisis between the two Countries soon."[64]

Goading Berkeley to act was an incident involving the *Driver,* one of the ships banned from U.S. ports because of the *Leander* affair. On May 2 she had anchored in Charleston harbor. Her captain, William Love, complained of difficulty in getting water and may have threatened the use of force. This created an uproar at Charleston, and Love was told to leave within twenty-four hours or face bombardment from the shore.[65] On May 31 Berkeley informed the Admiralty of the incident, enclosing copies of two American newspaper accounts. He recalled that on February 2 and April 29 he had requested Admiralty "directions how to act if such an aggression should take place, as also with respect to the demand of the American Seamen who had entered voluntarily and received the Bounty in His Majesty's Service, to neither of which I have received an answer."[66] Referring to the *Cambrian,* Berkeley said he had written Erskine that

> after the justice which Great Britain has shown, in instantly recalling the Officers engaged in that affair for trial, that I could not conceive that very unwise proclamation would be put in force against the Ships, commanded by other Captains, but that if it was, I must look upon it as a declaration of Hostilities and act accordingly. . . .[67]

Without waiting for word from the Admiralty, Berkeley issued his order of June 1, 1807, which led directly to the *Chesapeake-Leopard* Affair.

Historian Scott Jackson wrote that this order conformed to the letter of Admiralty standing instructions,[68] but it certainly stretched those instructions to the limit. Berkeley's order called on his commanders to search for British deserters from the listed warships. He excluded the *Melampus,* probably because Erskine had informed him of the shaky nature of the claim to its deserters. Berkeley's instructions also directed that there be reciprocity of search for the American captain of the *Chesapeake.* The order said nothing about the use of force in securing compliance; indeed, this was specifically prohibited in the Royal Navy's *Regulations and Instructions Relating to His Majesty's Service at Sea.*

Within ten days this order was on its way to the Royal Navy squadron in the Chesapeake aboard Berkeley's flag-ship, the fourth-rate *Leopard,* commanded by Capt. Salusbury Pryce Humphreys. It is doubtful that Berkeley anticipated an immediate armed clash or else he would not have issued orders recalling Douglas and his 74-gun *Bellona* to Halifax or allowed the *Leopard* to tarry in Halifax for so long before she sailed. It was certainly reasonable for him to believe that the *Chesapeake* had already sailed for the Mediterranean.[69] It is also reasonable to assume that, since Humphreys was Berkeley's own flag captain, the *Leopard*'s master knew exactly what the admiral intended.

The *Leopard* (52 guns), 1,044 tons burthen and 146.5 feet long by 41 feet abeam, had seen extensive service. Laid down at Portsmouth in January 1776, her frames went to Shereness Dock Yard on May 9, 1785, where she was launched on April 24, 1790. In 1804 she served as Rear Adm. Thomas Louis's flagship for a British squadron of nearly twenty vessels off the French port of Boulogne. Two years later she was sent to Halifax specifically to be Berkeley's flagship.[70]

British writers have depreciated the *Leopard*'s strength. William James classified her as a powerful frigate, with armament somewhat heavier than that of the *Chesapeake*, and John Marshall described her as "inferior in size, weight of metal, and men" to the *Chesapeake*.[71] The *Leopard* was in fact more heavily constructed and gunned than her American opponent.

In June 1807 the *Leopard* shipped 356 well-seasoned officers and men (including 25 boys and 13 supernumeraries). She carried fifty-two guns: twenty-two 24-pounder long guns on her main deck, twenty-two long 12-pounders on her upper deck, four 24-pounder carronades on her quarterdeck, and four guns (two 24-pounder carronades and two long 12-pounders) on her forecastle.[72] Total potential weight of shot was thus 960 pounds, or 480 pounds for a broadside. The *Chesapeake*'s weight of broadside metal was only 444 pounds. However, the American ship's twelve 32-pounder carronades were larger than any guns aboard the *Leopard*, so the *Chesapeake* should have had the advantage in close-in fighting; the *Leopard* had only six carronades, and they were 24s. In a long-range engagement, the *Leopard* would have had the advantage with her 24-pounder long guns against the 18s of the *Chesapeake*. In fact, the encounter between the two warships took place at very close range—150 to 200 feet, considered point-blank range in war at sea—but hinged on preparedness rather than gun specifications.

Comparisons of armament do not, of course, take into account crew effectiveness in serving the guns. The *Leopard*'s crew was well-trained and had been exercised at her guns, while the reverse was the case aboard the *Chesapeake*. As Lt. William Allen of the *Chesapeake* later put it: "we had on board a raw undisciplined crew, part of whom was never stationed at a gun in their lives before."[73]

It never will be known what might have happened had the *Chesapeake* been ready to fight. A battle on fair terms would not have been a certain British victory. The author of *British Naval Biography*, in praising Captain Humphreys, grossly overstated the case when he wrote that even though the *Leopard* was "inferior" to the *Chesapeake*, if the two warships had met again in the War of 1812 under the same commanders "there is very little reason to suppose that the result would not have been similar to that of their encounter in 1807."[74]

Capt. Salusbury Humphreys was born in 1778, the son of a minister; he entered the Royal Navy as a midshipman in 1790 and enjoyed steady promotion. Most of his early service, in a variety of ships, was on the Leeward Islands station. Promoted to lieutenant in 1796, he participated in the siege of St. Lucia and commanded the sloop *Fury*, which transported dispatches regarding an unsuccessful British attack on Puerto Rico in April 1797. He won special mention while serving in the British expedition against Holland in 1799 and was given command of the cutter *Stag*. Humphreys was promoted to commander in 1802 and raised to post captain two years later while commanding the bomb vessel *Prospero*. In May 1806 he received command of the *Leander* (50) at Halifax but was transferred shortly after his arrival to the *Leopard*, which was of similar size but a more efficient ship. Since Berkeley lived principally on shore, the *Leopard* "was employed as a private ship, in common with the rest of the squadron."[75]

It took Humphreys and the *Leopard* twelve days to reach the British Chesapeake squadron. Along the way she brought to and searched a dozen American merchant ships, most of which were involved in the Caribbean trade, and impressed seaman from some of them. Most notable was her June 19 seizure, off the Delaware Capes, of the schooner *Margaret K. Bailey*, bound for Philadelphia from Havana with a cargo of sugar and coffee. The crew was taken aboard the *Leopard* and the schooner sent to Halifax. A Norfolk newspaper reported that the schooner's crew had not been allowed "time to take their clothes or any other articles from on board the schooner. During the time they were on board the *Leopard* they were treated with much rudeness; their protections taken from then and torn. . . ." On the morning of the twenty-third the crewmen were transferred to the *Triumph* and then to an American schooner.[76]

At 8:00 A.M. on June 21 the *Leopard* ran up Lynnhaven Bay and anchored about noon in company with the ship-of-the-line *Bellona* and frigate *Melampus*.[77] It was only at this point that Captain Humphreys learned that the *Chesapeake* had not yet sailed; but within hours the U.S. frigate dropped down the bay and anchored. Since it was clear the *Chesapeake* would likely sail the next day, Douglas and Humphreys met to discuss the course of action.

Douglass shares some responsibility for what followed. There would have been no likelihood of the *Chesapeake* offering resistance to the 74-gun *Bellona*. Douglas did not send the *Melampus*, a frigate like the *Chesapeake*, whose Captain Hawker had been reported as threatening force against the *Chesapeake*, for the simple reason that she was of equal size to her and in a fair sea fight more likely to be defeated. In any case, Berkeley's order made inevitable the confrontation that followed.[78]

Barron, the *Chesapeake,* and the U.S. Navy

In 1807 the United States Navy was quite small and relatively new. The largest American warships of the Revolutionary War were frigates (a 74-gun ship under construction at the end of the conflict was turned over to France). Most of the Continental Navy's ships were captured or destroyed; after the conflict, the government sold off what remained. The effects of not having a navy were soon apparent; other nations imposed restrictions that severely hampered U.S. trade, and warships of the Barbary States of North Africa seized U.S. merchantmen.

The Barbary depredations reopened debate in the United States about the need for a navy. Advocates of a navy argued that it would protect overseas trade, safeguard American neutrality, secure U.S. dominance in the Western Hemisphere, be a useful diplomatic tool, help unify the country, and build the national economy.[1]

Many Americans, especially those in the interior and the South, opposed a navy. Some, such as Patrick Henry, saw it as an instrument of imperial ambition and a financial burden. Others believed it would benefit the North at the expense of the West and South and thought that the taking of a relatively small number of American hostages did not justify its expense.[2]

Rather than build a navy the United States initially chose to pay tribute, but depredations by the Barbary powers increased. In the fall of 1793 attacks on U.S. shipping, heretofore limited to the Mediterranean, were extended into the Atlantic. Federalists, supported by Jefferson, wanted to fit out a fleet; Republicans, led by Madison, were opposed.[3]

Another impetus to naval construction was the naval warfare between France and Britain that began in 1793. Advocates saw a navy as necessary to compel the two sides to respect American commercial interests.[4] After some debate, Congress passed a naval bill calling for the acquisition of six frigates: four 44-gun ships and two 36s. This bill, signed by President Washington on March 27, 1794, is considered the birth of the U.S. Navy. In order to placate those opposed to a standing navy, the bill contained an amendment providing that if peace was concluded with Algiers, construction would be halted.[5]

Although the act permitted the purchase of vessels for conversion, the administration opted for new construction. Although this would delay getting the navy to sea, it would ensure that its components were proper warships. The frigates were to be powerful enough to "overmatch double-decked ships in blowing weather, handle any frigate, yet light enough to evade action in light winds."[6] The frigates built to these specifications were three 44-gun warships: the *Constitution, United States,* and *President;* a 38, *Constellation;* and two 36s, *Congress* and *Chesapeake.* Extremely fast, they were also the largest of their classes in the world; they were as heavily built as some ships of the line and had more powerful batteries than their European counterparts.

Their construction was soon delayed. It took time for Naval Constructor Joshua Humphreys to produce their designs and secure the necessary live oak. Then peace with Algiers was declared, and work stopped altogether in 1796. Congress approved a supplementary appropriation permitting completion of the three most advanced—the *Constitution, United States,* and *Constellation*—but work on the other three was canceled and the yards shut down.

The *Chesapeake* was being built at the Gosport Navy Yard, which had been purchased specifically for her construction. A few miles south of Norfolk, this facility was later known as the Norfolk Navy Yard. The *Chesapeake* was the least advanced of the six frigates, and the order halting work canceled her construction.

The "undeclared war" with France resurrected the *Chesapeake.* Her keel was laid on December 10, 1798; she was launched on December 2, 1799, and in commission by May 22, 1800. Josiah Fox, assistant to Naval Constructor Humphreys until 1801, designed her and also superintended the building. The ship was to have been a 44, but Fox thought Humphreys's 44s too large (as did Capt. Thomas Truxtun and some others). He was also short of sufficient molded timber to build a 44 of the *Constitution*'s scale.[7] Secretary of the Navy Robert Smith authorized Fox to prepare a new design for a frigate of reduced size, and so the *Chesapeake* was built as a 36. Her principal dimensions were: length between perpendiculars, 152′8″; breadth, 41′3″; and depth, 20′1″. She weighed 1,244 tons and had a complement of 340 men. Her 1798 plans are in the Josiah Fox Papers at the Peabody Museum in Salem, Massachusetts.[8]

After the British captured her in 1813 the *Chesapeake*'s lines were taken and a model made of her. This 1813 plan, a copy of which is in Record Group 217 of the National Archives, gives her dimensions as: length of gun-deck, 151′; beam, 40′11″; and depth of hold, 13′9″. The 1813 British survey listed her displacement at 1,135 tons and rated her at 48 guns with a crew of 325 men. Howard Chapelle wrote that she was "considered both handsome and fast." James Fenimore Cooper said she was "a roomy and convenient vessel, but was thought to be weak for her dimensions, and her sailing was remarkable neither way." One of her captains, Stephen Decatur, reported in September 1808, "The *Chesapeak* as a Vessel of War Sails uncommonly dull." Whatever her sailing qualities, she was certainly an unlucky ship. This began with the death of a worker during her launching.[9]

The *Chesapeake*'s 1800 battery was thirty 18-pounders and twelve 32-pounder carronades. In 1807 she was rated as a 38-gun frigate. Her June 1807 battery was twenty-eight long 18-pounders and twelve 32-pounder carronades, for a total of forty guns capable of firing 888 pounds of shot (broadside weight, 444 pounds).[10]

Carronades were short, low-velocity, slight-windage, flat-trajectory weapons. First produced by the Carron Company of Scotland in 1776, they soon became popular in the world's navies and by 1800 were aboard U.S. frigates. They were particularly effective in yard-arm actions; their relatively light weight-to-projectile ratio enabled ships to mount heavier caliber carronades than would be the case with long guns. A 32-pounder carronade of this period was just over 4 feet in length and weighed approximately 1,918 pounds, considerably lighter than a 6-pounder long gun at 9 feet in length and 2,688 pounds.[11]

The carronade used approximately one-third the weight of charge for a long gun of comparable caliber. Its ball moved toward the target at lower velocity, and this produced an irregular hole and considerable splintering. This was desirable, since wood splinters were the chief cause of personnel casualties in sea fights.[12]

Samuel Barron was the *Chesapeake's* first captain. She saw service during the Quasi-War with France, mostly in convoy/patrol duties, and on January 1, 1801, while in West Indian waters, captured the French privateer *La Jeune Créole* (16).

One of the few ships retained in the navy after the Quasi-War, the *Chesapeake* was laid up at Norfolk in February 1801. She was reactivated with the declaration of war on Tripoli in February 1802 and sailed from Hampton Roads on April 27 for the Mediterranean, where she was the flagship of Commodore Richard Morris's squadron. She participated in the blockade of Tripoli and convoyed American merchantmen until April 1803 when she returned to the United States. After June 1803 she was in ordinary—in modern parlance, "mothballed"—at the Washington Navy Yard.[13]

Early in 1806 Secretary of the Navy Smith ordered the *Chesapeake* readied for the Mediterranean, where she was to be the flagship for the U.S. squadron. Work proceeded with dispatch; by mid-May she was completely rigged and nearly ready to receive her officers, crew, and stores. In late April 1806 Smith wrote Capt. James Barron: "You will hold yourself in readiness to go to the Mediterranean in the frigate *Chesapeake,* for the purpose of taking the command of the American Squadron in that quarter. . . ." Smith thought the frigate would be ready to sail at the beginning of June.[14] Barron would relieve Commodore John Rodgers. Capt. Charles Stewart was to be Barron's flag captain, and Smith ordered Stewart and a number of lieutenants and midshipmen to Washington to serve on the frigate. But Congress refused to authorize the men to man her and, at the end of May, work on the frigate was discontinued; Smith informed Barron that plans to send her to the Mediterranean were "suspended for the present."[15] The *Chesapeake* was kept in ordinary, her rigging removed. On May 29 Smith gave Barron superintendency of gunboat-building at Matthews County, Virginia.[16]

Finally on January 17, 1807, Secretary Smith again ordered Barron to the *Chesapeake* to prepare her for the Mediterranean. The frigate and sloop-of-war *Wasp* were to relieve the *Constitution* (Commodore Hugh Campbell), *Hornet* (Capt. John Dent), and schooner *Enterprise* (Capt. David Porter).[17]

James Barron was, at thirty-nine, one of the senior navy captains and at the peak of his career. He and his older brother, Samuel, were from a distinguished naval and maritime family. Their grandfather had come to America from Bristol, England, and ultimately commanded Fort George,

site of the later Fortress Monroe. At his death in 1750 he left three sons—
James, Richard, and William—all of whom became officers in Virginia's
Navy during the Revolution. James, youngest of the brothers, commanded
the Virginia state schooner *Liberty*. In 1779 Governor Thomas Jefferson
appointed him commodore and commander in chief of the state's navy.
James had two sons, Samuel, born September 25, 1765, and James, Jr., born
September 15, 1768. The Barron brothers were inseparable as boys and
remained close throughout their lives.

Samuel joined the Virginia navy at age fourteen during the Revolutionary War and soon distinguished himself under fire during the capture of a
Tory sloop. That won him promotion to lieutenant. Later he became
acting captain of a sloop. James also enlisted as a midshipman under his
father during the war, probably in 1781 at age twelve. It was a difficult time
for the Virginia navy. The British controlled the Chesapeake Bay, and at
the end of the war the Virginians had not a state vessel afloat. On the
return of peace Commodore Barron still commanded the navy, Samuel
was a lieutenant, and James, Jr., a midshipman. The father died in 1787.
With the abolition of the Virginia navy the following year, his sons entered
merchant service.[18]

In 1790, at age twenty-two, James married Elizabeth Armistead. A
daughter, Jane, was born the next year. Regarded as a young man with a
bright future in commerce, Barron worked his way up to captain for a
leading Norfolk firm. He was tall (over six feet), with broad shoulders and
dark blue (but short-sighted) eyes. Contemporaries described him in such
terms as "distinguished," "kind and amiable," and "charming." He seemed
"to have had a gift for making friends" and "the reputation of being the
courtliest of men."[19]

In March 1798, during the undeclared naval war with France, both
"web-footed Barrons" (as the family was known in Hampton) joined the
new U.S. Navy as lieutenants. Samuel commanded the brig *Richmond;* later
he was the first captain of the *Chesapeake*. James was commissioned on
March 9, 1798, to serve as third lieutenant on the frigate *Unites States* under
John Barry, ranking captain in the navy.[20] Among the midshipmen on the
frigate was Stephen Decatur, then twenty.

James Barron was an officer with an inventive frame of mind. He was
credited with developing the first U.S. Navy uniform code of signals and
was known for his seamanship and, ironically, in view of the charges
leveled by critics in 1807, his courage. During a cruise in the Gulf Stream
searching for French vessels, the *United States* fell victim to a nine-day-

long storm, in the course of which she sprung her bowsprit and her running rigging became useless. This threatened her masts. At some risk to his life as the frigate pitched in the storm, Barron managed to set the purchases on the shrouds and save the masts.

Barry commended Barron to the secretary of the navy, leading to his May 22, 1799, promotion to captain. Four others were also advanced to captain at the same time: Edward Preble, John Rodgers, George Little, and Christopher Perry. William Bainbridge, who felt he should have been promoted, had to be talked out of resigning from the service.

After his promotion Barron served as flag captain for Commodore Barry in the *United States*. In October 1800 he got his first independent command, the 20-gun *Warren,* and sailed to join Commodore Thomas Truxtun of the St. Kitts squadron in the West Indies. There Barron contracted yellow fever and in April 1801 went home in the *New York*. The same month word was received of the end of the Quasi-War. Barron had distinguished himself only in seamanship; there had been no opportunity for him to engage a French warship.[21]

One event of the Quasi-War needs mention here. Truxtun and the *Constellation* captured the frigate *L'Insurgente* in February 1799 in one of the major U.S. victories of the conflict. The prize was turned over to Capt. Alexander Murray. On her return from the cruise Barron examined the French-built frigate. Although *L'Insurgente* was to receive a new captain, Murray had the responsibility of readying her for sea. After a thorough inspection, Barron concluded that *L'Insurgente*'s refit was so poor that she might be endangered in a storm. He wrote as much to a friend, and this came to the attention of Murray, who was furious. (Barron's concerns may have been well founded. *L'Insurgente* was lost at sea during her second cruise, probably in a storm of September 1800.) No doubt Murray held something of a grudge. He was later president of the board of inquiry investigating Barron's conduct in the *Chesapeake-Leopard* Affair.[22]

Barron was one of only nine of the twenty-eight Quasi-War navy captains the Jefferson administration retained. During the war with Tripoli he commanded the frigate *President* in Commodore Richard Dale's Mediterranean squadron. His brother Samuel had command of the frigate *Philadelphia*. On a second Mediterranean cruise James Barron commanded the frigates *Chesapeake* and *New York* (with Decatur as his first lieutenant) under Commodore Richard Morris. In April 1803 he left the *New York* to return to the United States and spend a year superintending gunboat construction.

In September 1804 Barron was again in the Mediterranean in command of the frigate *Essex*, part of the American squadron his brother commanded in a blockade of Tripoli. In May 1805, just prior to the conclusion of a peace treaty with Tripoli, Samuel Barron fell ill and turned over command to the next senior captain, John Rodgers, who moved James Barron from the *Essex* to the *President*. Unfortunately for James, his efforts to see his brother prosper (he had urged Samuel, despite his lingering fever, to keep his command as long as possible) were interpreted by the Rodgers camp as being aimed at their leader. Rodgers termed a subsequent Barron letter wishing him success in his new post as "two-faced" and charged that Barron had urged his brother to keep command "while assuring me with the gravity of a Judas that he was prevailing upon him to resign." Rodgers also had differences with the Barrons over peace with Tripoli; the brothers favored negotiation, while Rodgers favored continuing the war. Barron later commented, "In the year 1806 . . . I had a difficulty with Commodore Rodgers. . . . It originated from some remarks of Commodore Rodgers respecting my brother's command in the Mediterranean." Regardless of the rights or wrongs, Barron had made another prominent enemy in Rodgers. Fame and glory had also again eluded him; his duties consisted of routine patrolling.[23]

At the end of June 1805 Barron served as president of the court of inquiry held at Syracuse, on Sicily, to investigate Captain Bainbridge's loss of the *Philadelphia*. The frigate had run aground before Tripoli and had been forced to surrender; later young Lt. Stephen Decatur won immortality in a daring raid to fire her. The deed won Decatur promotion to captain at age twenty-five, the youngest man to hold that rank in the history of the U.S. Navy. The Bainbridge court of inquiry was *pro forma*, something Barron no doubt remembered two years later when Bainbridge sat as a member of Barron's court-martial. It was a foregone conclusion that Bainbridge would be exonerated, and nothing was said about what his biographer has called his "thoroughly stupid decision" to send away a support vessel, his incautious pursuit of a Tripolitan vessel before the frigate ran aground, or the possibility that the *Philadelphia* might have been kedged off the reef. Bainbridge was found blameless.[24]

After the court of inquiry, Barron sailed the *President* from Syracuse to Malta and then to Gibraltar, where he arrived at the end of July. On August 2 he left for the United States, arriving on September 10. His return began a long shore leave, which according to navy regulations meant half pay of $600 a year. It was thus with some relief that Barron learned in the spring of 1806 that he would be appointed to command the U.S. Mediterranean squadron with his flag in the *Chesapeake;* but when it proved impossible to get the frigate to sea in 1806, he ended up again superintending gunboat construction.[25]

Despite his lack of an opportunity to prove himself in battle Barron seemed a man with a distinguished career ahead of him. One 1851 source lauded him in these words:

> James Barron enjoyed a high character in the service, being deemed one of the most ready and ingenious seamen that American had ever produced. No officer, indeed had borne a more conscientious part in the organization of our navy than he had done. He originated the first code of signals used by our ships, and early distinguished himself for his superior nautical science and skill. As a military officer, too, he was deemed accomplished and efficient, and one of the best disciplinarians in the service.[26]

While regarded as skillful in his profession, Barron also seems to have been reflective, introspective, and without the burning desire for glory that motivated so many of his fellow officers. Certainly he had prominent enemies in the service, some of whom questioned his courage.[27]

In the summer of 1806 Rodgers returned to the United States from the Mediterranean. Still upset with Barron, Rodgers believed that some unflattering references to him in the American press, about which he learned at Gibraltar, had come from Barron. On July 24 Rodgers fired off a letter to Barron informing him that he stood ready "to account to you at any time from the present"—in effect, a challenge to a duel. Barron replied from Hampton on July 29 that he was sick in bed but willing to fight. Both men appointed seconds (Rodgers chose Capt. Thomas Tingey, and Barron requested the commandant of the Marine Corps, Col. Franklin Wharton). Preparations dragged on into the fall; but after Rodgers's marriage at the end of October he lost enthusiasm for dueling, and the affair fizzled out. Secretary Smith may have prevented the duel by ordering the two captains not to leave their stations "without special orders from me."[28] Both captains agreed to print a circular stating the terms of their formal reconciliation, which was given to friends. Despite this formal resolution of their quarrel, Rodgers seems to have hated Barron the rest of his life.[29]

Decatur, who aligned himself with Rodgers, also was hostile. Although one of his biographers says Decatur had disliked Barron since serving under him in the *United States,* there is no evidence of this; indeed, there is every indication that Midshipman Decatur had learned much from Barron. More probably the falling out came over an innocent remark Barron had made about Decatur's relationship with Susan Wheeler (whom he married in March 1806), when Barron assumed Decatur was engaged to someone else.[30]

Barron's prohibition from leaving his post without prior permission of the secretary of the navy was lifted on January 17, 1807, when Smith ordered him to "make arrangements" regarding the gunboats he was then superintending and repair to Washington, where "You are to have command of the Frigate *Chesapeake,* to proceed with her to the Mediterranean."[31]

The Navy Department had been extraordinarily dilatory in ordering the *Chesapeake* into service. The *Constitution* had sailed for the Mediterranean in August 1803, more than three years before. Commodore Rodgers had managed to piece together a crew for the frigate of longer-term men from all the units about to return to the United States, including the gunboats, but the men were near mutiny.[32] The *Chesapeake* would have to be sent out as soon as possible.

On January 24, 1807, Smith ordered the *Chesapeake* made ready. That same month Smith called Charles Gordon, the youngest master commandant on the list, to Washington from Annapolis. Master commandant was the rank between lieutenant and captain, comparable to the modern rank of commander. Smith ordered Gordon to the *Chesapeake* to serve as flag captain of the frigate under Barron. Gordon returned the order because it did not specify the rank he was to hold and, on February 23, Smith sent a new one, informing Gordon: "You will immediately place yourself under command Com. Jas. Barron under whom you are to act as Captain of the frigate *Chesapeake* to which Ship you are hereby attached."[33]

One historian of the early U.S. Navy has described Gordon as "a foppish young man who strove for elegance in wit as he did in dress."[34] Certainly he had important social and political connections. A native of the Eastern Shore of Maryland, Gordon's exact birth date is uncertain; probably it was some time in 1778. He never married, but he was related to the important Republican Nicholson family. Congressman Joseph Hooper Nicholson was his mother's younger brother. More importantly, Gordon's aunt, Hannah Nicholson, was married to Secretary of the Treasury Albert Gallatin, the second-most powerful figure in the Jefferson administration. Gordon is also said to have been related to Capt. Alexander Murray, and his brother Joseph was a many-time officeholder in Kent County.

Gordon joined the navy as a midshipman in June 1799 in *L'Insurgente*. Although older than the average midshipman, Gordon was ambitious. Promoted to lieutenant in December 1800, he became a skilled seaman. During the Quasi-War he served in the *Constellation* and in 1801 was on the *Philadelphia*. On the navy list of that year Gordon ranked twenty-fourth of thirty-six lieutenants; nearly one hundred others were released from the navy in the downsizing following the war.

In 1801 Gordon sailed to the Mediterranean in the *George Washington* and then transferred to the *President*. In June 1802 he was allowed leave, and in August was ordered to Washington and posted to the frigate *New York*, commanded by James Barron, and returned to the Mediterranean. In September 1803 Gordon transferred to the *Constitution*. He commanded Gunboat No. 2 during attacks on Tripoli in August and September 1804 and was included in the resolution of thanks to Commodore Preble voted by Congress. In September 1804 Gordon was officer of the watch on the *Constitution* when a wind shift led to a collision with the *President*. His own ship was damaged in the bows, but he was "absolved of any dereliction of duty, the vagaries of the wind being acts of God."[35]

The next month Gordon transferred to the *John Adams*. She sailed for home in December and arrived at New York in February 1805. He assisted Preble in the construction of bomb vessels at Boston and in July 1805 was ordered to the *Adams* (Capt. Alexander Murray), which vessel he served on in home waters until 1807. Murray praised Gordon, finding him an "excellent and inspiring officer" and one "who merited the patronage of the Navy Department." He was promoted to master commandant in April 1806, and a year later he was still the youngest of that rank on the navy list.[36]

After his court-martial Barron was sharply critical of Gordon's appointment as captain of the *Chesapeake*. He noted that in 1806 Stewart, newly promoted to captain, was to have been the frigate's captain but that he was "otherwise disposed" and Capt. Joseph Tarbell had been appointed. The next year "to my great dissatisfaction I found Captain Gordon was substituted for Captain Tarbell, this induced me to request to be relieved from the command, for I knew Captain Gordon was too much addicted to pleasure . . . to bend his mind to business, I suffered myself, however, to be overruled in this important matter."[37] Despite this statement, there is no official record of Barron raising objections to Gordon's appointment at the time it was made.

Smith also ordered lieutenants, midshipman, and other officers to the frigate. In mid-February he ordered Lt. Charles Ridgely of the *Chesapeake* to Baltimore to enter forty able seamen competent to serve as quartermasters, boatswains, and other petty officers. They were to be entered at the rate of $12 a month to serve two years from the day the frigate "weighs anchor on a Cruise." On February 20 Smith directed Lt. Arthur Sinclair at Norfolk to enter an additional forty able seamen there for the *Chesapeake* on the same terms.[38] By mid-March Sinclair had signed them; thirty-eight were on the way to the frigate, one had deserted, and another was in jail.[39]

It proved more difficult to prepare the frigate for service than to secure officers and men. Smith ordered Captain Tingey, commandant of the Washington Navy Yard, to give the *Chesapeake* and the *Wasp* priority and if necessary suspend work on other vessels. On his arrival in Washington, however, Barron discovered that the frigate needed substantial repairs before she could be ready for sea, including new fore and main lower rigging.[40]

Barron spent two months at the Washington Navy Yard trying to get the *Chesapeake* ready and then returned to Hampton Roads to await her arrival and do final fitting out. Work on the frigate proceeded slowly. In addition to sail repairs there were alterations to be made to her quarterdeck to mount new carronades.[41]

While this was going on, Smith asked Barron to inspect cannon powder for the *Chesapeake* and determine whether it might be obtained at Malta or elsewhere in the Mediterranean. Barron reported to Chief Clerk Charles Goldsborough that the powder was not fit for service and asked that good powder be supplied. He was told that it was "not to be had." In his subsequent trial, Barron pointed to this as evidence that Smith did not anticipate problems with the Royal Navy when the frigate sailed.[42]

One reason for the delay in readying the *Chesapeake* was that the navy yard was at the same time preparing the *United States* and *Wasp* for service. When Tingey requested the services of seven or eight Philadelphia journeymen sailmakers, Smith chided him for delays with the *Chesapeake:*

> The *Chesapeake* has now been in commission two months. You were months before apprised of the intentions of the Government to send the *Chesapeake* to sea early in the spring to relieve the *Constitution* and from your frequent verbal communications to me I was under the impression that she would have been put to sea in two weeks from the time the officers could join her. You will inform me in

detail of the causes of this great delay that I may know where the blame attaches. We cannot but appear censorable in the eyes of the whole country on this occasion. Our means of keeping up a Navy appears feeble and contemptible indeed, if we require such a length of time to put a Frigate to sea after her Hull has been completely repaired. I really feel on this occasion extremely concerned and mortified, fearing as I do, that the Yard is exposed to just ridicule.[43]

Tingey replied in detail, citing weather problems and the need for new rigging and alterations to sails. He had not been present when the frigate had returned from the Mediterranean and did not meet with her officers. As a consequence he could not have known that her sails had been set daily for two or three years, and no one had informed him that they might need repairs. When the frigate had been readied for service in 1806 the officers who had been called to Washington for her had expressed no dissatisfaction with her rigging. At the end of that year the frigate had been dismantled and laid up, and when she was again ordered prepared for sea he had done all he could, Tingey said.[44]

Recruiting, meanwhile, continued in Philadelphia and Norfolk. In February Smith ordered Lt. Sidney Smith of the *Chesapeake* to Norfolk to enter forty additional able seamen there, relieving Lieutenant Sinclair of that responsibility. Few recruits were to be had in Philadelphia, and a rendezvous there was halted at the end of March. In late April Robert Smith ordered Lt. James Lawrence at New York to enter thirty seamen for the frigate there. He authorized pay of $12 a month and a bounty of not more than $20 if necessary; an advance of two to four months' pay was authorized if security was given as a safeguard against desertion.[45]

Lt. William H. Allen referred to the difficulties in recruiting men in a March 30, 1807 letter to his father. Allen had been ordered to the *Chesapeake* in late January and was recruiting men for her when he wrote from New York:

In the first place it is a duty of too much responsibility for Officers situated, as we are, our ship in Washington and the men to be procured at Newyork, Philadelphia and Norfolk, my orders were to ship as many seamen, ordinary seamen, and Boys (170) these you see are to be kept in the city where they are recruited 'till you get a sufficient number to send round under charge of an officer in chartered vessell (that is to make it an object to charter one) now what do you think of 60 to 80 Sailors, no doubt some of them wild

Irishmen let loose in this city, after you have advanced them from 18 to 70 dollars each, to be sure you are ordered to take good security for the money, but if it is not good you must be chargeable, I never had so much trouble with a pack of rascals in my life, now I'll just give you an account of my success—I have been here 25 days have entered for the service 57 men, and now what[']s become of them 47 I have on board a vessell under charge of an officer so far *good*. 1. I discharged because his wife *overpersuaded* me as the girl said, 1. I discharged as unfit for service. 1 I discharged because I could not hold him, another I must discharge because I cannot hold him and 6 have been given *leg Bail* for their honesty, however I don[']t think I shall lose by them.[46]

On April 10 Smith wrote James Barron, then at the Navy Department in Washington: "You will proceed to Hampton and on the arrival of the *Chesapeake* in that road, you will join her. . . ."[47] Tingey was finishing preparations and providing twelve months' of supplies. These included 60 barrels of flour, 63,875 pounds of bread, 1,500 pounds of butter, 3,900 pounds of cheese, 163 bushels of beans or peas, 650 gallons of molasses, 650 gallons of vinegar, 4,563 gallons of spirits, 225 barrels of beef, and 225 barrels of pork.[48]

Gordon formally assumed command of the *Chesapeake* at the yard in Washington on May 1.[49] One of Barron's biographers asserts that he "had been warned by the Secretary of the Navy to be careful not to take over the responsibilities of the captain but to give Gordon a chance to show what he could do. It was once more evident that the Secretary took a strong interest in this officer."[50] On May 1 Barron wrote Gordon from Hampton: "by no means advise your leaving the navy yard with any unfinished work, and depend on Norfolk. You will experience more difficulty and trouble there than you can conceive." On May 10, unaware that the *Chesapeake* had already sailed, Barron again wrote Gordon that it would be best not to have the frigate come "to this Road, before she was complete in all respects, and all the men ship't would expedite our sailing." He also wrote a third letter, dated only "May." Commiserating with complaints Gordon had apparently expressed about the Washington yard, Barron referred to his subordinate's letter, saying "the contents thereof would really astonish a stranger to that place, but I have long known the perverse disposition of the rulers of that establishment. . . ." Nonetheless, he urged Gordon to finish up work at Washington, for things were worse at Gosport: "But Sir let me entreat you to persevere, and on no consideration leave the yard, until you have the ship in all respects complete for sea (except by the express order of the Honble. Secretary of the Navy)."[51]

On the morning of May 9 the *Chesapeake* took on board a pilot and departed Washington in what turned out to be a tricky trip down the Potomac to the Chesapeake Bay and Hampton Roads. In order to keep her from grounding on leaving the yard she had on board only twelve 18-pounder guns of her aft gun deck armament.[52] Even so, the frigate was only two miles along the Eastern Branch when she grounded at Greenleaf Point. Gordon had to order all hands to heave her clear using her anchors and capstan. On May 10, to lighten her, Gordon transferred the bulk of the frigate's provisions and shot to the schooner *Vixen.* The next day the frigate slipped her cables and dropped down the Potomac to anchor near Alexandria. On May 13 and 14 the crew was employed in "discharging the *Vixen.*" On the fifteenth the ketch *Spitfire* came alongside, and the frigate took aboard eight 18-pounder guns to help trim the ship. On the seventeenth the crew "sent down the Top Gallt., yards in consequence of the Fore Top Gallt. Rope not being properly bent." In the course of this the *Chesapeake*'s fore topgallant yard came loose and the spar crashed to the forecastle, killing two of the crew and "very much injuring" another. While at Alexandria the frigate received additional guns. On the nineteenth she weighed anchor and stood as far as Broad Creek, seven miles from Alexandria. There she anchored again and took on supplies from a navy yard tender. The next day the frigate again weighed and stood down river.

At Mount Vernon Captain Gordon ordered the customary sixteen-gun salute while passing President Washington's grave.[53] The frigate had aboard only twelve of her guns. As with so much else on the trip down river, the simple salute proved to be far from routine: the crew discovered that a number of the cartridges were too large to fit in the muzzles of the guns and that some sponges were also too large. Gordon later wrote, "Had we been engaged in active War, I should have suspected the Officers of the Yard with having a design on my character. . . ." Gordon ordered Gunner William Hook arrested, but reinstated him when he learned that the cartridges had been issued to Hook by a Mr. Stevenson of the Washington Navy Yard. Gordon had the sponges "sheered and reduced to the proper size."[54] That same evening, as the frigate passed Mount Vernon, Seaman Gideon Winslow fell overboard and drowned.

On May 23 the pilot boat came alongside, bringing Dr. Bullus, his wife, their children and servants, and Captain Hall and his wife; the frigate again got under way and came to below Indian Head. Crewmen continued to join the frigate in her progress downriver, but some also left. On the twenty-fourth a seamen from the frigate deserted from her boat when it was on shore. The next day another seamen, William Barret, "departed his life" and was buried ashore. On May 27 the *Chesapeake*'s crew discovered the frigate's small launch missing from her moorings; the crew lowered the gig and it and the larger launch were sent off in pursuit. They returned empty-handed, but the errant launch was later recovered down river. On the twenty-eighth boats were put out to tow the frigate, but she grounded on Mattawoman Bar. The crew put out a stern anchor and tried to heave the ship free, but the hawser broke. Using the larboard (port) anchor, the crew finally managed to free the frigate. They then used the starboard anchor to warp the ship into deeper water.

On the thirtieth the ship again weighed and stood down river. The next day eight men deserted in the cutter. Gordon sent Midshipman Fitz Henry Babbitt and a small party of marines in the pilot boat to bring them back. He also sent some men in the small launch and jolly boat to look for the cutter, which was recovered about five miles away on the Maryland shore. Babbitt and the marines returned empty-handed, however. On June 2 the four-man crew of the jolly boat mutinied, seized control of her from her officer, and deserted. The cutter was sent in pursuit, again without success. Midshipmen Babbitt, Charles Norton, and John Pettigrew were put ashore to look for the deserters. That same day a wind enabled Gordon to hoist in the boats and sail past the French ship *Patriote* into the Chesapeake Bay and anchor. One crewman died the same day and was committed to the deep; another died June 3 and was also buried at sea. On June 4 the frigate again got under way and finally reached Hampton Roads.[55] On the frigate's arrival the three midshipmen returned with the four deserters from the jolly boat. Many men were sick during the passage down river. Gordon later reported that from sixty to eighty-five were continually on the sick list; only thirty-five had been sick when the frigate sailed.[56]

At Norfolk Lieutenant Sinclair had conducted a rendezvous to enlist men for the *Chesapeake*'s forthcoming cruise. He had been commissioned a midshipman in June 1798 and had entered the service the following November. He had served in the *Constellation, Insurgente,* and *Chesapeake* during the Quasi-War, had been discharged in the naval reduction of 1801, and was reinstated in May 1804. He then served in the *Essex, Siren,* and Gunboat No. *3,* and he commanded No. *10* in the Mediterranean. From mid-1806 Sinclair had charge of ships in ordinary at Norfolk and was in gunboat service there.[57]

It was Sinclair who signed up the Royal Navy deserters from the *Melampus* and other British ships.[58] One contemporary claimed that, while she was at Washington, the *Chesapeake* had on her rolls the five deserters from the *Halifax*, three deserters from the *Melampus*, and twelve other British seamen.[59] Four of the men from the *Halifax* deserted again on the *Chesapeake*'s passage down the Potomac. Ratford was the only *Halifax* deserter left on the *Chesapeake*.[60] In all, twelve seamen and a boatswain were taken aboard the frigate in Hampton Roads; another twenty-five men were discharged or deserted.[61]

Meanwhile, Captain Gordon struggled to get the *Chesapeake* ready for sea. The condition of the ship was technically his, not Barron's, responsibility. As commodore, Barron had responsibility for the entire Mediterranean squadron. However, Gordon was unusually junior to command a ship as important as the *Chesapeake* on his own. In naval custom both shared responsibility. Although Gordon had actual charge of the ship, Barron was senior officer and in command.

Both men were clearly more concerned with getting to sea than training their crew. Their decision to sail with a ship unprepared for action was not an unusual approach; however, it contrasted sharply with the style of Capt. Edward Preble, who had his ships ready for battle at any time.[62] It should also be noted that in a letter to Captain Rodgers just after the *Chesapeake*'s encounter with the *Leopard*, Captain Tingey pointed out its close resemblance to a scenario predicted by Rodgers.[63] The possibility that the British might use force to reclaim their deserters must have, or should have, occurred to other captains.

Barron wrote in 1813 that the *Chesapeake* "laid twenty-two days in Hampton Roads with her whole crew on board, and her orders ready."[64] During that period Barron, who was recovering from illness, visited the frigate only twice.[65] The first time was on June 6, when his broad pennant was hoisted and he formally assumed command. He stayed aboard only three hours at most, however, and was there only an hour or two on his second visit on June 10. On June 6 he and Gordon inspected the frigate's gun deck and the quarterdeck, but Barron did not look at the magazines. Much of his time aboard was spent in the cabin. That same day the *Wasp* came down from Craney Island and anchored near the frigate; she went to sea the next day.[66]

After his cursory inspection, Barron wrote a letter to Secretary of the Navy Smith that he would later have great cause to regret:

> I have just returned from visiting the *Chesapeak* [*sic*], and feel a particular pleasure in stating to you, that from the extreme cleanliness and order in which I found her, I am convinced that Capt. Gordon and his officers must have used great exertions. Capt. Gordon speaks in high terms of approbation of the lieutenants. The state of the Ship proves the justice of his assessment.—
>
> I am sorry that the Ship has arrived here in want of any thing that may occasion delay. Every possible means shall be used to procure expedientially such articles as I find her deficient of, and that alone shall detain us. Some men have effected their escape, the number has not yet been made known to me, but the loss of them is not an object to stop us. There is neither Carpenter or Boatswain on board, and I am doubtfull whether the gunner will be able to proceed or not. If we should not be so fortunate as to procure those officers here, I shall consider myself authorized to take them out of the remaining vessels once in the Mediterranean. It is not now in my power to inform you the precise time that we shall be in a condition to sail, but hope it will be in the course of the coming week.[67]

Barron's judgment on the fitness of the frigate and her crew in this letter stands in sharp variance with his testimony after the encounter with the *Leopard*.[68]

The *Chesapeake* arrived at Hampton Roads with only twelve guns of her main battery on board. The remainder were shipped from the Washington Navy Yard on other vessels.[69] On June 5 the ketch *Spitfire* came alongside and the men transferred 18-pound round shot and stands of grape to the frigate. The next day the *Chesapeake* received the carronades for the quarterdeck from the same vessel. Over the next week her crew was kept busy receiving stores and water for the upcoming cruise. The emphasis throughout was in preparing for sea, and nothing was done to train the men.[70]

On June 13 Gordon wrote Barron at Hampton to tell him that the frigate was delayed from sailing to fit half ports for the guns, secure carronade slides, and correct deficiencies in blacksmiths' work and procure items in the boatswain's and sailmaker's departments that should have been taken aboard at Washington. In addition, the new rigging needed to be overhauled because it had been fitted in cold weather. He hoped to be able to sail in three days.[71]

On June 15 the *Spitfire* anchored alongside and the *Chesapeake's* crew took from her twelve 32-pounder carronades, 204 barrels of bread, and "sundry Stores." The next day was spent transferring water and setting up fore and aft rigging. On the seventeenth the crew was busy receiving studding sails' gear, swaying the sky sails aloft, and crossing the royal yards. They also took aboard more water from the tender, and Dr. Bullus, Captain Hall, and their dependents, who had gone ashore on the frigate's arrival, returned on board.[72]

The next day crew members continued preparations for sea; they loosed sails to dry, furled them, and stationed the ship's company (each man went to his particular station). They also let go the larboard anchor. The weather was squally, with winds from the northeast. The nineteenth was also rainy. The men housed the topgallant masts; got the sheet anchor ready for letting go; let go the port anchor; '"veered away" the entire port cable and then hove it up again, "unbent the cable and bent a new one," and took on water. Armorers, sailmakers, and carpenters were all employed on sundry assignments. The crew was also again called to quarters.[73] That same day Captain Gordon reported to Barron on shore that "The weather has been such, that I have not expected you. We are unmoored and ready for weighing the first fair wind. All station bills are complete. The guns are all charged, and if possible, we have an exercise this evening."[74] On neither occasion when the men were called to quarters before sailing were they exercised at the guns, however.[75]

On June 19 Barron wrote to Gordon from Hampton that he "came to town yesterday with an intent to bid a final adieu to the shore, but the prospect of getting to sea being unpromising was prevailed on to stay a day longer. The moment I perceive an alteration I shall be with you." Noting that Secretary Smith had complained of officers not writing him as often as they should nor being explicit, he told Gordon to make an extract from the log of activities since the frigate's arrival at Hampton Roads and send it on. In a postscript Barron noted, "The herbs sent on board yesterday should be tied up in small bunches, and hung in some airy place. Tell the Dr. I sent the Potato vines off yesterday."[76]

On June 20 there was more rain, some heavy, and a wind out of the northeast again kept the frigate windbound. The crew housed the topgallant masts, got the sheet anchor clear for letting go, let go the larboard anchor, and veered out the whole of the starboard cable. They also hove up the whole of the starboard cable and the larboard anchor, unbent the old cable, and bent the new one. The tender came alongside, and the crew brought more supplies on board; they also secured the sheet anchor and swayed the topgallant masts.[77]

On June 21 the crew loosed sails to dry; they also sent the old bower cable on board the pilot boat to be returned to Washington. First Lt. Benjamin Smith mustered the ship's crew. The men finished transferring water from the tender, furled sails, and set up topmast and topgallant rigging, fore and aft. The ship weighed anchor, stood further down the roads, and came to. The crew then crossed the topgallant yards and were called to quarters. Barron, who boarded the frigate at noon, later reported to Smith that the wind was "still adverse" but "has the appearance of a change. The moment it takes place we shall depart."[78]

Secretary Smith's sailing instructions indicated no alarm. On May 15 he had written Barron: "as soon as the *Chesapeake* shall be prepared for sea, you will weigh anchor, and proceed direct to the Mediterranean." These instructions contain no hint of trouble with Britain.[79] Indeed, the expected pacific nature of the cruise is shown in President Jefferson's request that Barron purchase for him in the Mediterranean a pipe of Marsala Madeira, "if conveyance is available."[80]

June 22 began with a fresh breeze from the southwest and clear weather. As the frigate got under way Gordon began a letter to Secretary Smith: "I am happy to inform you every thing on board is now in order. The officers and crew perform to my satisfaction."[81]

The Threat of War

The *Chesapeake-Leopard* incident produced immediate outrage in the United States. As James Fenimore Cooper put it, "It was, perhaps, fortunate that the attack on the *Chesapeake* occurred at a moment when the relations between the two countries were rather more amicable than they had been for several years, or it might have led to an immediate declaration of war."[1] Even so, along the U.S. Atlantic coast there was fear of imminent British attack and, for about two weeks, acute crisis.

After the encounter the *Leopard* returned to the British anchorage in Lynnhaven Bay with her prisoners in irons and anchored in the midst of the squadron. All crewmen had been recalled to their ships, showing that Capt. John Douglas had anticipated the possibility of action.[2]

The *Chesapeake*, meanwhile, anchored in Hampton Roads at about 12:30 P.M. on the twenty-third. At 2:00 a boat came alongside with Commodore Samuel Barron; an hour later Captain Gordon and Dr. Bullus left the frigate in the pilot boat for Washington, and about 5:00 Capt. Stephen Decatur came on board. He and Samuel Barron left the ship about an hour later.[3] According to one of his biographers, Decatur had "first hand impressions that led him to believe that Barron had been grossly negligent of his duty. To this opinion he adhered ever afterward."[4]

Gordon and Bullus carried Barron's report of the incident to Washington. As one historian has noted, Barron's decision to send Gordon was a "terrible mistake. . . . Somebody was going to held at fault for what had happened, and if it was not Gordon, it would Barron himself. Allowing the politically seasoned Gordon to get his side of the story in front of the secretary of the navy first was an act of professional suicide on the part of James Barron."[5]

In his report Barron expressed no displeasure with his officers' conduct. Perhaps he assumed they would close ranks with him to protect their own reputations from the censure sure to follow. If so, he was sadly disappointed, for Gordon also carried a letter from the frigate's lieutenants to Secretary of the Navy Smith. Lt. William H. Allen composed the petition, which was signed by him and lieutenants Benjamin Smith, William Crane, James Creighton, and Sidney Smith and Sailing Master Samuel Brooke. Writing on board what they termed the "late U.S. Ship *Chesapeake*," the officers expressed themselves "deeply sensible of the disgrace which must be attached to the late (in their opinion) premature surrender." All had sought to be "worthy of the Flag under which they had the honor to service, by a determined resistance. . . ." They considered it their "duty" to request Barron's arrest on two charges: "1st, On the probability of an Engagement, for neglecting to clear his ship for action; 2ndly, For not doing his utmost to take or destroy a Vessel, which we conceive it his duty to have done."[6]

Allen was the most outspoken. On June 24 he wrote his father, Gen. William Allen, from the "Late U.S.S. *Chesapeake*." After relating what had transpired, he added:

In narrating to you the circumstances that led to the disgracefull surrender of this ship, I have not digress'd from the subject to give bent to my wounded feelings—Oh! that some one of their murderous balls had deprived me of the power of recollection the moment our colours were struck—I could have greeted it, received it to my bosom, with a kindred smile—nothing could equal so horrible a scene as it was, to see so many brave men standing to their Quarters among the blood of their butchered and wounded country men and hear their cries without the means of avenging them: and when we would have done it, to have our colour struck, yes in 3 minutes every gun would have been at work—My God is it possible. My countrys flag disgraced. You cannot appreciate you cannot *conceive* of my feeling at this moment, Was it for this I have continued so long in the service against your wishes.—the wish of all my friends; to be so *mortified, humbled.*—cut to the soul. Yes to have the finger of scorn pointing me out as one of the *Chesapeak*. But do not my friend think I feel for myself.—that I feel I have not done *my* duty.—*No*.—Perish the thought—I feel—Yes—I proudly feel, I would have willingly given *my* trifling life an offering for the honor of my country—Yes— give us a *Commander* give us a *man* to lead us to glory and there is not an officer in this ship that will not immolate himself to serve his country.

Then, in words marked "private," Allen wrote of Barron, "here we lay without a flag flying the Commodore still on board, he has a trifling wound in the Calf of his Leg—I was near cursing him—but I leave him to his own conscience, while he possesses the power of recollection *no curses* can add to its tortures."[7] In a later letter Allen characterized Barron's conduct as "Base and Cowardly."[8]

Ominously for Barron, when Smith acknowledged receipt of the petition he wrote the frigate's lieutenants that their communication "does you honor. It will be attended to."[9] On June 26 their version of events rather than Barron's was published in the pro-administration *National Intelligencer*. It would be three months before the U.S. press published the correspondence between Barron and Humphreys, and it came from British sources.[10]

Norfolk, meanwhile, was in immediate alarm. The *Norfolk Gazette and Publick Ledger* reported the encounter had "produced a degree of agitation beyond anything we ever witnessed or can attempt to describe."[11] On June 24 citizens of Norfolk and Portsmouth met at the town hall and unanimously adopted resolutions calling for an end to all communication with, or assistance to, British warships "now within our waters and on our coasts," for citizens to wear crepe for ten days in memory of those killed on the *Chesapeake*, for a subscription fund for the wounded and the families of those killed in the attack, and for Mayor Richard E. Lee to call out the militia.

Angry citizens of Norfolk destroyed some two hundred of the HMS *Melampus*'s water casks, critical for a sea voyage. Another resolution held this action "highly laudable and praise worthy." A few days later citizens of Hampton passed a resolution calling on Decatur to put gunboats in service.[12]

Decatur, commander of naval forces at Norfolk, did what he could to prepare for a possible British attack, but he wrote Secretary Smith that he had available only "four old gun boats" and needed 150 men to man them.

He reported several "insolent and menacing" British messages, and he believed the British might attempt a night boat attack to try to cut out the *Chesapeake* or the French frigate *Cybelle*. While confident he could thwart such an operation, he asked that new gunboats be brought into service as completed. He also recommended six frigates be fitted out and expressed the hope that, if this were done, he would "not be continued in Gun Boats."[13]

A clash with the British was only narrowly averted. On June 26, despite the mood in Norfolk, Captain Douglas pushed the matter of communicating with British authorities ashore by sending one of his dispatch schooners, the *Hope*, to the city. It anchored near Fort Nelson and sent a small boat to shore carrying Lieutenant Manderson of the *Bellona* with letters for Consul Hamilton to convey to the ambassador in Washington, Erskine. Hamilton, fearful for Manderson's life, went immediately to the courthouse and called on Mayor Lee and other government leaders to protect him. Although, as Hamilton put it, they "objected in the strongest Terms to his Advice Boat having been sent up," they agreed to go to Hamilton's house, where Manderson had just arrived. A crowd of some hundred people had gathered and was "insisting in the most clamorous and violent Manner that the British Officer should be given up to them, as an Atonement for the Blood shed on board the *Chesapeake*." As government officials sought to reason with the crowd, some of the mob dragged Manderson's yawl into the street to prevent his escape. Meanwhile, men armed with muskets and bayonets set out in boats for the schooner and were about to board her when the midshipman in charge, acting on Douglas's orders, hoisted a white flag of truce "and claimed the Protection of the Fort, the Commandant of which agreed to take the Schooner under his Custody." Some time later Decatur and city officials succeeded in convincing the crowd to let the British lieutenant depart.[14]

On June 26 Secretary Smith wrote to Lt. Benjamin Read at Baltimore to countermand an order for the sale of the schooner *Revenge* there and instead direct that she be fitted out for immediate service. That same day he ordered Decatur to take command of the *Chesapeake* "and prepare her for sea." Gordon would remain aboard the frigate as flag captain. Decatur received command of all U.S. Navy forces on the southern U.S. coast. Smith also wrote Barron that Decatur was succeeding him and instructed him to turn over to Decatur all correspondence from the department. Barron was to "remain at Hampton until you shall hear from me."[15]

The Americans strengthened the defenses of Norfolk. On June 24 Gov. William H. Cabell appointed militia commanders and ordered small arms sent to Norfolk. After President Jefferson called for restraint, Cabell instructed Brig. Gen. Thomas Mathews, commander of the 9th Brigade of Virginia Militia (composed of regiments from Norfolk, Norfolk County, and Princess Anne County), to avoid rash action; but he also ordered other militia units to Mathews's command.[16]

Mathews did what he could to repair Fort Norfolk and mounted nine 18-pounders there. He also ordered a detachment of the "Norfolk troop of horse" to the Capes to prevent the British from obtaining supplies ashore. By mid-July Mathews's brigade numbered some 1,600 men—infantry, cavalry, and artillery—and included militia from as far away as Richmond and Petersburg.[17]

On June 27 Captain Tingey at the Washington Navy Yard wrote to his close friend, Capt. John Rodgers, at Havre de Grace, Maryland. Noting that the *National Intelligencer* account of the incident was apparently "pretty much as it happened," he commented extensively on Berkeley's order but declined to pass blame, since "it is not improbable you or myself—or even both—may have to sit in judgement thereon." He did note, however, that Gordon was staying with him and that "from what I can learn his conduct will redound to his honor—as will that of the Lieut. &c." Tingey reported that the incident had "caused here, much perturbation. . . ." Jefferson had sent for the secretary of war, Maj. Gen. Henry Dearborn, and Secretary of the Treasury Albert Gallatin, and Tingey speculated that Decatur would receive Barron's Mediterranean command.[18] In a later letter to Rodgers, Tingey summed up sentiment among U.S. Navy officers when he wrote, "let us have peace if we can on honourable terms, but at all events Death before dishonor."[19]

Word of the incident also spread abroad. Commodore Hugh Campbell aboard the *Constitution* in the Mediterranean heard about it via a Boston newspaper account just as he was about to sail for Gibraltar "in the expectation of meeting the *Chesapeake* which Vessel I have frequently been informed was fitting out for this station." Campbell prepared for action with the British by arming the *Hornet* with four 32-pounder carronades from his ship, and he ordered the squadron to avoid Gibraltar and other British ports.[20]

On July 14 Smith ordered Capt. Isaac Hull of the schooner *Bald Eagle* to the Mediterranean with a letter for Campbell: "Sir, Hostile intentions on the part of Great Britain, have been manifested towards us, and in consequence the President of the United States has determined to call home immediately all our Publick Vessels of War. . . ." Campbell was to bring home stores at Malta and instruct agents at Leghorn and Syracuse in Italy and at Gibraltar to sell off theirs. "These orders you are to execute without one moment's delay. Disclose them to no one, not even to your most confidential officer, and you will manage to execute them that no one shall suspect your object." If the *Wasp* had not already arrived, orders were to be left for her return to the United States immediately. It was 1815 before the U.S. Mediterranean squadron was reconstituted.[21]

At noon on July 1 Decatur formally took command of the *Chesapeake*. Four hours later Commodore Barron left the frigate for Hampton, limping off past a line of his officers.[22] That same day Decatur informed Norfolk that he had to concentrate on reequipping the *Chesapeake* and was suspending work on the gunboats, which would, however, remain where they were "with every thing on board, ready for such measures as the government may direct or emergencies call for."[23]

A June 23 survey of the "late U. S. Frigate *Chesapeake*" found twenty-two round shot in her hull, all but one in the starboard side, but Decatur's report of July 4 put the number of shot in the hull at only fourteen, the damage from which "can be repaired in four days by six carpenters." Two 12-pound shot had rendered the spare fore topmast "entirely unfit for service," the second cutter was "much injured" by a shot that passed through her and cut both of her masts and oars, and the first cutter was "slightly injured." British fire had "irreparably" damaged both mizzen and main masts. The foremast had been struck by one shot but could be repaired. Shot had cut away seven of the fore and main shrouds as well as the main and spring stays, but these could be repaired. The mizzen rigging was beyond repair. The frigate could be completely repaired in three weeks.[24]

While Decatur exercised the *Chesapeake*'s crew at her guns on a regular basis, sometimes twice a day, Naval Constructor Josiah Fox, who arrived at Norfolk on July 2, supervised twenty-two shipwrights and mast-makers from the Washington Navy Yard in restoring the frigate to serviceable condition.[25]

As the Norfolk newspaper put it: "The *Chesapeake* is lying in Hampton Roads without any colours! And strange to tell the *Leopard* is triumphantly riding at anchor within our waters near the Capes!"[26]

Decatur had reason for alarm. The British not only kept their squadron inside the Capes but brought to all vessels passing in and out by firing warning shots. Douglas planned to deny passage of vessels to Norfolk until the citizen resolves were rescinded.[27]

As one U.S. historian put it, "Many British officers, with their paranoid attitude of whining superiority so common among them, chose to believe England the aggrieved party."[28] Indeed, Admiral Berkeley reported that "it was by the pertinacity of the American Captain [that Captain Humphreys was] compelled to use force."[29] He maintained that Jefferson was working the affair for political purposes. The admiral wrote Earl Bathurst in August 1807: "The violence of the American rabble still continues, and as it accords with the views of Jefferson and his party, it is not checked by Government, but is kept up by every means in the numerous newspapers that are published." Berkeley reported the Americans were fortifying their harbors, and he professed to believe that, when they had "secured themselves," they might avail themselves of a "secret plan," regarding which he said French emigré Gen. Jean Victor Marie Moreau had given warning, to attempt a *coup de main* against the dockyard and stores at Halifax. With "a few more ships," Berkeley would "be tempted to run up to New York with the squadron before the harbour is secured and wait there for the issue of negotiations, as having the city under the terror of destruction would insure a favourable issue to any terms you might propose." He advocated the creation of a squadron with a "flying army of 5,000 men in coppered fast-sailing transports"; it would be able to keep the entire U.S. coastline "in alarm" and thus prevent the United States from detaching forces to mount an attack on Nova Scotia or Canada. A few days later Berkeley even advocated a preventive attack on New York: The city had "so large a quota of the national wealth" that a *coup de main* there would "disable" Americans from going to war and "compel them to any treaty." He believed this could be accomplished by four ships of the line, two bomb vessels, four large frigates, and six or eight gun brigs.[30]

The British squadron in the Chesapeake, meanwhile, landed crews to get water despite the threats of the Americans. On July 3 there was almost a major naval battle in Hampton Roads, the deep-water anchorage immediately west of the Chesapeake Bay and connected to it by a channel between Old Point Comfort on the north and Willoughby Spit on the south. On the afternoon of the second, Captain Douglas took four British ships—the liners *Bellona* and *Triumph*, the *Leopard*, and the *Melampus*—

up from Lynnhaven Bay and anchored in the Roads. The next morning he sent a letter by boat to Mayor Lee of Norfolk in which he referred to the public resolution of June 29 prohibiting contact with the British ships. Characterizing this as "extremely hostile," Douglas threatened,

> if this infringement is not *immediately annulled* [emphasis in original], to prohibit every vessel bound either in or out of Norfolk, to proceed to their destination, until I know the pleasure of my government, or the commander in chief on this station. You must be perfectly aware that the British flag never has, nor will be insulted with impunity.

His squadron could "easily obstruct the whole trade of the Chesapeake." The matter of "deserters, lately apprehended from the United States frigate *Chesapeake*," was, he said, a matter to "be decided between the two governments *alone*. It therefore, rests with the inhabitants of Norfolk, either to engage in a war or remain on terms of peace." Douglas called for a response, "without delay." While this letter was being delivered to Mayor Lee, British tenders took soundings in the Elizabeth River channel almost to Crany Island.[31]

In order to bring maximum firepower to bear against any British attack, Decatur moved the *Chesapeake* and French frigate *Cybelle* to the narrows between Norfolk harbor and the channel, positioning them perpendicular to the channel. Between the two ships Decatur placed the four gunboats; they faced the channel so their bow guns could bear.[32]

Decatur commanded not only the Norfolk gunboats but also those recently constructed at Hampton and in Mathews County. Smith ordered Decatur to concentrate on preparing the Norfolk gunboats for service. Smith ordered the bomb ketch *Spitfire* readied and her sea mortar mounted, and he informed Decatur that he hoped to send her to Norfolk within ten to twelve days with muskets, pistols, cutlasses, battle axes, powder, and any other supplies Decatur might request. Decatur pointed out to Smith that the ketch would be of little use: she "can not render material Service at this place, nor can She, or any Morter [sic] Vessel, be used against Shipping to any advantage." He did, however, submit an extensive list of small arms and ammunition required.[33]

In addition to ordering preparations at Norfolk, Smith called for gunboats and bomb ketches to be made ready and concentrated at New Orleans, Charleston, Norfolk, and New York.[34] Fears that the British in Hampton Roads might attempt to destroy gunboats there led Smith to instruct Capt. Samuel Barron to keep those he had been superintending at Hampton and Mathews County in place until they could safely be moved to Norfolk. He urged Barron to rush them to completion and secure militia for their protection.[35]

Mayor Lee, meanwhile, met with the Norfolk aldermen, and they approved a reply sent to Captain Douglas on July 4. While the note was defiant in tone ("We are prepared for the worst you may attempt. . . ."), Lee pointed out "that the act of which you complain, is an act of individuals, and not of the government."[36]

The situation at Norfolk so alarmed Jefferson that on July 5 the cabinet decided to call on state governors to ready 100,000 militia: "The object is to have the portions on the sea-coast ready for any emergency; and for those in the North we may look to a winter expedition against Canada." Virginia's quota by the Act of April 18, 1806, was 11,563 men. Two days later, at another meeting, the cabinet decided to ask Governor Cabell "to order such portion of militia into actual service as may be necessary" to defend Norfolk and the gunboats at Hampton and Mathews County. Jefferson was being drawn into preparations for war.[37]

The crisis began to abate on July 5 when the prominent Norfolk attorney Littleton W. Tazewell, accompanied by his friend James Taylor, carried Mayor Lee's reply to Captain Douglas. Tazewell was invited on board the *Bellona*, met by Douglas at the gangway, and then conducted to his cabin for a meeting with the squadron captains. Douglas read Lee's letter and passed it to Capt. Sir Thomas Masterman Hardy, captain of the 74-gun *Triumph*, who gave it to the other captains in turn. Douglas did his best to defuse the situation by insisting that his letter had "contained no expression of menace which he recollected, and that it was certainly not his intention to use language which could be construed to convey such ideas. . . ." He said he "had no orders to commit any act of hostility" and was anxious to "preserve the relations of amity, which had existed between the two governments. . . ." He denied having made any insulting remarks and added that, if any had been made by his officers, they were not authorized. He had wanted only to be able to communicate with "accredited officers of his government"; the means by which this was accomplished was a matter of indifference. Tazewell thought Douglas sincere and said that his treatment was "marked by as much attention, politeness, and respect, as any gentleman ever received from others." In its July 8 edition, the Norfolk paper printed Tazewell's report to Mayor Lee of his meeting with Douglas.[38]

Norfolk was not alone in its alarm. A "Corresponding Committee of the Inhabitants of Norfolk, Portsmouth and its Vicinities" sent letters to other seacoast cities, and they responded. On July 8 a citizens' meeting at Wilmington, North Carolina, unanimously held that "our rights as an Independent nation" had been assaulted and that the "recent outrage committed at Norfolk" was "tantamount to a declaration of war, or a flagrant violation of our sovereignty." The citizens pledged solidarity with Norfolk and dedicated themselves to cooperate "in such measures of redress, vindication, or satisfaction, as the constituted authorities of our country may deem proper to pursue." They voted to halt provisioning of British ships of war and end pilot service for British warships and privateers on the Cape Fear River.[39] On July 15 a like committee at Charleston requested that gunboats there "be got in readyness to defend this Harbour against any attack which may be made."[40]

Secretary Smith took other steps. He ordered Captain Rodgers, then fitting out Gunboat No. 7 at Havre de Grace, to take command of gunboats and bomb vessels at New York. Rodgers increased his flotilla of one bomb vessel and fourteen gunboats by adding bomb ketches and seventeen gunboats (Nos. 29 through 45) from Portland, Newport, and Middletown.[41] The nine Portland gunboats arrived at New York under the command of Lt. James Lawrence. By September Rodgers had thirty-one gunboats and three bomb vessels, divided into two divisions of seventeen boats each, commanded by Lawrence and Lt. Oliver H. Perry.

One veteran of the Revolutionary War, concerned about the possibility of "surprize, ruin & destruction of our Cities which it is possible for them [the British] to approach, with their Ships of war . . . [and] . . . that we may not be injured more than we have allready [sic] been by them," wrote General Dearborn to suggest that "To keep them from our Rivers & Bays can only be done by red hot balls." He recommended construction of additional gunboats and portable furnaces "in which a 24-pound ball may be heated in 30 minutes with a bushel of Charrcoals."[42] Another citizen offered a plan for a moored floating battery, "Perfectly Round the sides to rise about 6 or 7 feet above the floor and Pierced at proper Distances with port holes for the Guns."[43]

Jefferson believed the situation was highly dangerous and wrote Secretary Dearborn on July 7: "The British commanders have their foot on the threshold of war." He was concerned the British might attempt to sail to Norfolk and possibly bombard it.[44] Dearborn wrote Governor Cabell that the president had authorized him to call on governors to have militia available "in readiness to march at a moments warning. . . ."[45]

On July 6 Captain Douglas sent a second, conciliatory, letter to Mayor Lee. He noted that "as every circumstance relative" to Lee's letter of the fourth had been fully discussed with Tazewell and Taylor, he "had only in addition to remark, that as far as I am individually concerned, every exertion shall be used that can, consistent with the honour and dignity of the British flag, tend to an amicable termination."[46] Two days later Smith ordered Decatur to allow transmission of Erskine's dispatches to Douglas.[47] That same day Erskine advised Douglas to avoid any hostilities until London sent instructions, and that evening Douglas ordered two of his four ships, the *Triumph* and the *Melampus*, back to the Lynnhaven Bay anchorage.[48] Five days later, on the thirteenth, the *Bellona* and the *Leopard* also left Hampton Roads.[49]

Erskine was not alone in urging caution on Douglas; Consul Hamilton did the same after the British ships had been withdrawn. Hamilton, who had been consul at Norfolk since 1789, was a tireless voice for conciliation and much appreciated by the citizens of Norfolk, judging from their subsequent testimonials.[50]

Secretary of the Treasury Gallatin did not believe a British land attack was imminent. He wrote his wife on July 8:

> They will not venture on any hostilities on shore until they receive orders from Great Britain; for their naval arrogance induces them to make unfounded distinctions between what is legal on land or on water even within our jurisdiction, and they have not really sense or knowledge enough to feel that their present conduct within the Chesapeake is as much actual invasion as if an army was actually landed. . . .[51]

In mid-July Captain Douglas sailed for Halifax in the *Bellona*, taking with him the four men from the *Chesapeake*. His successor was Captain Hardy of the *Triumph*, formerly Nelson's flag captain on the *Victory*. Hardy recognized the volatility of the situation and ordered his ships out of sight of land, where they could still maintain a loose blockade. Hardy also sent the *Leopard* to Bermuda. She never returned to an American port.[52]

Captain Hardy was in broad agreement with Erskine. He told Hamilton that the latter's appeal was full of

> moderation and Peace, which so fully accords with my ideas that nothing on my part shall be wanting (consistent with my Duty as an

Officer) to reestablish that friendship between the two nations so essentially beneficial to both, and as I trust that no insult will be offered to the British Flag, every conciliating measure shall be adopted.[53]

American defensive preparations continued, however. On July 9 a large quantity of gunpowder from Baltimore and shot and small arms from Washington arrived at Norfolk.[54] Smith also ordered Captain Hull to Norfolk to serve under Decatur and take charge of the gunboats there. He wanted gunboats at Hampton and in Mathews County moved to Norfolk "as soon as they can be taken with safety."[55]

On July 14 Decatur reported the *Chesapeake* was nearly ready: "the Hull is now compleated, the fore, & mizzen masts will be in today, & the main masts will be finished by the middle of this week, after which we shall be ready in a very short time for any service." A day later he had six gunboats in service: Nos. *1, 4, 58, 59, 68,* and *69.* Two of the Hampton gunboats arrived four days later, and Decatur sent officers to take charge of those in Mathews County when launched. Seamen were in short supply, however. At thirty men per boat, he needed 480. By July 19 only 11 had signed up; even at the end of the month, men were signing on at a rate of 1 per day, and Decatur sent Lt. Joseph Tarbell and two midshipmen to recruit at Baltimore.[56]

Withdrawal of the British ships from Hampton Roads returned the bay area to normal; although British warships regularly transited in and out of the Chesapeake, they made no attempts to land and, as the Norfolk paper reported, behaved "with great politeness to the vessels going out and coming in, giving them no interruption." The writer of the article regretted that Hardy had not been in command from the beginning: "We think he would never have written such a letter as that of Commodore Douglas, which had been productive of indignation scarcely short of that produced by the original outrage."[57]

Meanwhile Berkeley was seeking to justify his actions to London. On July 16 some of the crew of the British schooner *Vesta* mutinied. Twenty-five men escaped: eight "pretended" to be Americans, but the others were Irishmen and British West Indian subjects of the crown, Berkeley said. After this incident the *Vesta* put in to the Chesapeake Bay before proceeding to Halifax. Berkeley reported to London that she had brought

Confirmation of the *Chesapeak* Frigate's Crew being mostly English Seamen, as two English Vessels who were permitted to leave Norfolk, reported to the Captain of the *Leopard* that on the 16th Inst. 150 men of the Frigate went to the Captain on the Quarter Deck and refused serving under the American Frigate in the Event of Hostilities between the two Nations, and demanded their Discharge on The English Merchant Ships then quitting the port, which was refused by the Officers.[58]

On July 27, despite rainy weather, Fox finally had the *Chesapeake* ready for sea.[59] On August 1 Decatur moved the frigate and gunboats into the bight of Crany Island "to prevent desertion, & keep the crew healthy, neither of which could have been effected lying in the harbour of Norfolk."[60] Two weeks later, with more bravado than candor, he reported:

I fear we shall not be able to act offensively, without risquing more than would be justifiable. Gun Boats ought never to act against heavy Shipping, unless they have Shoal Water, or a place to return to, in case of a Breeze. Where the British now are there is neither, but should they return again to Hampton Roads, and we have Men, we will convince them our boats are Superior to their Ships.[61]

During this time there were some incidents with the British that might have had serious repercussions. On August 30 Lt. John Rowe's Gunboat No. *30* was at latitude 40° 36′ off New York when she encountered the HMS *Nimrod,* a 26-gun sloop-of-war bound for Halifax from the West Indies. The *Nimrod* fired seven shots in No. *30*'s direction, forcing her to heave to. At "the particular request" of James Pearse, the *Nimrod*'s captain, Rowe went aboard the sloop and was detained for an hour, although he reported that he was "treated with attention and politeness."[62]

Another incident occurred early in September. Two British warships— the frigate *Jason* and large brig *Columbine*—appeared off New York and anchored, the *Columbine* inside of Sandy Hook and the *Jason* near the entrance of the narrows. On September 4 Captain Rodgers, hoisting his flag in No. *8,* took five gunboats to force the British from U.S. waters. On the way he conferred with Secretary Gallatin at Governor's Island. Gallatin told Rodgers that the president did not want to use force and that the gunboats should not proceed farther, as they "might have the appearance of menace." Rodgers decided to await orders; before he received any, the British sailed.[63]

From mid-July the British squadron was anchored between Capes Henry and Charles. Near Cape Henry the British sent parties ashore to dig for fresh water. Militia surprised one such landing party from the *Triumph* and opened fire. The seamen ran into the woods but surrendered in the morning. The Americans took a master's mate, midshipman, and three seamen to Norfolk, not as prisoners of war but as "offenders against the law." Another volunteer formation, including a young lawyer cum lance corporal named Winfield Scott, took two midshipmen and six seamen, all unarmed. Another British party ashore put off when militia cavalry appeared.

The captured seamen were returned in early August. Captain Hardy wrote to General Mathews to thank him for the return of "The Midshipmen and three men that improvidently quitted His Majesty's Dispatch schooner *Hamilton* [tender to the *Triumph*] for the amusement of fishing. . . ."[64]

On July 27 the Norfolk paper reported that although some of the British ships in the bay went out and returned each day, the British had made no attempt to land. The story added, "Commodore Sir Thomas Hardy . . . behaves as far as we can learn with great politeness to the vessels going out or coming in, giving them no interruption. . . ."[65] The threat to Norfolk had eased to the point that the Petersburg and Richmond militia, commanded by Major Ambler, were embarked on two vessels to return up the James. They departed with salutes from Forts Norfolk and Nelson and cheers from seamen on the *Chesapeake*. On August 3 all of Mathews's land force was disbanded with the exception of a troop of cavalry (Capt. R. B. Taylor), a company of artillery (Captain Nelson), and a company of Princess Ann militia.[66]

This left defense of Norfolk to the *Chesapeake*, the French frigate *Cybelle*, gunboats, and Forts Nelson and Norfolk. The Norfolk paper thought this inadequate. The *Cybelle* would fight if attached but was a foreign vessel, and no "publick money" had been expended on Fort Norfolk. The paper believed the government "relies too much on the *volunteer system*, for both men and money. . . . We have had a short but satisfactory lesson on this subject. The *sixteen Gun Boats* would, no doubt, be a considerable acquisition. But where we ask are they?"[67] Even by August 27, despite recruits from Baltimore and Philadelphia and marines from Washington, Decatur could man just eight of his fourteen gunboats. It was not until November 19, nearly five months after the *Chesapeake-Leopard* incident, that sixteen Norfolk gunboats had commanding officers, and only five were lieutenants. Decatur arranged them in four divisions: 1st (Nos. *1, 60, 64,* and *66*), 2nd (Nos. *5, 61, 67,* and *69*), 3rd (Nos. *10, 58, 63,* and *68*), and 4th (Nos. *4, 59, 62,* and *65*).

On August 7 the Norfolk paper reported that the *Triumph* in the Chesapeake Bay and the *Columbine* in Hampton Roads were the only British ships "in our waters." In a gesture of goodwill, Hardy had returned some blacks who "had got on board the *Triumph*."[68] On August 25 Governor Cabell discharged Captain Taylor's cavalry troop, retaining in service only an infantry company commanded by Capt. John Reade and an artillery company under Capt. Peter Nestelle at Fort Norfolk.[69]

At the end of August Decatur reported to Secretary Smith that fifty-six men of the *Chesapeake*'s crew were sick from influenza. He thought a short cruise would "be of infinite service to them." The frigate was "now in high order, & the crew is well acquainted with the use of their guns, as I could wish them.— In fact, Sir, I would rejoice in an opportunity of risquing my reputation in her, along side one of their proudest ships of equal force—I feel confident Sir, if put to trial, the event would prove me, not a Vain boaster. . . ."[70]

By November relations between Britain and the United States had improved to the point that Smith ordered Decatur not to prevent British efforts to obtain assistance in refloating the schooner *Zenobia*, driven ashore about twenty-five miles south of Cape Henry in October 1806.[71]

Meanwhile, the Royal Navy dealt with the four men taken off the *Chesapeake*. All were tried at Halifax. On August 26, 1807, Jenkin Ratford (John Wilson) was found guilty of mutiny, desertion, and contempt (insolence to a British naval officer). He offered little defense, although he claimed that he and the other deserters from the *Halifax* "had been persuaded by the Boatswain to enter for the *Chesapeake*, to protect themselves," Lieutenant Sinclair "asking them if they did not have a second name." Ratford also claimed he had hidden in the coal hole from fear the Americans would make him "fight against his country, which he declared he would not on any account." He then threw himself on the mercy of the court. It sentenced him to death. He was hanged from the fore yard-arm of the sloop *Halifax* on August 31. In his last remarks Ratford declared he had been born in Yorkshire.[72]

The three deserters from the *Melampus* were charged with "having in the Evening on, or about the 4th day of January last while at Anchor in Hampton Roads taken a Boat from alongside and deserting." They were found guilty, but

> in consideration of their former good conduct, and the high
> character given them by their Officers as well as the contrition they

have shewn for their Offences, the Court doth only, adjudge the said William Ware, Daniel Martin and John Strachan to Corporal Punishment, and to receive each of them, five hundred lashes on their bare backs with a Cat of nine tails, alongside of such ships at such times and in such proportions as the Commander in Chief at this place shall direct.[73]

This sentence was subsequently remitted, and the three were merely subjected to "temporary" imprisonment. Ware died in captivity, but Martin and Strachan were later brought to Boston and, on July 11, 1812, formally restored to the *Chesapeake,* from which they had been taken five years before.[74]

Captain Humphreys was in a difficult position. Captain Douglas, aware that his subordinate might be made a scapegoat, defended Humphreys and obliquely criticized Berkeley when he transmitted Humphreys's account of the encounter with the *Chesapeake* to Berkeley: "I beg leave to state, I am perfectly convinced Captain Humphreys could not have fulfilled your instructions, without having recourse to the measures which he adopted."[75]

Berkeley in no way criticized Humphreys. On July 4, when he wrote to acknowledge receipt of his report, the admiral said, "as far as I am enabled to judge by it, you have conducted yourself most properly." He also said he had informed Humphreys's wife that the captain had "fulfilled my directions." Berkeley was quite unrepentant and seemingly oblivious to the storm his orders had caused. He noted, "I hope you mind the published accounts of this affair as little as I do. We must make allowances for the heated state of the populace in a country where every tie, both civil and religious, is treated so lightly."[76]

News of the attack on the *Chesapeake* reached London on July 26. On August 2, before the American minister could make demands for redress, London conveyed to Washington its disavowal of the right to search ships in the national service of any state for deserters and a promise of suitable reparation for an "unauthorized act." On October 16 London issued "A proclamation for recalling and prohibiting seamen from serving foreign princes and states," which declared that British naval officers could no longer claim the right to seize deserters from the national ships of other countries.

By September 14 the Norfolk newspaper had proclaimed the crisis at an end: "It is now certain that the attack on the *Chesapeake* was not only an act unauthorized by the British Government but that it is disapproved of, and that reparation is promised. It is therefore very probable, that this affair will be adjusted, and the nation remain at peace. . . ."[77]

In a gently worded order of August 24 Whitehall recalled Berkeley, making reference to the "unfortunate transaction." The Admiralty informed him that it had never given instructions to issue "such an order of so preemptory a Nature as that of 1st June, tending to produce . . . so decisive a cause of proceeding on a question between two Nations of such Magnitude and importance." It went on to state, "This unauthorized act in a Matter of such high Moment has induced their Lordships to think it will be expedient to appoint an Officer to succeed you in command of the American station." With no word from the U.S. government, the Admiralty was at a loss as to instructions to guide his successor, and that "may therefore delay his arrival for a time."[78]

It was not until October 3 that Berkeley received the recall order. He expressed profound disappointment: "I cannot sufficiently express my regret . . . persuaded as I am that my conduct will bear the strictest investigation, and confident that the orders I issued were not only necessary, but *specifically authorized*. I must therefore conclude my recall, to be a matter of political expedient, of which, at present, I will not complain, although I may be its victim." He also sought to reassure the Admiralty that "apprehensions of my proceeding to Hostilities" were unfounded and "their injunctions to the contrary" unnecessary.[79]

In December, before his departure, Berkeley ordered Captain Hardy and the *Triumph,* which had returned to Halifax, to sail back to the Chesapeake. Meanwhile he left Halifax in the *Leopard* (Captain Humphreys) for Bermuda. Hardy's return excited no anxiety at Norfolk.[80] Before he left Halifax Berkeley saw his eldest daughter, Louisa, marry Hardy.

Berkeley's family connections were undoubtedly behind William Grenville's reluctance to speak publicly of the *Chesapeake-Leopard* Affair. No actions were taken against Berkeley. In December 1808 he received command of an important naval squadron off the Spanish and Portuguese coasts during the Peninsular Campaign and in July 1810 was promoted to the rank of full admiral. He returned to England in 1812 and retired from public life. Berkeley died in 1818.[81]

Captain Humphreys, whose conduct the editor of the *Royal Naval Biography* characterized as "not only unimpeachable, but, in a very high degree, praise-worthy," returned to England with Berkeley in 1808 and was placed on half pay. Although he attained flag rank in 1840, Humphreys never again held command at sea. As he noted a few years before his death in 1845, "notwithstanding repeated applications for a ship, I have never obtained an appointment since. I have now the rank of Rear-Admiral, having been passed over in the promotion in consequences of not having served the requisite time; how could I do so if, to conciliate the United States, the Admiralty would not employ me?" Humphreys even sought command of the *Chesapeake* after her capture by the *Shannon* in the War of 1812, "but neither this nor any other application met with success." A few years before his death Humphreys changed his name to Davenport, the result of an inheritance from his second wife. He did have the consolation of wealth, was named a Companion of the Bath, and received a knighthood (Knight Commander of the Guelphic Order of Hanover).[82]

In the last days of 1807 Captain Hardy returned with this bride in the *Triumph* to the Virginia Capes. Louisa noted in her diary that she went

> to the Bay of Chesapeake in N. America, and as Mr. Rose came out to settle the quarrel, we spent from December 1807 to April 1808 in that gloomy, desolate Bay, not allowed to land, as the Americans were in such an exasperated state that they might have been disagreeable.[83]

When Hardy returned the justification for the British presence was gone. The two French warships, blockaded for nearly sixteen months, took advantage of the absence of the British ships to sail into the Atlantic, the *Cybelle* on October 25 and the *Patriote* on December 16. The *Norfolk Gazette and Publick Ledger* noted on the departure of the *Cybelle*:

> This furnishes us with an evidence of the impolicy of depending upon any other, than our own means for defence. Our government some time since calculated upon this Frigate as part of the defence of Norfolk, and reduced another part of the force then employed in consequence, behold, she is gone without leave or notice, having taken what we used to call *French leave*. We wish Monsieur a good passage to France.[84]

The departure of the French warships was accompanied, somewhat ironically in view of the *Chesapeake-Leopard* Affair, by an exchange of notes between Decatur and French Captain Cuilur. On December 4 and 5 four seamen deserted from Norfolk-based Gunboat No. *1*. One was discovered with French officers on a pilot boat at Norfolk that served as a tender to the French warships, and Decatur insisted on his return. Several other deserters got aboard the *Patriote*. The seaman who was the subject of the exchange of notes had been in the crew of the destroyed French warship *L'Impétueux* and had entered the U.S. Navy in Baltimore. The French released him and he was removed to the *Chesapeake*, but the *Patriote* sailed away with two other deserters. In reporting the incident the Norfolk newspaper noted that "the employment of foreign seamen, particularly *deserters*, will generally be productive of mischief." The editor expressed approval of what had happened, however:

> The *Patriot* [sic] carried off two seamen belonging to the service of the United States, which had deserted and went on board that ship, and with the perfect knowledge of the French officers. These men it is true were Frenchmen, but according to the American principle, having become citizens of the United States, and actually in their service, they were to be considered as American citizens. Is there any man mad enough to say, that we ought to quarrel about these men? The French commander having regained his men, not *by force*, was justified in retaining them against the claims of this country. We were the original wrong doers.
>
> The case of the other seaman is differently circumstanced, for in that instance there was an open attempt to take the man from under the authority of his officer, by a positive refusal to deliver him up when demanded, and this within our own jurisdiction.[85]

Discussions continued with the British government over deserters. In more desperate naval straits than ever, the British were even more reluctant to back down on impressment. After the *Chesapeake-Leopard* Affair the British position was that the U.S. government had failed to enforce its own orders prohibiting British deserters on U.S. warships, and London questioned whether there was in fact any sincere effort to do so. The British asked why Jefferson had not ordered an immediate court of inquiry to learn why orders had been disobeyed regarding British deserters on the *Chesapeake*. There was even a suggestion that this might have been a deliberate effort, at a time "when the great mass of the inhabitants . . . sincerely wish to be at peace with each other" on the part of the administration "to push the public mind, blind folded, to extremes."[86]

In order to remove any ambiguity on this score, Secretary Smith ordered Englishmen removed from U.S. ships. On July 16 he informed Decatur that Chaplain William Petty, said to be an Englishman, was to be removed from the *Chesapeake* and sent ashore, where he would report to Smith.[87]

Certainly there were other Englishmen in the *Chesapeake*'s crew on June 22. Henry Harvey had deserted from the Royal Navy gun brig *Ferreter* at North Yarmouth in January 1807, made his way to America, and entered for the *Chesapeake* at Norfolk on April 4. On June 22 Harvey—who had twice deserted from the American frigate—was in irons under her half deck. When a lieutenant from the *Leopard* asked him his country, Harvey replied that he was an Englishman, but he was not asked if he was a deserter. The same happened to Boatswain William Brown and Seaman Thomas Addison. Not deserters, both admitted to being English by birth but were not taken.[88] According to Brown, about two weeks after the incident there were some 60 to 70 British seamen on board the *Chesapeake*. These men, including Brown, John Bradley, Edward Gill, Thomas Tool, John Watson, Alexander Brown, a man calling himself Henrick Lewis, and John Robinson, petitioned Decatur "for leave to quit the American service, in consequence of their apprehending a War with England." Decatur told them that having "entered for the *Chesapeak,* they should not quite the service, but, if a War did take place between Great Britain and America, they should fight whether they were willing or not. . . ." Brown and fourteen other British subjects then sent a letter to Consul Hamilton identifying themselves and expressing a desire to leave American service, but Brown later said he did not know whether Hamilton received the letter.[89]

The issue continued to trouble relations between the two countries. In September two British "dispatch schooners" suffered mishap in the neighborhood of Hampton Creek, and a launch from the *Chesapeake* was sent to investigate. On the twenty-fifth Capt. Sir Robert Laurie of HMS *Milan* wrote U.S. Army Major Newton at Norfolk to point out that in the launch's crew were two deserters, "both native-born British subjects,— George Curtis from the *Triumph* and John Birk from the *Bellona* and some other Englishmen, and who related that there were several more on board the *Chesapeake* (one of whom is now second Captain of her Fore-top and bore so indifferent a Character on board the Ship he was on that he would have been turned on Shore)."[90]

This prompted Secretary Smith to inquire whether there were still British deserters aboard the *Chesapeake*. He asked specifically about Curtis and Birk. Smith wanted to know the circumstances of any deserters' recruitment, including any alias employed, and their capacity in the crew. On November 16 Decatur mustered the crew of the frigate. Her log states:

The Commodore then addressed himself to the Crew as follows.—
'I have Recd. a letter from the Secy. of the Navy requesting to
Know if there are any British Subjects.—Deserters from the British
Service, if there Were for them to Walk forward.' No One Came
forward.—The Commodore then Mentioned the Names of 2 Men,
Jno. Burke and George Curtis, and Enquir'd if they were on board.—
George Curtis, alias Thos. Powers, Came forward, and Acknowledged
his Name was Curtis, and that he Was a British Deserter, and that
he was an American born in Pasquatank North Carolina, that his
Parents Moved to England, When he was 3 Years Old, and that he
was impressed from the Brig *John,* On her Voyage from N. Brunswick
to Port Royal in Jamaica. . . .[91]

Decatur reported to Smith that Curtis/Powers undoubtedly was a deserter from the *Triumph.* He relayed the circumstances of his having been
pressed into British service and noted, "It is a well known fact Sir, that a
vast majority of our Seamen have, at some period of their lives, been
impressed into the British service." Decatur was unable to locate anyone
on the frigate named Birk (presumably he had entered under an assumed
name), and Madison later told Erskine he had no knowledge of him.[92]
Smith requested that Decatur provide information on Curtis's birthplace,
names and residence of his parents, and whether there were people in his
birthplace who could vouch for him through sworn testimony: "We want
the fact of his being a native American Citizen clearly substantiated."[93]

In December Smith sent out a circular to commanders at Norfolk, New
York, Charleston, and New Orleans, ordering the discharge from the U.S.
Navy of any foreigners "who may have deserted from a Publick Vessel of
war belonging to the foreign State of which such Deserter is a subject." On
December 25 Decatur discharged two deserters, one from the French navy
ship *Eole* and the other from the *Triumph.*[94]

Much of the negotiation between the British and Americans over impressed seamen was carried on by Capt. R. H. Bromley of the frigate
Statira, which had brought British special emissary George Rose to the
United States and remained in Hampton Roads during the three months
he was in the country. Bromley negotiated first with Larkin Smith, the
collector of customs at Norfolk, and then with Decatur.[95]

The Americans opened the exchange in January 1808 when Larkin
Smith demanded the release of George Fox, an alleged American citizen

impressed on board the *Statira* at Portsmouth, England, the previous September. Although Bromley replied in a conciliatory tone, he held that the ship's records showed Fox's claims to be a tissue of "impudent false-hoods." At the same time Bromley called in a separate letter for the return of three British subjects serving on the *Chesapeake,* all of whom wanted to take advantage of a royal proclamation of October 16, 1807, extending pardon to all Royal Navy sailors who returned "to their allegiance."[96] Decatur told Hamilton that the three men were indeed on the *Chesapeake* but that "they all deny having applied, or wished to be placed under the British Flag, one of them however acknowledges that he did inform you he was an Englishman, and wished to obtain his discharge from the United States' service."[97] There seems to be justification for questioning Decatur's answer. British seamen on the *Chesapeake* later stated they had been de-nied application to leave American service and had been held on the frigate against their will.[98]

Before the failure of Rose's mission and his return to Britain on the *Statira,* Bromley and Decatur exchanged additional notes and requests for the return of seamen. "British subjects" identified by Bromley as serving on the *Chesapeake* included Henry Harvey, George Brookes, and John Derman or Deerman.[99]

Secretary of the Navy Smith continued to resist pressure from British captains for the discharge of seamen they claimed were deserters.[100] However, on January 8, 1808, he wrote commanders of the major con-centrations of American naval vessels—Decatur (Norfolk), Isaac Chauncey (New York), and Samuel Elbert (Charleston)—ordering them to "ascertain with as much precision as may be in your power how many British & French Subjects there are in the Vessels under your com-mand. . . ."[101]

The reports from Gosport and Charleston lack sufficient data for mean-ingful analysis, but Decatur's report stated that he had sixty British seamen and thirty-four Frenchmen. Few of the French sailors had been in the United States longer than two years; the majority of the British seamen had been in America from five to twenty years and some longer. Of twenty-nine men manning three gunboats at Charleston, however, twenty were natives of the British Isles, and the remaining nine had been born in continental Europe. Of 305 naval enlisted men in Chauncey's report, 126 were said to be native-born; another seven said they had lived in the United States twenty-five years or longer (thus qualifying as citizens, even under the British definition, because they had been in the country at the time of the peace treaty ending the Revolutionary War), and sixteen produced documentary evidence of being naturalized American citizens (which, under an act of 1808, required five years of residence). As historian Christopher McKee wrote, the fact that at least two of the sixteen had lived in the United States for a year or less casts doubt on the integrity of the naturalization process. Six of the foreign-born seamen carried protections, at least one of which was suspicious. Deducting the 155 men in the categories above from the 305 leaves 150 seamen, all of whom were foreign nationals; they represent more than forty-nine percent of the total. McKee noted that if all 305 men had been placed in a merchant ship and sent to sea to be stopped by a British warship intent on impressment, the British would have recognized only the 133 men in the first two categories as U.S. citizens entitled to protection. McKee also stated that the foreign nationals who comprised nearly half of the U.S. Navy enlisted ranks at New York had probably "been knowingly recruited." He concluded that the U.S. Navy was, and for several years had been,

> dependent on recruiting foreign seamen—predominantly British nationals—for about half of its enlisted manpower. Britain's frustration with this situation as it tried to find the men to fill its ships to fight a seemingly endless war with Napoleon is understandable. That this frustration would exacerbate Anglo-American tensions and manifest itself in incidents of harassment of United States warships was only to be expected. That it would one day explode in such unauthorized and high-handed violence as the *Leopard-Chesapeake* incident of June 1807 was virtually inevitable.[102]

The information supplied to Smith helped bring a change in policy. In February 1808 the Navy Department ordered the discharge from U.S. Navy vessels of all foreigners (able and ordinary seamen, and boys). The directive specified "all persons who have come to this country since the Peace of 1783, and who have not been duly naturalized according to law."[103] In June Smith ordered commanders to enlist "none but American Citizens"—that is, "Citizens by Birth, or Foreigners who resided in the Country at the Peace of 1783, or who have been naturalized according to Law."[104] McKee noted that this policy change was probably as much to "ensure jobs for native-born seamen thrown out of work by the Embargo as to eliminate provocations to the European belligerents." After 1808 a number of British seamen remained in the U.S. Navy; it is impossible to say how many, but it is clear they were not blatantly recruited for U.S. service.[105]

Smith's order led Decatur to muster the *Chesapeake*'s crew and "tell all foreigners, that they might have their discharge." He discharged from the frigate alone twelve Frenchmen and sixteen Englishmen and Americans. Six of them were paid off on the *Chesapeake* but sent on Gunboat No. 5 to be discharged at Baltimore, probably so they would not enter on board the *Statira*. Among them were Curtis, Thomas Garnett, Harvey, and Thomas Addison. The latter two were apparently able to take advantage of the October 1807 royal pardon. Both did make it to the *Statira* and were separately interrogated on board while at sea about their time on the *Chesapeake*. Each claimed personal knowledge of about a dozen Englishmen on board the American frigate at the time of her encounter with the *Leopard* but implied that the true number was considerably greater.[106] In an affidavit of March 26, 1808, William Brown, English-born boatswain on the *Chesapeake* at the time of the encounter with the *Leopard,* stated "that he supposes full half the Crew of the *Chesapeak,* (about 200) were British Born Subjects, although may of them had American Protections. . . ."[107] Decatur provided some confirmation of this when he informed Smith in mid-April 1808, "We have discharged since the 18th. of Feby. 175 men 150 of whom were foreigners."[108]

SEVEN

President Jefferson's Dilemma

"War has nothing terrible in it, when compared to the *surrender* of our maritime rights. . . . The insurmountable barrier which England can place in the way of the American intercourse with the whole of Europe, Asia, and Africa! They cannot stir from their harbours without our leave. . . ."[1] If the American people wanted war, the London *Times* starkly stated the dangers of challenging the mistress of the seas.

In the first flush of rage over the *Chesapeake* incident, most Americans seemed willing to take that risk. Demands for war against England came from all sides as public anger at the *Leopard*'s audacity spread throughout the United States. Many Americans wanted a war to end once and for all the years of the Royal Navy's continuous insults to the dignity of their country.[2] Their president shared in the anger and branded the attack an "outrage," that created a "state of excitement in this country not seen since the battle of Lexington."[3] Robert Erskine, Britain's minister in Washington, taken aback by so much anti-British fury, warned Foreign Minister George Canning that "the indignation of the People of the United States has been excited to the most violent Extent." And he was convinced that if Admiral Berkeley acted under orders from the Admiralty "there can be no redress for what they term a national insult."[4] John Hamilton, the consul at Norfolk who had experienced firsthand the wrath of an irate mob, told Canning a few days after the incident that "it is impossible to describe the popular agitation and irritation which have prevailed at this place since the return of the *Chesapeake* to the Roads."[5]

Phineas Bond, England's consul at Philadelphia for over twenty years, had been in the United States long enough to understand Americans better than most Englishmen. He suspected the outcry was momentary public bravado that would dissipate quickly. Yet even Bond, noting results of town meetings at Richmond, Baltimore, Philadelphia, and Norfolk, cautioned Canning that "this event has excited a universal Ferment here, and it will undoubtedly pervade the whole nation. . . . The most moderate men assert, they consider their ships of War as a part of their national territory, and any Intrusion upon that Portion of their territory, as an attack upon the Sovereignty and Independence of the United States."[6] During the rest of that hectic summer of 1807 war with Great Britain seemed the only way to satisfy American national pride.

There was also fear that the attack on the *Chesapeake* was the prelude to more British military action against the United States. Rumors spread that Royal Marines had landed in Virginia and were heading for Norfolk and that British troops in Canada were poised for an invasion of New York. Some American newspapers claimed "on good authority" that England's government itself had issued the orders to stop and search ships of the U.S. Navy. Others published reports that dozens of American merchant vessels had been captured on the high seas and that hundreds of American sailors recently had been impressed into the British navy.[7]

Rumors were not limited to the western side of the Atlantic. Distance and time merely added confusion to the dangerous misunderstanding that had been developing between Jefferson's administration and the Portland ministry. For months war continued to be a very real possibility in the minds of the people of both countries as each government wondered and worried what the other might do next. When the first reports of the incident trickled into London in late July most Englishmen refused to believe that the Royal Navy could have committed such an act. The *Times* commented cautiously "we have not been able to determine whether this unfortunate rencontre was the consequence of some premeditated insult, on the part of the American frigate, or whether it arose from some circumstances capable of future accommodation."[8] But when the English press began reprinting excerpts from the most bellicose American newspapers the English reacted angrily, blaming the United States for all the problems between the two countries. The *Times* claimed the American press was "filled with invectives" and represented the "inflammable nature of the *active citizens* of the United States." Many English newspapers predicted war with the United States. The *Times* was less hostile but nevertheless prepared its readers for that eventuality. Even while hoping for peace, however, its editors were condescending: "If the Government of the United States were to take its tone from what seems to be the habitual pettishness and impetuosity of the myriads of adventurers of all nations who have inundated that country, it would be impossible to preserve peace with America for six months together."[9]

In Washington President Jefferson felt as vindictive and angry as the most contentious of his fellow citizens. It would have been quite understandable if he had truly wanted a war with England in July 1807 after all the years of frustrations from a series of British ministries. The *Chesapeake-Leopard* incident was an excellent catalyst for uniting public opinion to support a war. And had Congress been in session, public anger might have forced a war declaration. But regardless of Jefferson's own emotions, common sense dictated that he act with caution and wait for more information before determining official policy. In the meantime, he had scarcely more accurate information for assessing the rumors of British military activity than did the average citizen. The best he could do for the moment was to issue what orders he felt necessary for the defense of his country, even if this meant sending out militia to chase phantoms, and call his cabinet into emergency session to discuss ways to meet the crisis.[10]

There was too little accurate information for intelligent, informed discussion in Jefferson's cabinet. Steps had to be taken in case some or all of the rumors of British activity turned out to be true. Secretary of War Henry Dearborn, already in New York City on other matters, was ordered to remain there and organize the city's defenses.[11] Since Erskine had already protested the isolation of Royal Navy ships by the people of Norfolk and the threat of British troops landing in Virginia was a strong possibility, the president directed Virginia's Governor William Cabell to call up state militias in the region "for the defense of Norfolk and protection of the country."[12] Secretary of the Treasury Albert Gallatin was quite pessimistic about chances for peace. He felt war would be "calamitous," but he was convinced it had been forced on the United States and began to lay plans for it.[13] He particularly feared "an efficient [British] fleet on our coast late this autumn." He cautioned Jefferson they might attack New York, Norfolk, Charleston, or possibly New Orleans.[14]

Having dealt with the more immediate problems of national defense, the cabinet turned to the thornier question of how to treat with the British government. There was agreement that the United States should require from the British both an apology and an explanation for the *Leopard*'s attack. Along with the apology America should expect the return of its citizens forcibly taken from the *Chesapeake,* compensation to the families of the men killed during the attack and for damages to the ship itself, a court-martial for Captain Humphreys, and the recall of Admiral Berkeley. These were reasonable and obvious demands from a country that had suffered an unprovoked attack on one of its national ships. Presumably a reasonable government responsible for that attack—unless it had warlike intentions—would be willing to give satisfaction. And so Secretary of State Madison instructed the U.S. representatives in London, James Monroe and William Pinkney, to present these demands to Foreign Minister Canning.

Two things were quite obvious to the cabinet. Given the anxieties of the American people, the British navy could no longer enjoy the hospitality of America's neutral ports. The debate turned on how best to rid U.S. territorial waters of the ubiquitous Royal Navy. With the example of the citizens of Norfolk in mind and with the agreement of his cabinet, Jefferson on July 2, 1807, issued a proclamation ordering Britain's naval ships in U.S. ports and territorial waters "immediately and without delay to depart from the same, and interdicting the entrance of all the said harbors and waters to the said armed vessels."[15] The other obvious point was that only Congress could declare war. The president had been mindful of this when he reminded Governor Cabell "whether the outrage is a proper cause for war, belonging exclusively to Congress, it is our duty not to commit them by doing anything which would be to be [*sic*] retracted."[16]

Gallatin and Secretary of the Navy Robert Smith wanted to call Congress into session as quickly as possible. Jefferson and Madison thought this premature, but they agreed to add 100 gunboats to the coastal fleet as a precaution against a possible British invasion.[17] After considerable cabinet discussion, the president decided to wait—some said procrastinate—until October for a special session of Congress. This would not only allow time for the British government to respond to the claims Monroe and Pinkney were to present at Whitehall, it would also permit American merchantmen still at sea to return home in the event war was imminent.

Jefferson also made another momentous decision. He moved his government's insistence on redress from Great Britain for the attack on the *Chesapeake* one step farther than necessary. He decided to use the affair as an opportunity to end years of frustration over British practice and force a solution to the most irritating problem in Anglo-American relations. Over the objections of Gallatin, Dearborn, and Smith, Jefferson stipulated that Madison's instructions to Monroe and Pinkney for the American demands should include, as an equal part of the whole, the British government's disavowal of impressment from American merchant vessels as well as from U.S. naval ships. In the formal July 6, 1807, orders to his representatives in London, Jefferson tied together the specifics of the *Chesapeake-Leopard* incident and the generalities of what Britain considered a time-honored practice essential to its national defense.[18] In so doing he committed a diplomatic blunder that would haunt the rest of his presidency. His detailed instructions to Monroe and Pinkney backed Whitehall into a diplomatic corner, leaving it little room to maneuver.

It would be a nervous wait of several months before the president received Britain's response. The longer he waited, the more pessimistic he became. By August he was convinced that authority of the attack on the *Chesapeake* had come directly from the British government and therefore that "they will not give the reparation for the past and security for the future, which alone may prevent war."[19] Facing the very real probability of war, he was forced to rethink the relationships the United States had with other countries, particularly France. By now he distrusted Napoleon so much that he could not attempt some diplomatic grand design to defend the United States by isolating Great Britain. In fact, he complained, "it is really mortifying that we should be forced to wish success to Bonaparte, and look to his victories as our solution."[20]

Yet Jefferson certainly could not ignore France. As he commented to James Bowdoin, "friendship with France, and peace at least with Spain, become more interesting."[21] France was now important enough that he wanted John Armstrong, U.S. minister in Paris, to let the French know exactly the preparations Americans had taken for war with Britain. Nor did he forget to promote once again American acquisition of Florida by adding his own fillip to goad Napoleon: "England will immediately seize the Floridas as a *point d'appui* to annoy us."[22]

Fortunately, time eased the tensions. July brought no confirmations of serious British military activity in Virginia or elsewhere. And British men-of-war gradually left American ports, although often only after considerable verbal abuse of local authorities. With no invasions to confront, President Jefferson reduced land defenses along the Virginia coast to a roving cavalry patrol. His anger mellowed enough for him to permit port officials to supply British armed ships with water and food "on giving their assurance of immediate departure from our waters."[23] Significantly, as the Royal Navy reduced its presence, the pervasive public anger dissipated. If Jefferson truly wanted war in the days immediately following the *Leopard*'s attack, he had missed his opportunity. Public tempers had cooled a month later.

During that month the unfortunate Robert Erskine was trapped in the dual roles of placating an irate American government and at the same time protecting the health and safety of crews on Royal Navy ships. He was as uncertain of the actual course of events as everyone else and kept insisting to Secretary Madison that he could not believe the incident was the result of any policy of the British government: "His Majesty cannot have caused any order issued with a hostile spirit towards the United States." On the other hand, he complained to Madison about the protests he received almost daily from Royal Navy officers unable to get necessary supplies for their ships because of Jefferson's proclamation of July 2. He argued incessantly that the proclamation was a most unneutral act and an insult to the dignity of Britain's navy and should not be enforced.[24] His greatest difficulty, however, was trying to restrain angry ship captains from instigating some new incident—several did anyway—that might disrupt the unstable calm in relations between the two countries. He warned Captain Douglas, still in command of the British squadron in Chesapeake Bay, to maintain a "friendly disposition towards the United States . . . until His Majesty's Commands upon the Occassion shall be known."[25] And in two strong letters to Berkeley, Erskine suggested the admiral apologize—unless, of course, he did have specific orders to stop armed vessels of the United States—and offer definite proof that the men taken from the *Chesapeake* were British subjects. He predicted that unless the United States was assured its national ships were immune from all search "I cannot doubt War must ensue."[26]

Neither Douglas nor Berkeley helped Erskine's position. Douglas had already distributed his circular letter to the people and mayor of Norfolk protesting the order cutting off supplies to his ships and threatening to prevent ships leaving or entering Norfolk if it were not annulled immediately.[27] Berkeley was just as arrogant. His response to Erskine insisted that Commodore Barron knew all along that the men taken from the *Chesapeake* were deserters and that this "proves a tacit acknowledgement of the usuage and justice of searching for Deserters." He made no mention of an apology.[28]

Erskine's nervous dispatches were on Canning's desk soon after the first reports of the incident reached London in late July. He described how the citizens of Norfolk had cut off all contact between the shore and the British squadron and how Captain Douglas's insulting letter had increased the "Ferment which was excited throughout the United States." And he feared war as a "strong possibility."[29] By the end of July he felt a bit more hopeful. If the king apologized for the attack on the *Chesapeake*, Erskine suggested, "it would have the most powerful effect not only on the minds of the people of this Country; but would render impossible for the Congress to bring on a war upon the other points of differences at present under discussion."[30] Phineas Bond, who had never been as pessimistic as Erskine, would not have recommended such a humiliating step. More realistic than his youthful colleague, Bond predicted in early August there would be no war because "America is in no condition to wage war with Great Britain . . . the Consequence of a Rupture would be serious to us, but ruinous to the United States."[31]

George Canning responded to the incident with his usual measured contempt for the United States. Only after several vague reports trickled into London did he send a note to Monroe expressing his private regrets.[32] His politeness cooled when the dispatches from Erskine and Bond arrived, and with them copies of the most vehement American newspapers. Then he temporized and entered a nonconstructive debate with Monroe over whether the men taken from the *Chesapeake* were British or American. Canning was obviously more concerned over the nationality of the men involved than with America's reaction to the insult to its flag. He ignored Monroe's argument that nationality made no difference and that the real issue was "that, on principle, a ship of war protected all the people on board and could not be entered . . . for any purpose . . . without violating the sovereignty of the nation whose flag she bore."[33] If Canning was surprised at the boldness of Admiral Berkeley's action, he did not show it. The Admiralty certainly must have made him aware of the complaints of deserters from the Royal Navy in American merchant and naval service that poured in from British officers and consuls. Berkeley himself had insisted there were at least 10,000 such seamen and angrily notified the Admiralty he would take steps to stop the practice.[34] With such reports on his desk, Canning evinced little sympathy for the U.S. position.

Yet he had his own risks to consider. England's coalition against Napoleon had just fallen apart. He could ill afford to fan the war spirit in the United States into an open flame. At the same time, he had to avoid a political backlash if the ministry made concessions to the Americans that British public opinion would not support. There was growing popular anger against the United States after the publication in many English newspapers of the sentiments expressed in the American press. The Opposition, however, particularly the Grenvillites, demanded an explanation for the *Leopard*'s attack and argued strongly that war with America would be equally disastrous for both countries.[35] Even within the ministry there was serious division on how to deal with the Americans. Canning had to walk warily and keep a balance between defending what Britons claimed were their rights and appeasing the Americans outraged over the violation of theirs.

Even before Monroe and Pinkney had received Madison's instructions, at Canning's request King George formally apologized for the attack on the *Chesapeake*. Both the king and the foreign minister publicly stated that the Royal Navy should never stop the national ships of a neutral country and certainly not fire upon them.[36] His Majesty's Government also offered compensation to the families of the American seamen killed during the attack. To the ministry, all of this seemed a reasonable response. The government had taken responsibility for an unauthorized action by one of its naval officers and offered redress; as far as Whitehall was concerned, that should have ended the matter. But with the presentation of the formal U.S. demands in early September, the ministry's attitude changed dramatically.

When he overcame his own anger, Canning finally convinced his colleagues to make additional concessions. After considerable debate among cabinet members—all of whom believed the officers had acted correctly—Admiral Berkeley was recalled and Captain Humphreys ordered home. There was even a begrudging hint that three of the men taken from the *Chesapeake* were perhaps Americans after all and could be returned. But this was all Canning's government was willing to do. Canning refused to discuss abandoning the practice of impressment from U.S. merchantmen that Jefferson had insisted must be part of any settlement of the affair. He adamantly informed Monroe and Pinkney that it was in "the last degree hazardous, if not absolutely impractible, to stipulate for the abandonment of a practice to which the navy and the people of England attach so much importance."[37] England's foreign minister saw clearly that the U.S. government had made it impossible to ease tensions between the two countries. He confided to a friend:

> *They* insist upon mixing two questions which *we* insist upon separating. We are ready to atone where we were wrong, but

determined to maintain our rights. If they had taken our atonement by itself as we offered it, they would have appeared to have gained something. But they have so managed matters that we shall now appear to bully them even in making reparation. Nothing could be more advantageous for us than the course which they have taken.[38]

Opinion in England divided over the course that Canning took. Most newspapers and most members of Parliament grudgingly accepted the ministry's concessions as necessary to avoid a pointless confrontation with the Americans, although they were embarrassed that the king apologized. If anything, the ministry was criticized for being too conciliatory, especially in the recall of Admiral Berkeley. When the *Times* finally published Berkeley's order that had caused the whole affair, it commented only that "there was no violation of the jurisdiction of the United States; the search was not to be made unless the *Chesapeake* was found without the limits."[39] Public and press opinion throughout Britain saw nothing wrong in the Royal Navy searching the national ships of a friendly nation; most people failed even to perceive the cause of collective American anger. And when it published in an "Extraordinary Edition" the full text of Jefferson's Proclamation of July 2, the *Times* expressed shock, shared by many Englishmen, at what it labeled this "unneutral act" by the American administration.[40] But the *Times* was more moderate than most of the English press and the only newspaper in England to admit later, with some embarrassment, "it turns out to be too true" that a British frigate fired on a harmless United States revenue cutter carrying Vice President George Clinton and his daughter from New York to Washington.[41]

Week after week William Cobbett's *Political Register* was the most American-baiting journal in Great Britain. Cobbett, spokesman for the most extreme British nationalists, insisted that "we claim also a right to take our *seamen*, whether deserters or not, from on board the ships of any other nation, when we find such ships at sea . . . a right that cannot be given up without giving up that superiority at sea, which alone can give us even a chance of remaining an independent people." He called the protections granted by American consuls "a device quite novel in the affairs of nations." And he was delighted, as were other Englishmen, that American "arrogance has received a severe rebuke" from the *Leopard*'s attack.[42]

Cobbett was also playing politics when he branded as "traitors" the editors of a very small minority of moderate newspapers who had criticized the Royal Navy's actions in America. In page after page of diatribe against the United States, he accused the *Independent Whig* and the *Edinburgh Review* in particular of endangering "British liberties by want to concede American liberties."[43] Both these journals had supported the previous Grenville ministry and its moderate policies toward the United States. Cobbett wanted to dull the Grenvillite opposition in Parliament to the stringent policies of Portland's cabinet. Cobbett's perception of Britain's rights was shared by the vast majority of the English press. Even the staid *Gentlemen's Magazine* defended Berkeley's order, contending that "no course was had to compulsion, until all conciliatory measures had failed" to persuade U.S. authorities to return British deserters to their own ships.[44] Cobbett was probably correct that "the public mind seems to be made up to war with America, rather than yield the smallest particle of our rights to her."[45]

These expressions of press opinion in England indicated clearly that Jefferson had committed a serious blunder by insisting the British government disavow impressment. Even the most moderate consensus regarding the United States considered impressment so vital to national security that it would insist on the removal of any ministry making such a concession. If Jefferson wanted to fight Britain over the issue, so be it. Indeed, general planning for war in North America continued well into 1808.[46]

Canning hoped that his mild concessions to the United States would avoid a war with America so that he could turn the full attention of his government to far greater problems in Northern Europe. Napoleon had broken up the coalition of great powers arrayed against him and again brought British foreign policy to the brink of disaster. Through a series of brilliant military and diplomatic coups, the French emperor made a vassal of Prussia and forced the czar to accept French peace terms at Tilsit. France and its new-found allies were now in a position to threaten Sweden and Denmark, Europe's last remaining neutrals. Napoleon so dominated Europe that he now could tighten his "Continental System," a total blockade of the European coast intended to bankrupt and starve England into submission.

One key to the success of Napoleon's system was Denmark's navy. Not only could it block Britain's access to Baltic trade, it could be used with other fleets under French control to challenge the Royal Navy on the high seas. Britain could not tolerate such threats, and her government demanded that the Danes surrender their fleet for safe-keeping in England. Caught between the land power of France and the seapower of Britain, the Danes hesitated. While they delayed, a British army landed on the peninsula and a squadron of the Royal Navy swung into Copenhagen's harbor. When the Danes finally refused the British demand, the combined forces bombarded the city, killing hundreds of civilians and destroying a third of its buildings. The Danes had no alternative but to surrender the remnants of their fleet. Britain had removed a threat to its national security, but at a terrible price to its reputation. "Copenhagen" struck fear of England in other small countries and earned the bitter enmity of generations of Danes.

This blatant violation of Danish sovereignty stimulated anti-war liberals throughout England and encouraged the long-simmering peace movement among its working classes who had suffered the heavy burden of years of warfare. An embarrassed growl of protest came from the Opposition. Yet in general the public supported the action and believed it necessary, if unfortunate.[47]

The lesson of an adamant British ministry's callous treatment of such a small neutral could not be lost on other irksome neutrals. Would Britain hesitate to ignore the claimed rights of the United States?

Despite its arrogant stand toward Denmark, Britain's cabinet knew it was necessary to resolve the *Chesapeake* crisis. It had made all the concessions to Jefferson's administration it could. Having already earned public censure for the king's apology and the recall of Berkeley, the ministry dared not risk further public criticism that could undermine its support in Parliament.[48] (In fact, it mollified some of the critics by giving Berkeley command of the British fleet off the coast of Portugal—in effect promoting him).

Canning became furious when James Monroe pushed too hard and implied that impressment of American sailors indicated Britain's continued lack of respect for the United States. The foreign minister accused the U.S. government of using the crisis to extort a denial of impressment; to that he promised "an unqualified refusal."[49] After consultation with the cabinet he decided "it would be useless to prolong discussion" if Monroe and Pinkney could not separate the general issue of impressment from the specific problems rising from the *Chesapeake* crisis.[50] He informed the two Americans that he preferred to negotiate directly with Jefferson and Madison and therefore would send a special emissary to Washington. Much to Monroe's disgust, Canning also told them he was now unwilling to reopen the moribund discussions to negotiate a replacement for the expired Jay Treaty. For Monroe this meant an end to his mission; he returned home and left to William Pinkney the responsibility for representing the U.S. government in London.

Canning's motives are unclear. He may have honestly desired conciliation. However, his choice of the young and relatively inexperienced George
Rose as his special emissary may indicate he only intended to pay lip
service toward reaching a solution. Or he may have believed the United
States simply had not the courage to fight for its proclaimed national
rights, and when confronted with the adamant refusal to discuss impressment Jefferson would back down.[51] At any rate, the uncompromising and
inflexible instructions he gave to Rose doomed the mission before the
emissary sailed from Portsmouth. Regardless of his motives, Canning's
contempt for the United States made impossible any reasonable settlement
of differences between the two countries.

Although Rose was permitted to admit that Berkeley's order was an
"unauthorized act of hostility," he was to stress that it was the natural
result of "instances of insult towards the Officers of H. My's Ships, and of
Seduction of the crews." And even though the king had recalled the
admiral from command at Halifax he would show no "further mark of
displeasure towards Adml. Berkeley." Because the king had disavowed the
Leopard's action immediately, Rose was to explain that Jefferson's Proclamation of July 2 was unnecessary, a "hostile act" that must be revoked as a
precondition for further negotiations. Additionally, if Rose were "delayed
beyond a reasonable time" because of the proclamation he was to return
home at once. Above all else, Canning forbade Rose "to enter into any discussion respecting the question of Impressment from merchant vessels."[52]

When Rose's ship dropped anchor at Hampton Roads in late December
American authorities, somewhat to his surprise, allowed it to remain while
he awaited permission to proceed to Washington. Until he could leave for
the national capital, the bored young diplomat interviewed the few remaining British officers in the area and read some still-hostile local newspapers. Then from the narrow confines of his shipboard cabin he sent
London his hasty observations of the American situation. Almost as con-
temptuous of America as his master, Rose actually did a disservice to his
government. His first dispatches were full of exaggeration and misinfor-
mation, and they certainly misrepresented the public attitude within the
United States.[53] They added to the growing animosity and contempt of the
British toward the United States, its people, and particularly Jefferson's
administration.[54] Worse still, they indicated his own uncompromising
mindset before he even met with the secretary of state.

Rose was already too late to affect the drift in American policy. When
Congress convened in late October other strong forces were influencing

Jefferson's thinking. For one thing, the French were now enforcing Napoleon's Berlin Decree against American shipping. They had tacitly ignored American violations of their continental blockade for months, but in early autumn they started seizing American ships. Congress was still angry enough at the British to direct the president to start applying to their commerce the Non-Intercourse Act of March 1806, but obviously not angry enough to sustain a vote for a war declaration. Its timidity disgusted Sen. John Quincy Adams of Massachusetts, who complained of "an obvious strong disposition to yield all that Great Britain may require, to preserve peace, under a thin external show of dignity and bravery."[55] Even Gallatin had lost some of his summertime enthusiasm and cautioned Jefferson that he would be open to public censure if he urged war "whilst so unprepared against attack."[56]

Now President Jefferson had to confront his dilemma: how best to preserve the dignity of the United States in the midst of Europe's ever-expanding conflict? Canning already had made it clear that England would not disavow general impressment. Jefferson could opt for war. Indeed, he had hinted at this in his message to Congress shortly after it convened in October. But the risks were great, the example of Copenhagen too ominous. Or he could do nothing, wait for Canning's special emissary, and hope that a settlement of the *Chesapeake-Leopard* incident would be satisfactory enough so that he could ignore the larger question of general impressment. This would certainly ease the tensions in Anglo-American relations. Doing nothing, however, would be a severe embarrassment for his presidency. After all, it was he who had insisted the British disavow impressment as an essential element in their offer of satisfaction for the *Leopard*'s attack. And it was he who had rejected out of hand the potentially beneficial Monroe-Pinkney treaty a year earlier because it ignored the issue. To ignore impressment now would be disastrous for Jefferson's personal prestige.

Between war and acquiescence, Jefferson found another course, but one that proved just as dangerous to his reputation. After a series of cabinet discussions he opted for the long-held American practice of economic embargo, a tradition that began when colonists refused to purchase British manufactures during the Stamp Act Crisis in 1765. His decision was made easier after learning that the British were soon to issue new restrictions on neutral commerce in Europe. Lord Percival, Britain's chancellor of the exchequer, issued in late November the new Orders-in-Council that in effect licensed all neutral ships that wished to trade with the European continent. The rules were obviously directed at Americans, whose merchantmen would be forced by the Royal Navy into English ports where they would pay a fee for English permission to proceed to a continental port. Napoleon's reaction made matters worse; his Milan Decree, issued in December, declared any such licensed ship to be British and therefore an enemy vessel whose cargo and crew faced capture and imprisonment. What Jefferson feared might happen was reality by the start of the new year. U.S. merchant ships, regardless of their destination, were stopped, searched, and often confiscated by the British or by the French and their allies.

Congress waited with mounting impatience for Jefferson to respond. While it waited, Secretary Madison sent it affidavits describing continued insults and violations of American jurisdiction by British naval officers. All of them indicated contempt for U.S. laws and public sensitivity. One British captain, for example, haughtily dismissed a directive from local authorities to leave U.S. waters, saying, "by the threat [the order] contains, you appear, like your Government, to have something to learn." (Despite his defiance, his ship sailed the next day.)[57] Such insults fanned congressional indignation. Had he wanted it, Jefferson's influence in both houses was strong enough to get a war declaration as late as mid-December. But merchant groups, fearful that war would destroy their businesses, began sending memorials requesting that Congress be cautious in its deliberations.

As late as December 12 the British consul at New York still thought war "inevitable."[58] Rather than a request for war, however, Jefferson asked Congress to levy a total embargo of all American shipping to foreign ports. His reasoning was quite simple. Given the increasing ruthlessness of all of the European belligerents toward neutral—by now almost entirely American—ships, the only way to protect U.S. merchant vessels, their cargoes, and their crews was to withdraw them totally from foreign commerce. Jefferson hoped denial of American food and raw materials would cause increasing shortages in European economies and force their governments to reassess their attitudes toward American national rights. Congressmen accepted presidential reasoning and, with a sigh of relief that he had made up his mind, hurried the necessary legislation through both houses in a matter of days—probably crossing their fingers that his premise was correct. Despite vague criticism from congressional Federalists, who viewed the embargo as appeasement of Napoleon, at the end of 1807 the United States by its own law had cut itself off from all international trade carried in its own ships.[59]

Since the start of the war in Europe in 1793 the United States had faced continuous interference with its overseas commerce and increasing impressment of its seamen into some other country's navy. Despite years of continuous protest, retaliatory non-importation legislation, and brief embargoes, the United States could never free itself from this pressure. Finally, when the insults to national pride became unbearable, drastic action was necessary. And the Embargo of 1807 was truly drastic action, probably more so than war itself. But the United States had never really prepared for war, and a war against Great Britain could have thrown the country into an unwelcome alliance with France; Americans now distrusted Napoleon as much as they disliked the British. For President Jefferson the Embargo, as unpopular as it would become, was the lesser evil.

It would be difficult, therefore, for George Rose to reach a satisfactory settlement of the *Chesapeake* Affair, for Jefferson had cast his die well before the young Englishman arrived at the national capital in mid-January of 1808. Nonetheless, Secretary of State Madison was willing to work with Rose on the specifics of the British offer for redress and compensation for the attack. The stumbling block was Rose's insistence that the United States revoke the July proclamation, which ordered British ships out of U.S. waters, before any discussion could take place. And Rose hampered the negotiations by slowly revealing other demands that were in Canning's instructions. Even a compromise that would have revoked the proclamation simultaneously with American acceptance of British compensation failed.[60]

During all these discussions Madison was in a difficult political situation. He had been selected by the Republican congressional caucus as the candidate in the next fall's presidential election, but now he drew opposition from a small group of dissatisfied Republican congressmen promoting the candidacy of James Monroe. Calling themselves the "old Republicans" and headed by the vociferous John Randolph of Virginia, they had broken with the administration as early as 1805 over the methods of using France to acquire the Floridas. They promoted Monroe as much to embarrass Jefferson as to thwart the ambition of Madison, whom they did not trust.[61] In addition to this opposition within his own party, Madison was closely identified with the increasingly unpopular Embargo. If he did not reach a settlement with Rose, his reputation as a statesman would be seriously damaged, and with it his presidential aspirations. Unfortunately for Madison and his country, the mission failed, and Rose returned to England in early March.[62] There would be no British compensation for damages and no British commitment to release the three remaining Americans taken from the *Chesapeake.*

Jefferson's administration now waited for its policy of national self-denial to coerce the European powers to respect American neutral rights. But many Americans were unwilling to wait long. Enterprising ship captains soon were evading the restrictions and defiant traders were smuggling goods into Canada by way of Lake Champlain.[63] Congress had drafted the original Embargo legislation hastily and was forced to amend it several times to increase the president's authority to enforce it. Jefferson had insisted all along that the Embargo was an honorable way to avoid war and, if given a chance, could accomplish its goals. He willingly exercised these new powers that some found to be "dangerous and odious." In doing so he quarreled with state authorities of his own party, often threatened the personal liberties or property rights of individual citizens, and endangered the entire national economy.[64] By mid-1808 ships were rotting at their docks, there was widespread unemployment in maritime industries, and commodity prices were falling throughout the country. No wonder most Americans hated the Embargo and tried to ignore it or get it repealed.

No one knew for sure how the Embargo affected the English and the French. Too many other factors beyond U.S. control worked against it. When the European war spread to Spain and Portugal, their colonies in the Americas opened markets to British merchants who easily made up their lost trade with the United States.[65] And bumper harvests in England in 1807 and 1808 eased the shortage of wheat, while lax enforcement of Napoleon's Continental System allowed English manufactured goods to enter Europe.[66] Yet England's textile industry did feel the impact of diminished imports of American cotton; prices on the Liverpool cotton exchange doubled before the end of the year.[67]

When Canning tried to get the embargo on cotton lifted, Pinkney refused to forward his request to Washington unless the Orders-in-Council were revoked as they applied to the United States. The foreign minister stubbornly replied that "could not be acceded to."[68] Despite the impasse, Pinkney optimistically informed Madison that the Embargo was "felt with more severity everyday" in England. He was certainly encouraged in December when Canning offered to modify the Orders-in-Council; Pinkney rejected the offer, insisting that the orders must be repealed, not modified.[69] Time might be working for the Americans after all.[70]

But time was running out for Jefferson's administration. The burden on Americans was too great too maintain the "great experiment" long enough to wait for British capitulation. Federalists in New England, suspecting that Jefferson had sold out to the French, found their advantage in growing discontent. During the April 1808 state elections they gained control of the lower house of the Massachusetts legislature and successfully maneuvered to force the resignation of Sen. John Quincy Adams, a moderate Federalist who had supported the Embargo. In the fall congressional elections much of the Northeast defected to the Federalists. Even in those areas remaining loyal to the Republicans the outcry against the Embargo was pervasive.[71] Although James Madison did win the presidential election, he would not come into office with the solid Republican support that accompanied Jefferson in 1801. It was obvious that the Embargo was an embarrassment for the incoming administration. By February even Jefferson recognized "a sudden and unaccountable revolution of opinion" in Congress, where many members wanted to repeal the Embargo before Madison's inauguration. Jefferson finally admitted that "after fifteen months' continuance [the Embargo] is now discounted, because, losing $50,000,000 of exports annually by it, it costs more than war, which might be carried on for a third of that."[72] In February Congress repealed the Embargo, effective March 4, 1809, the last day of Jefferson's term. To replace the Embargo, "non-intercourse" acts directed at both Britain and France were passed.

For President Jefferson 1808 was a bitter year. What should have been the climax of a long and successful public career was shrouded in failure. Even though he had survived the vituperative attacks of John Randolph's dissident Republicans, his leadership of his own party was weakened. In that weakness the Federalist opposition gained renewed strength. In the last months of his presidency Jefferson seemed to abandon any personal direction of policy, leaving control to Gallatin and President-elect Madison.[73] He had to recognize that the drastic policy of economic coercion had failed to gain from the Europeans the respect for his nation that he so desperately wanted. Instead he had plunged the country into an economic depression that brought widespread suffering to his people, damaged his personal popularity, weakened his party's control over national affairs, and had brought the *Chesapeake-Leopard* crisis no closer to resolution.

EIGHT

Assessing the Blame

Although Barron's seven wounds were described as "slight," he had lost a portion of his right calf and remained confined to bed for four months. On July 3 he wrote Dr. Bullus that he was not able to sit up and had to "Lay on my side," but "the worst wound" was that "shot by my Country men without knowing the Merits of my Case."[1] He probably expected that his junior officers would close ranks and support him, as had been the case with those aboard the surrendered *Philadelphia* at Tripoli.

Any hopes of this were misplaced; Barron early emerged as the scapegoat. As James Fenimore Cooper put it, "There is little question that the government, nation, and we might almost add, the navy, felt a predisposition to condemn Commodore Barron, previously to the trial, for it is the nature and most common refuge of masses of men, to seek a victim whenever they find themselves in any manner implicated in their characters or conduct."[2] Henry Adams put it prosaically: "Public sentiment required a victim."[3]

The general public and Barron's own junior officers demanded his court-martial. It is safe to assume that the lieutenants were at least in part motivated by a desire to exonerate themselves. This is shown in a remark by Lieutenant Allen after the verdict against Barron: "'tho I cannot exult in any thing so unfavorable to any officer yet I cannot but feel happy at the acquittal of Officers Commdg divisions that so intimately concerns myself. . . ."[4]

Barron's initial report to Secretary of the Navy Robert Smith had noted "our unprepared and unsuspicious state" when the *Leopard* opened fire.[5] Later he said the *Chesapeake* seemed "intended then rather as a store ship, than one which was supposed to meet and engage an enemy."[6] The initial report also had indicated no displeasure with his officers or men. That also changed. After the fact he found that the frigate lacked "the Principle [*sic*] officer necessary to Prepare a Ship for defense, the gunners Worthless Cowardly and trifling to the Extreme no Boatswain no Carpenter and a variety [?] of other necessary persons deficient or not appointed, never did I Set Sail in a Ship so totaly [*sic*] unprepared for defense in my life."[7]

The *Chesapeake* was certainly unprepared for a fight, but this fact was perhaps not surprising. Asked during the subsequent court of inquiry, "Was your gun deck lumbered at this time?" Gordon replied, "Not more than is usual in ships of war shortly after getting under weigh." The frigate's lieutenants also said the crew was as well disciplined as could be expected from men recently recruited. Barron expected to train the men during the voyage to the Mediterranean. As he put it: "you know that Since the Peace with France, and the war with Tripoli, that the training of the People to a Knowledge of the exercise of the guns, has been Left for the outward Bound passage."[8]

Barron was soon aware that his officers had turned on him, and he accused them in turn of cowardice and incompetence. He heaped scorn on Lieutenants Benjamin and Sidney Smith, William Crane, and John Orde Creighton as well as Sailing Master Samuel Brooke. Either because of his unfamiliarity with his officers or his poor spelling, Barron identified Brooke as "Brook," Creighton as "Craton," and Crane as "Crain." He was especially critical of Lt. William Allen:

> Allen I am told stood his ground with more obstinacy than any of them but this is all he did, for it was out of his division that the one gun was fired he is the most infamous and the most Vindictive Rascal of them all he came to that Ship with all the Prejudices that his friend Comdr R [Rodgers] could inculcate and I am induced to believe that all the Reports now in circulation Prejudicial to me have originated with him.[9]

Allen was indeed a protege of Barron's enemy, Capt. John Rodgers. Allen had served under Rodgers in the Mediterranean in 1804 and was his "favorite lieutenant."[10]

One junior officer, Midshipman Jesse D. Elliott, received only praise from Barron. Without Elliott's presence in the after gun division, "I have Reason to believe there would have not been one man Remaining," Barron wrote.[11]

The finger-pointing became increasingly public. When Gordon returned to Norfolk from Washington he demanded to know whether Barron was responsible for stories making the rounds that the commodore believed him guilty of "delinquency." Barron wrote Gordon, "I have done you all the justice in my power. I attach no blame to you." Even in his reply to Gordon, however, Barron continued his attack on the lieutenants, calling them "the greatest cowards that ever stood on a ship's deck." He said much the same in a letter to Dr. Bullus. None of his officers had obeyed his orders, Barron charged, except when he ordered the flag struck. It was only when the ensign had been lowered and the broad pendant still flew that "all those heretofore dumb fellows bawled out to the topmen to haul it down." This letter also contained criticism of Gordon, who, Barron contended, remained too long on the quarterdeck when he should have been below quelling the "panick."[12]

The growing acrimony took a deadly turn. Lieutenant Allen privately accused Barron of cowardice. Midshipman Richard Crump, who thought the same, fought a duel with Midshipmen James Broom, who defended Barron's conduct and had, on June 22, been wounded by Barron's side. In the duel Broom wounded Crump in the thigh. Doctor [Bolling?] Stark, a relative of Barron, called out Gordon, who made Lieutenant Crane his second. Dueling procedure held that if either principal fired too soon the opposing second was authorized to fire. In the duel between Gordon and Stark, six shots were exchanged, but on the seventh, Crane believed that Stark fired too soon. Crane fired at Stark, wounding him in the arm. A. J. McConnico, Stark's second, claimed the doctor had not fired too soon. Gordon fought McConnico to settle this affront, and both men were wounded.[13] Alarmed, Secretary Smith ordered Stephen Decatur to end the dueling. In November 1807 Decatur wrote Smith: "I am happy to inform you that Captain Gordon has entirely recovered from his wounds—all differences between the officers & gentlemen at this place I am informed are adjusted."[14] According to Lieutenant Allen, however, between June 22, 1807, and August 27, 1808, there were seven duels between officers of the *Chesapeake*.[15]

On June 26, 1807, the same day he relieved Barron of command of the *Chesapeake*, Secretary Smith moved to convene a court of inquiry. Capt.

Edward Preble declined to serve as its president because of poor health (he died on August 25), and on September 12 Smith named Capt. Alexander Murray president and ordered him to convene a board at Norfolk on October 5. Reportedly a cousin of Gordon, Murray had additional cause for bias: Barron's 1800 criticism of his reconditioning of *L'Insurgente.* Smith chose Capt. Isaac Chauncey and Capt. Isaac Hull, both then in command of gunboats at Norfolk, as the two other members and hired a civilian, Littleton Waller Tazewell, to act as judge advocate.[16]

Tazewell, born in Williamsburg, had been a congressman from Virginia before opening a law practice at Norfolk in 1802. By 1807 he was a well-known local attorney and militia captain. After the *Chesapeake-Leopard* incident he had played a prominent role in reducing tensions with the British squadron (see Chapter 6). His biographer writes that Tazewell had "no relish" for the Barron case. Although not close to them, he had known the Barron family for years. Tazewell wrote Smith that serving "would occasion some sacrifices of my feelings as an individual." He had no experience in such proceedings, it would lead to neglect of his own practice at a busy time, and he had hardly seen his young son. Despite these misgivings, he accepted the post as an obligation "I owe my country."[17]

The delay in holding the inquiry resulted from Preble's death and Barron's pleas of ill health.[18] Tazewell, who kept in close touch with Smith on procedures, was concerned about the possibility that war would halt the inquiry. He wrote Smith: "Events not improbable, may at any moment suddenly deprive the United States of all testimony." He did lose one important witness when, on October 14, 1807, after a week's illness, 1st Lt. Benjamin Smith died of "a bilious fever."[19]

The court finally convened aboard the *Chesapeake* in Norfolk harbor on October 5. It then adjourned, probably because Tazewell was not then in Norfolk, and met three days later. Informed that Barron was still sick and unable to attend, the court adjourned again until October 16.[20] It reconvened on that date with Barron present and met until November 5.[21]

The object of the hearing was "to enquire into the causes of the surrender of the *Chesapeak,* a Frigate of the United States, then under the command of James Barron Esq., a Captain in the Navy of the United States, to a British vessel of war called the *Leopard.*"[22] Entered into the record were Barron's sailing orders, his report to Smith, the exchange of notes with Captain Humphreys, records of those killed and wounded, damage reports on the frigate, the appeal of her junior officers for Barron's court-martial, and an extract from the frigate's log. The court granted

Barron's request that his cousin, prominent Norfolk attorney Robert Bar-
raud Taylor, act as his counsel.

Midshipman Peter Muhlenburg was the first witness. Muhlenburg, who
had been stationed on the quarterdeck on June 22, reported that none of
the breechings of guns there had been "cast off." Even so, the guns could
have been fired if there had been anything to fire them with. In cross-
examination Taylor established that Barron had joined the ship only just
before she sailed, that the gun deck was heavily "lumbered," and that none
of the officers had indicated that the *Leopard*'s approach signified hostile
intent. Taylor repeated these same questions of other witnesses and established that the crew had been quartered only a few times before sailing. His
intent was to shift blame for the ship's unprepared state to Gordon and to
prove that none of the officers had been concerned about the possibility of
action up to the time Lieutenant Meade had come on board.[23]

The next witness was Midshipman John T. Shubrick of the Second
Division. He was helping move the last of the sick crewmen to the cockpit
when the *Leopard* opened fire. Lieutenant Allen then sent him to the
magazine for powder horns, where Shubrick was told none were filled.
After a few minutes he was given two, which he then carried to Allen, who
told him the ship had struck.

Shubrick estimated that only about half the men of his division were at
quarters but said some guns were ready to fire within five to ten minutes of
the British opening fire. When the frigate struck all his division's guns
except one were ready to fire. They had not fired because there were no
filled powder horns. Shubrick asserted that from March 17 or 18 to June 22
the crew was quartered only once (when Barron came on board).[24]

Midshipman Glen Drayton was the next witness. He testified that after
Lieutenant Meade left the ship he heard Barron tell Gordon: "You had
better get your men to quarters, Sir. I don't know what they mean."
Gordon then went to his cabin to get his sword and on the way down met
Lt. Benjamin Smith at the after hatch and ordered him to get the crew to
quarters, "but without any hostile show." Drayton heard Gordon tell
Smith, "Don't let them beat to quarters." But as Gordon came out of the
cabin the drummer was beating, and Gordon "immediately went up to
him and struck him with the hilt of his sword. . . ." Drayton heard Barron
say to those below, "For God's sake fire one gun for the honor of the flag."
Shortly after this the colors were hauled down. As they struck the taffrail a
gun was fired from the second division. Drayton held that the *Leopard*

"fired a broadside into us after our colours were down." The pendant was then hauled down, and firing ceased.

Drayton also testified that some guns on the quarterdeck had no sponges or handspikes. Although some guns were finally primed, there were no loggerheads with which to fire them. He believed there was a fire in the galley but said that the loggerheads were not heated. He heard Captain Hall tell Barron that the marines were ready to fire. The two ships were within musket range. (Musket balls were found on the *Chesapeake;* they presumably came from the *Leopard.*) The crew had been quartered "two or three days" before the frigate went to sea, but the guns had never been exercised, the witness said. Drayton did not hear any officers suggest before the British lieutenant came aboard that the *Leopard* might have hostile intent. When asked by Taylor about the condition of cannon on the gun deck, Drayton reported that he saw four or five that were not forelocked and that one had a cap square that did not fit over the trunnion, but this was discovered after the encounter.[25] Taylor asked Drayton about Barron's position during the action. The midshipman replied, "He was much exposed, in the gangway." Asked by Taylor if Barron appeared "firm and collected, or alarmed, and agitated," Drayton said, "He appeared to me to be very firm."[26]

Captain Gordon was the next witness.[27] He gave his position at the time of the incident as "Master Commandant, acting as captain under the Commodore." He then gave a detailed account of the encounter with the *Leopard* and his role in it. While Barron had "visited" the ship at Washington in February it was not until the afternoon of June 6 that he had come aboard again: "I showed him the two decks, the gun and quarter deck throughout, and offered to show him below, but he declined it." Barron "expressed to me great satisfaction at the situation and afterwards communicated to me a letter which he wrote to the Secretary of the Navy." Gordon then produced the letter and attempted to read a portion, but Taylor objected to an extract and called for it to be read in its entirety into the record. This was done.[28]

Gordon said Barron was aboard the ship only one other time before they sailed, and he did not recall him then examining the frigate or giving any orders regarding her. Tazewell's questions made it clear the commodore had paid only two brief visits to the ship and had not carried out a thorough inspection of her. Tazewell also got Gordon to state that Barron knew there were men on board the frigate who the British claimed were "deserters from their service." Gordon said, however, that it had been "proved to the satisfaction of the British Minister that they were Americans." He said he was not alarmed by the approach of the *Leopard* because she was a ship of the line and "I did not expect an attack upon us was the object." He claimed to have been distracted by the responsibility of running the frigate. He did report, however, that he thought the *Leopard*'s "movements suspicious, and this remark was made by Commodore Barron himself at dinner."[29]

If an order had been given when Barron "first remarked that the movements of the *Leopard* were suspicious," Tazewell asked, would the frigate have been ready for action when the British ship came alongside? Gordon replied, "Perfectly so." Asked about cable on the gun deck, he said that at dinner he had asked Barron if it was customary in leaving the *Chesapeake* for vessels to unbend their cables and stow anchors before their pilots left. "He said no, and said I might get the ranges below, and stow the anchors. The people were doing this when the *Leopard* hailed us."[30]

Gordon also testified that the *Chesapeake*'s cannon locks had not yet been fitted to the guns.[31] These locks, a recent innovation aboard ship, allowed more instantaneous, and hence more accurate, fire. More importantly in this case, had they been in place that day the *Chesapeake*'s guns could have been fired quickly without the use of match rope or loggerheads.

Murray asked why, when it was clear the British might have hostile intent, Gordon made no effort to "make sail, to give time to prepare for action." Gordon said this was not possible: "We were then immediately under the *Leopard*'s guns, she had the weather gauge of us, and was so near us that she would have discovered our movements immediately. Besides at that time I thought it more essential to prepare to fire than to make sail." Gordon also testified that he did not know of anyone telling Barron that the frigate had three feet of water in her hold before he struck.[32]

Gordon said he thought the colors had been hauled down prematurely because "at the time the colours were struck, I believe we were in a situation to return the enemies fire." Gordon said, "I am of opinion he never had an idea of continuing the action, further than to fire a few guns, and to surrender the Ship." He added, "I do not impute to Com. Barron a want of spirit. . . . But I entertain the opinion, I have before stated, because he struck after only one gun was fired, and because he knew the British Ship to be superior to us."[33]

Gordon said he was not aware before sailing that some of the guns did not fit in their carriages. He had not reported the *Leopard*'s approach to Barron since the commodore "was upon deck himself with his glass in his hand, the whole time and I observed he was attending to her movements particularly." After the action Bullus had informed him that Barron wanted to mention him in a letter to the secretary of the navy "as approving of his conduct." He said he told Bullus "I did not wish this done, because I did not approve his conduct in all respects, and that I wished my name not be mentioned at all in the letter." Barron then sent for him and told him that he had not authorized Bullus "to say any such thing to me." Barron told Gordon he had ordered the colors to be struck and "then again repeated, that he held himself alone responsible for what had happened, and that he should not mention my name in that dispatch. . . ."[34]

Gordon testified that he was headed aft immediately after the encounter when Barron

> took me by the coat and said, 'Do Gordon tell me what you think of my conduct.' This being a question which required of me an immediate charge of cowardice or the expression of something to alleviate his apparently agitated feelings, I thought myself justified to say, 'I think your conduct correct while in my presence,' not meaning by my reply that I approved of the two essential points of his conduct, by these I mean first not going to quarters in time, and secondly his hauling down the colours when I conceived we were ready to return the fire.[35]

Under cross-examination Gordon admitted the crew had not been exercised at the guns prior to sailing; all guns were not aboard until the fifteenth, and bad weather prevented practice after that, he said. The crew had been quartered at least twice. Gordon maintained he thought the *Leopard*'s movements suspicious, resembling those "I supposed an enemy would have pursued, having an intention to attack a ship to leeward of him." He said it was normal for a ship wishing to speak with another to take the weather quarter "unless they adhere to rank, when the Senior Officer generally takes the weather side. Besides this her ports when she rounded were all open, even her lower deck ports. . . ." Taylor asked whether it was customary for two-deckers in smooth water and light winds to open their lower ports, and Gordon replied, "They are sometimes open, but generally they keep them in when at sea." But Taylor got Gordon to admit that the water was smooth and wind light, meaning the ports could safely be left open.[36]

Taylor elicited an admission that Gordon had not expressed his concerns about the *Leopard* to Barron or anyone else. He said this was because "Commodore Barron had a much better opportunity of judging her than I had, because I was engaged in working our ship, and he in looking at the *Leopard* frequently, and moreover he had declared to me at dinner, as I have before stated, that he himself had suspicions of her." Taylor then asked who else was in the cabin when Barron said this. Gordon replied: "Dr. Bullus and his lady and Captain Hall and his lady messed with us; some of them were present but whether all or when, I cannot recollect." Pressed to recall the precise dinner conversation, Gordon said, "I cannot recollect it. I should not have recollected this particular declaration of Commodore Barron's if the affair with the *Leopard* had not have happened. But I cannot recollect what lead [*sic*] to it, and only remember his expressing suspicions such as I have stated."[37]

When Taylor asked why, if he was suspicious of the *Leopard*'s movements, Gordon had not ordered the ship cleared and her crew to quarters, he said that Barron was on deck and gave him no orders to do so. Taylor then asked Gordon if he saw an enemy vessel intending attack whether he would wait for orders to clear the ship. He replied: "Any unusual lumber in the way I consider myself bound to clear away, without orders but not to clear the Ship for action, or call the men to quarters." Taylor then asked why he did not ask Barron "that the men might by his order be called to quarters." Gordon said, "There are circumstances under which I should feel myself bound to give him my opinion, but this was not such a case, because the Commodore had a much better opportunity of judging correctly than I had." He had not been disturbed by Meade's list of deserters because in the Mediterranean it was "common to apply for deserters in a polite way, but never to demand them if refused."[38]

Taylor pressed the witness regarding his conversation with Barron following the encounter. Hadn't he expressed "the most entire and unqualified approbation of his whole conduct in the affair"? Gordon said no. He had only told Barron "that no person could purposely attribute his conduct to Cowardice."[39]

The next day Taylor resumed his cross-examination. He asked Gordon whether "it would have been more to your credit to expose the lives of your Crew by a continuation of the attack, when there was no hope of success or escape." He replied, "Yes. I should under such circumstances have exposed the Crew."[40]

Pressed as to whether Barron had told him that differences between the British and U.S. governments regarding deserters on board the *Chesapeake* had been resolved, Gordon said, "it had been proved to the satisfaction of the British Minister that these men were Americans" and Barron gave no indication "that these men would be demanded of him."[41]

Taylor suggested Gordon could hardly have been apprehensive about the *Leopard*'s approach because of the leisurely manner in which the crew was stowing cable, and Gordon admitted there was still a range of cable on deck when the *Leopard* came alongside: "This I suppose was not got away at that time for want of proper exertion, the Petty Officers and people employed having no suspicions that more exertion was necessary." But the ship could have been cleared for action in "less than forty minutes."[42]

Taylor then asked Gordon about a letter to Secretary of the Navy Smith begun on June 22 as the ship passed out of Hampton Roads and finished after the frigate had passed the British ships. A copy of this was introduced. In it Gordon noted the "serious" deficiency in the gunner's department discovered when the frigate was passing Mount Vernon and went on to write, "Had we gone to sea without trying our guns as we did, and some unforeseen occurrence brought us to an engagement with those Englishmen off the Capes, my saying the Cylinders and Sponges were too large, would not have been a sufficient excuse to you, for our not giving a good account of her. . . ." This was, of course, precisely what happened. Damning also was Gordon's concluding statement: "I am happy to inform you every thing on board is now in order. The Officers and Crew perform to my satisfaction."[43]

Captain Chauncey asked why Gordon had returned to the quarterdeck before carrying out Barron's order to get the gun deck guns firing. He said this was because he thought everything was in order to fire.

Gordon told the court that he had heard prior to sailing, probably from Bullus, that the captain of the *Melampus* "designed to demand these Seamen, and from the manner in which it was expressed to me, it was my impression that force would be used if the deserters were refused." He said he had not reported this to Barron because he had understood from Bullus that the doctor had told Barron himself.[44] In a statement damning to himself Gordon said the presumed British threats had led him to order the *Chesapeake*'s guns loaded while she was in Hampton Roads, but this possibility did not occur to him again until he was shown the list of men the British sought.[45]

Gordon testified that he believed the frigate's colors had been prematurely struck in part because Barron had not yet received his report on the condition of the gun deck when he ordered fire halted. He was convinced Barron thought one return shot was sufficient. Barron had also failed to order the marines to fire "when it was evident they could have done great execution from the commencement of the attack." While Gordon was trying to get the gun deck guns to fire Barron should have been doing the same with the quarterdeck guns "rather than standing in the gangway hailing the *Leopard*," Gordon contended.[46]

Gordon concluded with a statement that while there was not much prospect of the Americans "carrying the *Leopard*," he did not want to

> convey the impression that as a national ship there was nothing left
> for us but to strike. In such situation I conceive that altho' we may
> be a little inferior, it is expected, and a Commander ought to exert
> himself to do his enemy all the injury in his power, and notwith-
> standing we could not expect to succeed in taking the *Leopard,*
> yet we had it in our power to retaliate, by injuring her very
> materially and very probably to have killed as many of her men.[47]

Lieutenant Crane followed Gordon on the stand.[48] As commander of the First Division he had received no orders to prepare for action until several minutes after Lieutenant Meade had departed. When he reached the gun deck he found the two bower cables and a few fathoms of the end of the stream (or sheet) cable there. In the Second Division a number of sick men were in hammocks suspended over the guns. Crane described all the clutter in his division and his efforts to deal with it:

> Immediately on my arrival at my quarters, I ordered to clear away
> and cast loose the guns, take out your half ports, quarter gunners run
> for your matches and powder horns, boys for your cartridges, and to
> the people at the guns, middle your breeching and hook on your
> train tackles.[49]

Crane said the presence of the cables did not materially affect getting the guns ready to fire and his division was ready immediately after the *Leopard*'s first broadside except for the absence of "Powder horns to prime and matches or hot loggerheads to fire off the guns." The powder horns arrived just as he learned the ship had been surrendered. He testified that he had seen the *Leopard*'s "lower deck ports triced up [i.e., open], she then being distant from us between four and seven miles." He said he was aware the

British had threatened to take deserters from the *Chesapeake,* and he suspected this was the reason for the hail from the British captain that he had "dispatches or communications." He admitted, however, that he did not share these apprehensions with Barron or any other senior officer because he saw Barron "examining the *Leopard* frequently with his glass." Crane believed the *Chesapeake* could have been made ready for action during the time Meade was on board if that order had been given as soon as he arrived. The fact that the drummer beat "a few taps" and then stopped produced "A great deal of confusion," he said. (In their testimony all the lieutenants gave the same response to this question.) Murray asked Crane whether the *Chesapeake* "might have avoided speaking the *Leopard* if you had kept under steady sail." He replied, "I think we might have run away from her. I think we might have done this even after she commenced her fire." When Hull later asked what led him to believe the *Chesapeake* could outsail the *Leopard,* Crane said: "I discovered we could outsail her in going out and her appearance induces me to believe she was a dull sailer."[50]

Crane believed that the *Chesapeake* might have been cleared for action in twenty minutes after Meade had arrived. He reported that Gordon said after the encounter "that no doubt the Commodore has saved the effusion of blood" by striking but that Gordon regretted "we had not fired a few broadsides into her."[51]

The next witness was Lieutenant Allen.[52] He said that in his division there were

> a range of the bower cable on the starboard side, extending as far aft as the after part of the Main Hatch way, two or three beef or pork barrels (one of them I believe full) and the grog tub between the guns, nine sick men hanging in their hammocks over and about the guns, with their bags sick necessaries and utensils between the guns.[53]

Allen said his guns were not completely ready to fire at the time the ship was surrendered. He needed both matches and powder horns, but Gordon had brought two of the latter. "This was every thing that I wanted. I had no wads it is true, but I should have used grape shot in lieu of them, unless I could send my quarter gunners for them. . . ." Only two of his guns were primed and one other had just been fired. Probably another four minutes would have sufficed to have his guns completely ready, he testified.[54]

Allen said that at Washington he had learned of the British demand for return of deserters from the *Melampus,* and he repeated Crane's story of hearing from Bullus on the way down the Potomac that the British captain had threatened to take them by force. Telltale danger signs Allen noted were the signals by ships of the British squadron as the *Chesapeake* passed, the *Leopard* immediately getting under way, her shortening sail when the wind became baffling, and "tacking when we tacked." As Allen put it, "I was induced to believe she intended something serious."[55] If an order had been issued to prepare the frigate for battle when Meade had come aboard, the *Chesapeake* "could have been completely prepared, in *every respect*" by the time he left (emphasis in original), Allen said.[56]

In July Allen had written his father:

Now had the men been beat to Quarters by the drum or piped by the Boatswain in 20 minutes they could have been in complete readiness for a fight (altho we had on board a raw undisciplined crew, part of whom were never stationed at a gun in their lives before) *But NO it was the wish of the Commodore.*

Allen felt Barron should have:

detained the Lieut. [Meade] and his boat until he was ready for action and then said *here is my answer!* But no, he did not do this but gave a positive refusal and in dictating, penning and copying, detained the English boat *half an hour!* Here you see a plenty of time had elapsed for us to have been prepared; but he never gave any order to clear the ship until the boat had left the side. . . .[57]

In his testimony to the court of inquiry Allen said that stopping the drumming "produced at first much confusion," but he admitted that many of the crew were "raw recruits and unskilled." He said no effort had been made to avoid the *Leopard*, which could easily have been done after the *Chesapeake* had passed the Capes, but he did later concede that he did not think the *Chesapeake* could have outrun the *Leopard*.[58]

Questioned about Barron's leadership, Allen had this to say:

I do believe that the surrender of the *Chesapeake* was principally owing to Commodore Barron's want of courage and want of conduct. . . . Com. Barron knew he had on board his ship, persons said to be deserters from the British Squadron in Hampton Roads, I believe he also must have heard the reports in circulation, and the threat made use of by the Captain of the *Melampus,* to take these men out of us; he saw the movements of the *Leopard* after our getting under way on the 22nd of June which under such circumstances, ought to have induced him to believe that an attack upon us was meditated, yet he did not call his men to quarters even after this or after the *Leopard* had hauled her wind on our weather quarter, had sent her boat on board of us with a positive demand, to which he must have known he was compelled to give as positive a refusal. Besides, when he did order his men to quarters, he did not do it in an efficient manner. During the fire of the *Leopard* too, after his flag had been insulted, his hailing her frequently, saying he would send his boat on board—His attracting the attention of the men stationed at the guns on the quarter deck from the guns to lowering down a boat—His ordering the first Lieutenant from his quarters into the boat—His directing him to go to the English Captain with a message saying he would answer his letter, when he had before answered it—His observing in the presence of the men on the quarter deck, that we should all be cut to pieces—and lastly his hauling down his flag before a gun was fired without even paying the compliment to his Captain to say, 'By your leave' are all strong reasons to satisfy my mind, that the surrender of the *Chesapeake* was principally owing to his want of conduct and want of courage—.[59]

Allen knew of only one deficiency in guns of his division: one cap square secured by means of a spike rather than the proper forelock. He thought that if the drummer had continued to beat the men would have all been at quarters "in the usual time for a green crew."[60]

The lieutenant said that at the time of the surrender the half ports lids were out of his gun ports but not the tompions from the guns, except for one "which had been blown out of the gun we had fired. The others we had been ordered not to take out, but I intended to fire them out." He was forced to admit that, given the crew, the outcome would have been the same even with an "Officer of skill and courage." But it would have been "after a brave resistance," Allen insisted. As he had informed his father, he told the court that the ship could have been ready for action after Lieutenant Meade came on board in "not more than twenty minutes." When Chauncey inquired "what situation did you consider Captain Gordon as holding on board," Allen said, "I considered him to be acting as Captain of the Ship under the Commodore."[61]

Tazewell next called Lt. John Orde Creighton, commander of the Third Division during the encounter.[62] He too said stopping the drumbeat produced "confusion." His division was encumbered by a large screen for the cabin servants forward of the cabin bulkhead, and behind it trunks, a table, a cask, and a locker for the cabin furniture. In the cabin there was a large sideboard near the mizzen mast. After five or six minutes the men managed to clear the deck save for the locker and the cabin bulkhead. But there were no powder horns, matches, or heated loggerheads. After a boy finally brought a half-filled powder horn, Creighton used it to prime all his guns. A loggerhead was brought but was not hot enough to fire them. Creighton said Gordon came to the division twice and asked why he was not firing. "I replied I had nothing to fire with. Captain Hall then came down the after ladder and said . . . 'Cant you fire one gun?' Captain Gordon then came a third time, and told me to cease firing, that the colours had been struck." Elliott was about to fire a gun, but Creighton said he took the loggerhead from him "or put my hand upon it to prevent his firing."[63]

Creighton said that he told pilot Charles Nuttrel that he thought it was suspicious when the *Leopard* got under way because of Bullus's remark about threats made by the captain of the *Melampus*. He said he had expressed this apprehension to Lt. Benjamin Smith. Asked why he had not mentioned it to Barron, Creighton said that "it was not my duty to do so, and it might have been considered disrespectful to him. Besides the Commodore was frequently on deck himself, observing the *Leopard* with a glass."[64]

Creighton was less certain than the other lieutenants that the frigate could have been made ready for action while Meade was aboard, replying only "I think she might." He did say he thought twenty minutes would have been sufficient. Asked whether his division could have been ready to fire in that time, he said, "I think so."[65]

Creighton said that while the British officers were mustering the crew after the encounter he went to Barron and asked whether he should secure his guns. Barron replied, "I have nothing more to do with the ship, she is surrendered. . . ." The commodore then asked about damage to the ship, noting that the main and mizzen masts were badly damaged. Creighton told him, "Yes Sir, The foremast wounded too." Creighton said Barron reacted as if he had not known this.

> I then told him I had not observed attentively the injuries the hull had sustained. During this conversation or immediately afterwards, Captain Gordon came in, and conversing with Com. Barron said, that he did not think any person during this affair could be charged

with cowardice, but added (striking the table with great warmth) I regret we had not gone to quarters, that we could have returned the *Leopard*'s fire, or words to that effect.[66]

Creighton testified that Barron replied, "Gordon my dear Fellow, say nothing of that here, we may have to speak of it elsewhere," adding, "I am the Victim, and nobody else is to blame." Creighton believed Barron had shown "great irresolution and indecision," citing his failure to order the men to quarters early, preventing the drummer from beating, and efforts to send a boat to the *Leopard* during the firing. Creighton did not believe that the *Chesapeake*'s surrender resulted from a lack of courage, however.[67]

Lt. Sidney Smith was next to the stand.[68] He had been the fifth lieutenant, stationed on the quarterdeck in charge of signals. Smith provided information on Barron's efforts to hail the *Leopard* during the firing and the lowering of the gig. He testified the quarterdeck guns had been cleared "in a very few minutes" but could not be fired for want of powder horns. He said Barron "appeared much agitated and confused, which combined with the other circumstances, induces me to believe it was the result of fear."[69]

Marine Capt. John Hall was the next witness.[70] Hall had gotten to the quarterdeck just after the first British gun fired and was close to Barron during much of the action. After the first broadside he "went aft, and finding my marines with their guns in their hands, I asked if they were all loaded, and was answered that they were." He reported to Gordon that his men were ready. After the firing began Barron "went aft, stood on the after starboard gun on the quarter deck hailed the *Leopard*, and said he would send his boat on board of her." Barron then ordered a boat lowered and hailed a second time. Getting down from the gun he said, "addressing himself to the Officers of the quarter deck, 'For God's sake Gentlemen, will none of you attend to your duty.'" He then pointed to rigging that had been cut away and said, "Look at that brace, and those shrouds, why dont you put stoppers on them?" Hall then reported to Barron that the marines were ready to fire, but the commodore merely replied, "Very well." Barron then sent him to the gun deck "to direct them to fire one gun for the honor of the flag, that he intended to strike." When he arrived there Allen was trying to fire a gun with a loggerhead, but it was not hot enough. Hall "delivered this order as loud as I could speak. A gun was fired when I was upon the gun deck and when I came up I heard the colours struck."[71]

Asked why his men had not been quartered before sailing, Hall said he had received no orders to do so. He did not know for certain that marines on the *Leopard* had fired but believed they had. Because of the proximity of the *Leopard* his men "could have fired with some effect," but he did not think it his duty to open fire without being so ordered. He was uncertain of the number of rounds each marine had, although he knew their cartridge boxes "were not full, and of the rounds we had all of the cartridges were too small." Hall said he had never been ordered to have the cartridge boxes filled and had never requested cartridges. Hall did not "believe that the surrender of the *Chesapeake* proceeded in any manner from want of courage or presence of mind in Commander Barron."[72]

Seeking to counter the lieutenants' testimony, Taylor asked Hall if he had heard any of the officers "express any opinion that an attack would be made upon you." Hall said, "They did not." Taylor also asked Hall about the dinner conversation; he said he had not heard Barron or anyone else "express any suspicion of hostile movements on part of the *Leopard*." Tazewell asked whether such a conversation had taken place, and Hall replied that "such language was not used in my presence at dinner. Nor do I believe that such language could have been used at that time without my hearing it." Tazewell asked if he had seen the *Leopard* from the ports, and Hall said he had. The judge advocate then asked: "Did the appearance of the ship cause no remark from any person at that time?" Hall replied, "Yes it did. A remark was made relative to her sailing and Com. Barron then observed he thought we out sailed her. These were the only remarks which I heard." When Tazewell asked Hall if he had been in the cabin the whole time that Barron and Gordon were there together he said that he was at the table during the entire time of dinner but that "after dinner while they were drinking wine I left the table." He did not know if Gordon had remained longer.[73]

Tazewell then called Sailing Master Samuel B. Brooke.[74] He was asked about the ship's log, which was kept by Midshipmen Babbitt and Pettigrew. Brooke said that both anchors had been stowed instead of only the harbor anchor and that the firing had lasted not more than ten minutes, instead of the thirty minutes reported in the log. He said that he thought the *Leopard*'s movements "suspicious"; it was "very uncommon to see a line of battle ship with her lower deck ports open, and her tompions well out, unless she intends something serious, and this was the situation of the *Leopard* before she came alongside of us." He had heard someone on board "say that we had men who had been claimed as deserters by the

British Officers, and that the Captain of a British ship had said he would take them from us, and when the *Leopard*'s boat came along side of us I was sure that the Officer came to demand these men, and if they were refused we should have something serious." He had reported his suspicions to Sidney Smith and told him "that if these men were not delivered up, we should have Hell to hold."[75]

Brooke agreed with the lieutenants that the ship could easily have been ready to return fire if an order had been issued when Meade had first come on board. He believed no gun had been fired before the flag was ordered down but admitted that he might have been mistaken on that point. Brooke said that Barron did not order him to attend to any rigging during the firing. Asked about Barron's conduct, Brooke replied, "I was certainly doubtfull [sic] of his courage in one respect, from his not clearing his ship for action in time. During the firing however I saw no mark of fear about him. He appeared a good deal confused."[76]

The next witness was Gunner William Hook.[77] Gordon had ordered him to the magazine after the *Leopard* fired her first gun, and the first broadside was fired before he got there. Hook said he had not learned that the sponges and cartridges did not fit the guns until Captain Gordon told him so during the ship's trip down the Potomac. Sponges and cartridges were then altered. Hook said he had filled eight cartridges and reported this to Gordon before the frigate sailed. All gun deck sponges had been altered before the frigate went to sea, but Hook had not examined the quarterdeck gun sponges. These fit rather tightly but could have been used, he said. They were, however, altered after June 22.[78]

Hook said that the day before sailing Lt. Benjamin Smith had ordered him to fill fourteen powder horns. He had gone to the magazine and had filled five, but then was ordered on deck. He said he reported to Smith that there were only five horns filled. Hook denied having told Captain Gordon before sailing that he had filled seventeen. He admitted he had not tried the wads before sailing to see if they were the right size; they were "delivered to us at Washington and brought down without examination," he said. They were afterward found "rather too large, that is they would go in the calibre, but fitted rather taught." Horn had not primed matches before sailing because he had received no orders to do so. He said he had not heard all hands ordered to quarters: "I heard the drum beat a few taps, but it was stop'd. I was then waiting at the Cabin door for the Keys to the Magazine, expecting to go to quarters but had not been ordered." Under questioning Hook admitted that he had made some wads himself. A few of them were too large, he said, explaining, "and these were knocked about a good deal, and got wet and then became too large in consequence of it."[79]

Asked why matches had not been passed up, Hook said he was in the magazine and the matches were kept forward and so he did not know about them. As for powder horns, he said he filled fourteen or fifteen, but they were not passed up because there was no one in the magazine passage to do so. "They were all sent at last, however, but too late." Likewise, cartridges were not passed up because nobody came for them. "They were all ready."[80]

Hook said he was delayed in getting to the magazine by some chairs and tables in the cockpit. He had examined the guns after they had been placed in their carriages and noted that eleven did not fit or allow cap squares over the trunnions, but he had reported this before the frigate left Washington. Nearly all cap squares (which held down the trunnions of a long gun, thus securing it to its carriage) would fit closely enough to allow nails to be driven in to secure them, but not enough to be forelocked. He believed the guns fit well enough in their carriages to be used. All implements were in place for the guns on both decks, save rammers and sponges on the quarterdeck, Hook said. Wads were ready in the storeroom, but only a few were on deck.[81]

Tazewell next called Midshipman Fitz Henry Babbitt.[82] He had been stationed on the quarterdeck and was there the whole time of the encounter except for several minutes when he went below to get the surgeon. Asked by Tazewell if he had heard any remarks by Barron "calculated to dispirit his crew," Babbitt said, "I saw Com. Barron walk aft during the time of the attack of the *Leopard,* and observing some men standing on the guns, he ordered them to keep down, saying 'We shall all be cut to pieces.'" He also said Barron had hailed the *Leopard* frequently while she was firing and had ordered the jolly boat down.[83]

Taylor sought in his cross-examination to offset the impression of Barron's lack of courage. Babbitt admitted Barron had shown "anxiety" only in getting "the boat lowered down."[84]

After Babbitt's testimony Tazewell informed the court that he had called all his witnesses and that Taylor was free to call any other member of the crew. Taylor said he believed that testimony by the midshipmen, particularly Jesse Elliott, might be useful, and Elliott was called.[85]

Elliott, who remained the most prominent of Barron's defenders, had been in the Third Division. Taylor asked him about the state of the division, and Elliott listed obstructions: "a tub containing beef, the harness cask, two trunks, a locker, and a canvas screen, before the cabin bulkhead. In the cabin a table and several chairs between the guns. . . ." Not all this "lumber" had been cleared before the *Leopard* had ceased fire, although the crew cleared away "everything necessary" to allow working three of the four guns on the starboard side of the division.[86]

Elliott said that part of his division was ready to fire before the colors were struck but the men lacked powder horns and matches. Asked about the call to quarters, he said that the halt in the drumbeat "confused me, and I did not suppose any resistance was intended. Lieut. Creighton however afterwards observed, 'By God we will have our division clear at all events,' and we then went to work."[87]

Asked by Tazewell whether, had the drumming continued, all the men would have gone to their stations, Elliott said he believed this would have been the case, "but it is impossible to answer for a green crew." He did believe the guns of his division would have been ready to fire by the time Meade left the frigate if the crew had been called to quarters immediately after he came on board. But Elliott also said, "I don't believe the guns would have stood more than one broadside, for I have since discovered that three of the guns in my division were not secured in their carriages. The carriages were too small for the guns." He admitted that he did not know this at the time.[88]

When questioning resumed the next day (October 30), Taylor asked Elliott if he believed "the surrender of the ship proceeded from want of firmness or presence of mind" on Barron's part. The midshipman replied, "I do not believe it did." Elliott did not see Barron until after the firing ceased, but "He then appeared calm and collected, and his orders which I heard during the firing were given plainly, distinctly and easily understood."[89]

Taylor's next witness was Midshipman James Wilson.[90] Save about half a minute, Wilson was on the quarterdeck during the entire encounter. Wilson said he did not hear Barron's reported remark about being "cut to pieces" or hear him say anything "calculated to dispirit his Crew." After the colors were struck he heard Barron ask Gordon "if he was satisfied." Gordon replied, "'Commodore, we ought to have some compassion on the men.' The Commodore again asked if he was satisfied. Captain Gordon made no reply. The Commodore then asked him the third time if he was perfectly satisfied, and Captain Gordon replied 'Yes Sir.'"[91]

Wilson said he saw no "agitation or confusion" on Barron's part. His orders were clear and distinct, and he made no effort to hide during the engagement—in fact, he was "generally much exposed." Wilson did not believe the ship's surrender "proceeded from want of firmness or presence of mind on his part." Wilson also testified that "only three men of those who were stationed with me ever appeared at their quarters at all."[92]

The next witness was Midshipman Robert Steele.[93] Never having been quartered, he was unsure of his station. Another midshipman told Steele he should be at the maintopsail braces on the quarterdeck, and he went there. The only orders he remembered from Barron were to officers on the quarterdeck: "Gentlemen, why don't you have the rigging repaired?" Steele had seen "no want of firmness" in Barron and had not heard him order the men to get down.[94]

Taylor then called Midshipman James Broom.[95] During the encounter he had been acting midshipman and one of Barron's aides. Broom was wounded in the first broadside while standing by Commodore Barron in the starboard gangway, and then went below. He described Barron as "firm and collected."[96]

Broom was the last witness. Taylor announced to the court that he "deemed it unnecessary to offer any defence for Commodore Barron." Having heard the evidence, the court was "well capable of judging correctly upon it, without any comment upon his part." The court then adjourned until the next day.

In the proceedings many of Barron's accusers used virtually the same words in their answers, as when they characterized the halt to the drumming as producing "confusion." Were they rehearsed? We will never know.

On October 29 the board met at Mrs. Street's Norfolk boarding house. It then adjourned until the next day at the same place. This happened daily until November 3, when it met aboard the *Chesapeake*.

On the third Tazewell began by reading the proceedings' minutes. This continued into the next day, after which the court was cleared for deliberation. "After some time spent in deliberation" the captains came to a unanimous opinion.[97]

The board's detailed and lengthy report was unfavorable to Barron.[98] In nineteen particulars it found him negligent in fitting out the frigate for service. He had visited the *Chesapeake* only twice while she was in Hampton Roads, "on neither of which occasions did he examine particularly into her state and condition." Her guns "were never exercised before she proceeded to sea" and her crew had not been called to quarters more than three times before sailing, not even once after Barron came aboard. The board also found that it was "generally known on board" that the captain of the *Melampus* had threatened to take deserters on the frigate. Barron "had full knowledge of the facts that such men were on board his ship, that they had been demanded by the British Government, and had not been delivered up." The court could not determine, however, whether Barron knew of the reported threat by the captain of the *Melampus.*[99]

The court found the *Leopard*'s movements suspicious. It did not appear "there was any vessel in sight, or any other object to induce her to go to sea but the *Chesapeak.*" Her mirroring the movements of the American frigate and having gun deck lids triced up and tompions out of her guns

> were in themselves so suspicious as to have furnished sufficient warning to a prudent, discreet, and attentive Officer of the probable designs of a ship of war conducted in that way and ought to have induced Commodore Barron to have prepared his ship for action; especially with the information he possessed of the situation of his crew generally, of those who had been demanded by the British Government particularly and of the general state of the ship at that time.[100]

The message borne by Lieutenant Meade clearly conveyed at least the possibility of the use of force. Barron failed to utilize the thirty-five to forty-five minutes Meade was aboard to prepare for action. The court concluded this was "a direct breach of the fourth article of the rules and regulations for the government of the Navy of the United States" of April 23, 1800.[101]

Even after Meade had left the frigate and Barron "was himself satisfied that an attack upon his ship would be made, he did not take prompt, necessary, and efficient means to prepare his ship for battle." His first order was "merely to clear his gundeck." His second, "given after the lapse of some time, was to get his men to quarters secretly, without beat of drum; although with such a crew as he had on board, and in such a situation as the ship then was, it was not to be expected that such orders could be effectively accomplished."[102]

The captains also found that during the attack Barron had:

> manifested great indecision, and a disposition to negotiate rather than a determination bravely to defend his ship. That he repeatedly hailed the *Leopard* during her attack upon him. That he drew his men from their guns to lowering down boats to send on board of the attacking ship. And that he ordered his first lieutenant from his

quarters during the attack, to carry a message on board of the *Leopard* at that time firing upon him.[103]

The court found "that during the attack, Commodore Barron used language in the presence of his men calculated to dispirit his Crew, by ordering them to keep down that they would be all cut to pieces." He had ordered the colors to be struck "before a single gun of any kind was fired from her, and that at the time they were so struck, her main deck battery was in a situation which would have enabled the return of a broadside in a very short time." The court concluded that "the *Chesapeak* was prematurely surrendered, at a time when she was nearly prepared for battle, and when the injuries sustained either in the Ship or Crew did not make such a surrender then necessary." This was a violation of Article 6 of navy regulations of April 23, 1807.[104]

The members of the court believed

that although the *Chesapeak* might and ought to have been better defended than she was, yet that she was not in a situation at the time of the attack made upon her, to have enabled so gallant a defence being made as might be expected. Some of her guns were not securely fitted on their carriages, some of her sponges and wads were too large, but few of her powder horns were filled, her matches were not primed, some of her rammers were not in their proper places, her Marines were not supplied with many cartridges, and none of those which they had were of the proper size. These circumstances however could not have influenced Commodore Barron in striking his Colours because they were not known to him at the time.[105]

The court determined that although Barron's conduct reflected "great inattention to his duty, and want of decision," during the attack "he exposed his person, and did not manifest either by his orders or actions, any personal fear, or want of courage."[106]

The court also found "the conduct of all the other Officers of the *Chesapeak* (except those whose duty it was to have remedied the deficiencies before stated) and of the Crew generally, was proper, commendable and honourable." Surprisingly, there was no mention of Captain Gordon.[107]

These findings led President Jefferson to order a general court-martial for Barron, Gordon, Captain Hall, and Gunner Hook. On October 7 Secretary Smith appointed Captain Rodgers president of the court-martial.[108] On December 7 he ordered Rodgers to convene the court on

January 4. Its eleven members included five captains; at the time there were only thirteen in the entire navy, and all other captains and master commandants were unavailable.[109] Aside from president John Rodgers (the only captain on the court senior to Barron), the other captains were William Bainbridge, Hugh Campbell, Stephen Decatur, and John Shaw. There were two master commandants, John Smith and David Porter, and four lieutenants: Joseph Tarbell, Jacob Jones, James Lawrence, and Charles Ludlow.[110]

One of Barron's biographers thought it an "evil practice" to bring a senior officer to judgment by his juniors, some of whom might have been disciplined by him: "To vote for his conviction would be an ideal way to take revenge." There was also the potential for personal gain, since "every man who was a junior stood to gain a step on the ladder of promotion by the dismissal of a senior."[111]

Certainly Rodgers and Decatur disliked Barron. Rodgers, his chief judge, had recently challenged Barron to a duel. It was also irregular for Rodgers in the course of the trial to tell Lieutenant Allen, Barron's chief accuser, that he hoped to be able to offer him "a situation on his station." Allen also said that another, unnamed member of the court told Allen he hoped to make him his next first lieutenant.[112]

One of Decatur's biographers asserts that Decatur "felt only disgust" for Barron's actions and quotes him as saying that he would have "fought the *Chesapeake* to the last man and if that had not availed touched off the magazine to carry the Englishman down with him."[113] Decatur at least gets high marks for his candor. He asked Secretary Smith not to include him in the court-martial:

> When the unfortunate affair of the 22nd of June occurred, I formed and expressed an opinion that Commo. Barron had not done his duty—during the Court of Enquiry, I was present when the evidence of the officers was given—I have since seen the opinion of the Court, which opinion I think lenient.—It is probable that I am prejudiced against Commo. Barron.[114]

Smith replied that, although the request "does you honor," without his presence "I should not be able to form a Court. Other applications have been made, to which I have given a similar answer." He expressed confidence in the members' "honor and judgment" and would not "excuse any of you. Already there are fewer Captains on the Court than I would have wished."[115]

When Smith refused his request, Decatur provided Barron's counsel a record of this correspondence with Smith. Strangely, Barron did not formally object to Decatur's appointment.[116] But after the trial he wrote that "Two of the members of this court were my enemies, and I had no confidence in their justice. . . ."[117] Regardless of the scarcity of captains, it says a great deal about the Jefferson administration's prejudgment of Barron that it allowed Rodgers and Decatur to serve.

While there is no evidence of prejudice on his part, Porter was, according to his biographer, "a crony" of Rodgers and Decatur. Bainbridge's position was ambiguous. He was close to Rodgers, Decatur, and Porter, but Barron had been president of the court that cleared him in the loss of the *Philadelphia,* and he had three times surrendered "without the slightest flourish of opposition, twice during war." This may explain why he asked only four questions during the court-martial.[118]

Despite his experience with such proceedings, Barron declined to exercise his right to challenge the appointments. Proud and convinced of his innocence, he may also have thought the matter already settled, particularly in light of the board of inquiry. It may also have been Robert Taylor's influence. According to one source Barron was "all for" acting to remove Decatur and Rodgers, but his counsel "saw things differently. The participation of men *known* to be hostile would serve to emphasize Barron's final vindication, an outcome which Taylor professed not to doubt. . . ."[119]

The court convened on January 8, 1808, in Barron's former cabin on the *Chesapeake.* Among those crowding into the cabin was his brother Samuel. The weather was cold and damp, and on occasion the court met at Mrs. Street's house.

Barron was the first to be tried, on four charges: "for negligently performing the duty assigned him" (the failure to inspect the *Chesapeake* while she was at Hampton Roads preparing for sea); "for neglecting on the probability of an engagement to clear his ship for action"; for "failing to encourage in his own person, his inferior officers and men, to fight courageously"; and "for not doing his utmost to take or destroy the *Leopard,* which vessel it was his duty to encounter." Beneath all these issues, however, was the question of Barron's courage.[120]

Secretary Smith wanted Tazewell to continue as judge advocate. His reappearance was certainly irregular; he had written the court of inquiry opinion critical of Barron. Tazewell said he preferred not to serve but was willing to do so if the court-martial could be held when his private legal responsibilities would allow; he specified between mid-December and the first of March. This may have been the deciding factor in the trial's timing.

Tazewell's role remains ambiguous. His biographer wrote that the trial "in its motives and impartiality, was considered a model for others to emulate"—certainly an exaggeration. She has nothing to say regarding Tazewell's role, if any, in the court's decisions.[121]

Tazewell opened the proceedings by reading the charges against Barron. He then read into the record the findings of the court of inquiry, a questionable procedure but one to which Taylor did not object at the time. (It is hard to understand why Tazewell's biographer characterized Taylor's performance in the court-martial as "brilliant."[122])

Barron regarded certain witnesses as vital to his defense. He particularly wanted Dr. Bullus to testify, but Smith had excused him from attending, unless Barron requested it.[123] Barron also wanted both Secretary of State Madison and Attorney General Caesar A. Rodney as material witnesses. Although British Minister David Erskine had publicly stated before the *Chesapeake* sailed that he was not happy with the resolution of the issue of British deserters from the *Melampus,* Barron maintained that he had been led to believe the case was settled and that he "was so informed before he went to sea." Publicly at least Tazewell supported this request, although he asked Barron to allow depositions instead—something the commodore refused.[124]

The court allowed wide latitude to Barron's accusers. This was shown in the testimony of the first witness, William Crane. Asked if he had any knowledge of Barron having heard threats by British officers to take men by force from the *Chesapeake,* he replied: "I do not know it of my own knowledge, although I have reason to *believe* [emphasis in original] that he did." Taylor objected to the admission of this statement, but the court allowed it to stand.[125] On other occasions testimony remained in the record despite having been disallowed.[126]

Porter was by far the court's most active member; he asked more than sixty questions of both defendants and witnesses, honing in on whether Barron's conduct tended to "dispirit" either officers or crew. Rodgers, Decatur, and Campbell also were aggressive questioners.[127] Tazewell's questions centered on the lack of readiness for battle; whether Barron knew there were Royal Navy deserters on board, and if so why he did not anticipate trouble; why he had not cleared the ship for action; and whether he had ordered the flag struck prematurely.

Apart from Gordon and the five lieutenants who had asked for the inquiry, most witnesses, including Sailing Master Brooke and Captain Hall, were more favorable to Barron than not. Gordon was also on trial and hardly a disinterested party. The more blame he could fix on Barron the less would fall on him: "Barron's conviction would mean Gordon's acquittal," one biographer noted.[128]

Crane made liberal use of hindsight when he said that, had he been in command, the *Leopard*'s shadowing of the *Chesapeake* and tricing up of her lower deck gun ports (in "so much sea") would have led him to order the ship prepared for action. Under Porter's questioning he admitted that he learned only after the fact that the *Bellona*'s signal had caused the *Leopard* to get under way. Crane admitted his division was not ready to fire when the frigate sailed but contended that it was not his responsibility to clear the guns until ordered. He also admitted that the crew was not "well disciplined" and that the British had the advantage of the weather gauge had the Americans attempted to escape; nonetheless, Crane felt that when Barron ordered the flag struck the frigate might still have fought for "a long time." All guns of his division were clear and would have been able to fire about a minute after the *Chesapeake* struck, he said. When Porter asked if Barron had acted in any way "unbecoming the character of an American officer," Crane cited stoppage of the drum beating to quarters, which "threw the crew into confusion; they did not know whether to go to quarters or not."[129]

Crane was followed on the witness stand by Lieutenant Allen. His letters reveal he believed himself on trial; only the proven guilt of Barron would erase the shame. He had written his father, "If I am acquitted honorably, you may see me again. If not, never."[130] Allen held that the *Leopard*'s coming up to windward led him to believe she intended trouble; normally ships passed to leeward when wishing to speak to one another. Under Porter's questioning, Allen was forced to admit that this did not mean that every ship coming up to windward harbored hostile intent. He agreed with Crane that halting the drumbeat impeded preparations for action. Allen and Crane both testified that, except on smaller vessels such as gunboats, the normal procedure for calling a crew to quarters was by drum. Allen also testified that Barron was not aware of the amount of water in the *Chesapeake*'s hold when he ordered her flag struck. And he said it was "general custom" to have matches primed when going to sea.[131]

On January 8 Tazewell, acting on Barron's request, wrote Secretary of State Madison to ask that he appear as a witness. The reluctance of Madison and Secretary of the Navy Smith to testify at Barron's trial suggests they may indeed have misled Barron on whether the matter of the British deserters had been resolved, but no written evidence settles the question. Certainly Madison and Smith did not want to get involved, and Tazewell's letter to Madison may have been prompted by political motives. Jefferson had announced he would not run for a third term, and Madison was his personal choice as successor. A movement in Virginia supporting Monroe was gathering steam, however, and Tazewell was one of those pushing it. Madison on the witness stand at Norfolk might well have worked to Monroe's advantage. In any case, Madison refused to accede to Tazewell's request, replying, "My memory does not apprise me of any circumstance which could be of importance to the trial."[132]

Tazewell's third witness was Lieutenant Creighton. He said he did not think the *Chesapeake*'s casualties and damage warranted her surrender. Tazewell asked if Barron's conduct was unbecoming an officer of the navy; Taylor objected, and the court recessed to consider this. Tazewell argued that he had asked the question of the other witnesses without drawing an objection from Taylor. The court allowed Tazewell's question. Creighton's response was: "Yes, I do think his getting his crew to quarters secretly was unbecoming the character of an American officer."[133]

Lt. Sidney Smith was next to the stand. He said that he and Sailing Master Brooke had noticed about 2:00 that the *Leopard* had her lower deck ports triced up "and was taking in water through them." Porter asked Smith whether he or any other officer had reported to Barron suspicions concerning the *Leopard*'s intent. Smith said he had not and could not speak for the others. Porter asked whether Barron's conduct indicated that he had not meant to make a serious defense of the frigate. Smith answered: "It did. From the moment of his secretly going to quarters, his not subdividing his marines, not having his gun deck cleared up during the time the British officer was on board, which was fully forty minutes, I was induced to think he did not intend bravely to defend the ship." He also said that Barron "appeared to me to be much agitated." When Taylor asked if he believed the agitation was the result of fear, Smith said, "I thought it was."[134]

Marine Captain Hall was next to testify. His answers were unhesitating and supported Barron. This testimony came, however, from one under accusation himself. In answer to questions from Taylor, Hall said that Barron had evidenced only "great anxiety" rather than agitation or fear, that his orders were distinct, and that "Every thing which he did, I thought was calculated to encourage them.—I never saw a man manifest more courage." Even while Meade was aboard Hall had no anticipation of an attack; nor, he said, did Lieutenant Crane, with whom he talked in the gangway. Hall also stated that during the firing he had seen Sidney Smith, sword drawn, sheltered "on the larboard side of the mizzen-mast."[135]

The same day Hall finished testifying, January 12, Sailing Master Brooke was called to the stand. He too was a strong witness for Barron, but he was not a naval officer. Brooke told the court he had observed the *Leopard* when she was about a quarter of a mile away. The two ships were on different tacks, and he could see that the *Leopard*'s lower deck ports were triced up, tompions out of the guns. There was not much sea and the wind was moderate, but her captain was careful to keep "her main yards square."

Brooke was in an excellent position to testify as to Barron's conduct during the action. Before the firing Gordon had ordered him to the gun deck to assist in stowing cable; but with the start of firing Brooke returned to the quarterdeck and remained there until the end of the attack. He said that Barron was in the gangway "at the height of the fire. . . . I thought he behaved very well there." He also opined that even if the crew had been ordered to quarters before the *Leopard* had opened fire the ship would not have been able to make much of a defense. She "had but few powder horns filled, and not enough cartridges filled to carry out an engagement." Based on his two sea fights, aboard the *Constellation* against the French frigates *L'Insurgente* and *Vengeance,* Brooke believed there was little prospect of the *Chesapeake* escaping from the *Leopard,* let alone destroying her: "I think she would have sunk us in a little time, perhaps an hour or half an hour. I don't think this ship can bear half the battering that the *Constellation* can." Brooke did damage Barron's defense, however, when he said he told Sidney Smith as the *Leopard* approached "that they were coming to demand the men we had on board, said to be deserters, and if they were not delivered up, they would fire into us."[136]

The next witness was Gordon; he began testimony on January 13. Gordon was not represented by an attorney, but both Tazewell and Rodgers instructed him to be aware of the possibility of self-incrimination. He refused to answer many of Taylor's questions for that reason.

Taylor asked Gordon whether he had reported to Barron the *Leopard*'s movements. Gordon said, "I did not," then immediately corrected himself by saying that he had told Barron in his cabin about signals between the British ships and the *Leopard.* He did not report after that, he said, because

Barron was then on deck. During dinner all could see from the forward port that the *Leopard* was shadowing the *Chesapeake*. Barron "then observed, (addressing himself to no particular person at the table that I recollect, but generally to the company,) that her movements appeared suspicious, but she could have nothing to do with us."

Gordon said he did not notice whether the *Leopard* had her gun ports triced up or tompions out of her guns until Barron called him to the gangway after Meade had left the ship, and then noticed it only when Barron pointed it out. Barron told him to clear the gun deck, but Gordon said this was not "a decisive order. Rather a request." Asked if Barron had encouraged "his officers and men to fight courageously," Gordon replied, "He did encourage them in my presence."[137]

Taylor asked Gordon if he had known of any irregularities in the gunner's department. Gordon declined to answer, and Tazewell reminded him of possible self-incrimination. When Taylor asked that Gordon be compelled to answer, Tazewell refused. Taylor then took another tack, asking Gordon if he had not encountered difficulty in firing a salute while passing Mount Vernon. Again Gordon refused to answer. He also refused to answer when Taylor asked whether he had reported to Barron that the frigate was ready for sea. Nor would Gordon discuss the contents of his June 18, 1807, letter to Barron stating that the vessel was ready for sea; the most Taylor was able to get from Gordon was acknowledgment that the signature on the letter was his.

Later in his testimony Gordon said that in Washington he had conversations with Barron regarding the British deserters and was left with the conviction that if the *Chesapeake* encountered the *Melampus* at sea the British would demand them. This was quite different from his testimony during the court of inquiry, when he said that Barron had told him at Washington that he believed the issue was settled. Gordon admitted he did not expect an attack from the *Leopard*. He claimed that it was Barron's remarks at dinner that had alerted him to the possibility of trouble. He could not recall any others at the table sharing Barron's apprehensions, and he said that he saw no need to issue an order to clear the gun deck and had not gone there to check its condition. He refused to answer whether he had asked Gunner Hook about the condition of the magazine.[138]

Gordon said he believed it would have been possible to have gotten the frigate ready for action while Meade was on board without making the British officer aware of this, and that the frigate could have been ready for action in fifteen to twenty minutes. He said he had assumed Meade was merely making "polite application" for return of seamen "such as I had before seen made in the Mediterranean, and that it had been refused, as had invariably been done there, and that nothing more would ensue."[139]

Gordon admitted that the *Chesapeake* could not have escaped from the *Leopard* but hedged on whether there was a chance the *Chesapeake* might have gained the advantage: "It is difficult to answer that. No one can calculate on the event of a battle. The *Leopard* was superior to us in force, and had the advantage of us in situation." He also claimed to have disapproved of Barron's conduct at the time, specifically in "not going to quarters in proper time, and hauling his colours down at the time he did." He said nothing akin to his court of inquiry testimony that asserted flatly that Barron "never had any idea of continuing the action, further than to fire a few guns and to surrender the ship." When asked by Barron after the surrender what he thought of his conduct, Gordon said he had first turned away and then, when pressed, only remarked that his superior's actions had "prevented bloodshed."[140]

Midshipman Glen Drayton was the next witness. In his cross-examinations of Drayton and other defense witnesses Taylor asked about the frigate's readiness. Drayton testified that the first station bills were not made out until a few days before the frigate sailed and that her guns had not been exercised while he was on board.[141]

After Drayton's testimony Tazewell informed the court that Dr. Bullus and Midshipman Fitz Henry Babbitt were "hourly expected." Barron very much wanted Bullus's testimony. He had been at the dinner table that fateful day, and Barron believed that Bullus had been told in Washington that the British regarded the matter of the deserters as settled. Tazewell wanted Babbitt on the stand; reportedly he had publicly aired views that might be useful to the prosecution. Tazewell had written Robert Smith to request both men's presence.[142]

While awaiting the two witnesses Tazewell sought to introduce written evidence. The court ruled this admissible but adjourned until Monday, January 18. When it reconvened Tazewell read into the record Secretary Smith's May 15, 1807, sailing orders to Barron, Barron's June 23 letter to Smith describing the attack, copies of Captain Humphreys's letter to Barron, Barron's reply and surrender of the ship, Humphreys's rejection of this, and reports of casualties and damage to the frigate.

This evidence was particularly damaging to Barron. Since Meade had taken Berkeley's original letter back to the *Leopard*, Barron had relied on memory for his report to Smith. He represented Berkeley's order as having stated that "each and every vessel of the British squadron should take, by force if they could not be obtained by other means, any British deserters found on board the *Chesapeake*." The actual order, subsequently made available by British Captain Douglas to Barron at his request, nowhere stated that force would be used; even the implication of force was not clear. Yet if this was Barron's assumption, why had he not ordered immediate preparation for action?[143]

On January 19 Taylor began calling defense witnesses, beginning with a number of midshipmen. Taylor's questions were designed to bring out the lack of any sign of hostile intent on the part of the *Leopard* before the *Chesapeake*'s crew was ordered to quarters and the unreadiness of the frigate and her crew for battle.

Taylor's first witness was Jesse Elliott. He and subsequent midshipmen testified that they had no suspicion of hostile intention on the part of the *Leopard* and had heard no one express such apprehensions. Elliott also provided testimony about the unreadiness of gun deck cannon to return fire.[144]

Next was Midshipman Charles Norton of the First Division. He seconded Elliott's testimony and described the cowardly actions of two men in the division.[145] Midshipman Alexander Wadsworth of the Second Division testified that he had seen no evidence of hostile intent and that not all his men were quartered during the attack. Wadsworth also told of the appalling state of the frigate's magazine. He said it would have been impossible for the *Chesapeake* to have maintained an action with the *Leopard*. When questioned by Tazewell as to whether it was the state of the magazine or the gunner that was the problem, Wadsworth said, "The gunner appeared to be deficient. I did not pay particular attention to the magazine." He believed the *Chesapeake* could not have sustained fire because the gunner was unable to "find the cartridges readily." When "opening a locker he did not know what sized cartridges were in it, and appeared to have forgotten his arrangements," Wadsworth said.[146]

Midshipman James Wilson was next. He too had detected no sign of the *Leopard*'s hostile intent. Wilson said only three men were at his station during the engagement when there should have been fifteen or sixteen. Throughout the engagement Barron "appeared very cool and collected," Wilson felt. He also provided testimony damaging to Gordon. Wilson related that after the surrender Barron asked Gordon if he was satisfied and Gordon replied that "we ought to have some compassion on the men." Barron then asked Gordon if he was "perfectly satisfied," and Gordon replied, "yes, sir" and then immediately turned and went aft. Wilson said that he remembered the exact word "perfectly." He refused, however, to be drawn into a judgment of whether Gordon approved of Barron's conduct. When Porter asked if there was any indication that Gordon might have been of a different opinion than his reply, Wilson said that "he appeared displeased."[147]

Taylor next called Gunner's Mate Thomas Garnett (or Garnet), who testified about the magazine and gunner's department.[148] Taylor then said he had no more witnesses to call until Dr. Bullus's arrival. The court adjourned.

The court convened the next day, January 21, at Mrs. Street's house. Because of extremely cold weather that froze the Potomac, the court met each day until January 29 only to adjourn.

Bullus was not to testify. Secretary Smith wrote Rodgers that when Bullus had returned from his diplomatic mission to England to deliver the U.S. demand for indemnity he found his family in financial straits, and Smith had decided to grant the doctor's "earnest entreaties" that he be excused from testifying. Smith did add that if his testimony was deemed essential Bullus would appear. Bullus did provide a brief and guarded deposition describing the conversation with Meade in Barron's cabin, but it shed no new light on events.[149]

When Rodgers informed the court that Bullus would not be coming, Taylor—after stating his desire to have the secretary of state, attorney general, and Bullus all testify—said that "after keeping the court waiting for so long a period," he would not ask for further delay.[150] It was strange that Taylor acquiesced. Bullus was the only individual, apart from Meade, who could have testified about Barron's reaction to Berkeley's circular letter and Humphreys's communication.[151]

Bullus remains an enigma. He had emigrated to the United States from England after the Revolution and studied medicine under Dr. Benjamin Rush. In 1798 he became surgeon's mate aboard the frigate United States, and when her surgeon literally "missed the boat," Bullus found himself responsible for the health of more than 300 men. On this cruise he apparently became friends with Midshipman Stephen Decatur. Capt. John Barry recommended Bullus for full surgeon, and he received the promotion in July 1799. That August he sailed to Europe aboard L'Insurgente, meeting Alexander Murray and Charles Gordon. He left the frigate on her return the next year and was assigned as surgeon at the Washington Navy Yard. He and his wife were regarded as socially prominent in the capital. In 1806

Bullus sold a pharmacy he had established. The next year he was able to secure the lucrative appointment as navy agent for the Mediterranean. After Bullus carried news of the *Chesapeake-Leopard* affair to Washington, Jefferson sent him across the Atlantic in the schooner *Revenge* to deliver dispatches to Monroe in London. He returned to the United States to receive another sinecure, navy agent at New York, which post he held until 1818. Did the Jefferson administration owe Bullus a special debt of gratitude?[152]

On January 29 Midshipman Fitz Henry Babbitt finally was on hand to testify. Babbitt, who had been stationed on the starboard side of the quarterdeck during the action, testified that Barron had spotted some of his crew "standing on the weather guns" and had ordered "us, to keep down [or] we should be cut to pieces." Babbitt admitted that this was not necessarily a sign of cowardice and that the men standing on the guns were away from their stations and unnecessarily exposed to enemy fire.[153]

Taylor then called Lt. Arthur Sinclair to the stand. He admitted that the forty seamen he had recruited at Norfolk included one man who was said to be a deserter from the *Halifax*. Taylor asked Sinclair if he had informed Barron of this before the frigate sailed, and Sinclair said he had not. Tazewell then asked Sinclair if he had known his recruits included three deserters from the *Melampus*. Sinclair said, "I did." Barron burst out, "I admit that I knew these men were on board before I sailed, and that they were said to be deserters from the *Melampus*."[154]

Elliott was recalled at Taylor's request. He testified that shortly after the encounter he had condemned the conduct of two officers on the quarterdeck and that Babbitt had warned him to be silent "until I knew which way the thing turned." Elliott said that he interpreted Babbitt's remarks as meaning that his testimony should coincide with that of other officers so "I might stand a better chance of being promoted." Elliott also reported that Babbitt had "expressed himself in the most favourable terms of Commodore Barron's conduct on that day, while on the quarter deck." Under questioning by Tazewell, Elliott admitted that Babbitt's remarks to him had ended their friendship. Elliott also said that Babbitt had told him privately that Lt. Benjamin Smith had not done his duty and that Lt. Sidney Smith "had screened himself from the fire of the *Leopard,* by getting under the lee of the mizen [*sic*] mast." Elliott asserted these remarks had been made in the presence of Midshipmen Drayton and Shubrick.[155]

On January 30 Tazewell called to the stand two quarter-masters mentioned by Babbitt, James Parker and John Watson, with the aim of establishing Babbitt's veracity. Parker testified that Barron had said to the men as he walked aft, "men stand in to your quarters, if we can't make no resistance strike the colours, or we shall all be cut to pieces." Watson quoted Barron as saying, "haul down the colours, she will cut us all to pieces." Parker said he saw no men standing on the guns. When cross-examined by Taylor, however, both men said Barron seemed calm throughout the incident and showed no fear.[156]

Taylor then recalled Captain Hall. He said that during dinner Barton had not expressed any suspicions as to the *Leopard*'s movements; nor had any others.[157]

The next witness was the pilot, Charles Nuttrel. He said that the sea was smooth on June 22, contradicting Crane's testimony. There was a fresh wind, Nuttrel said, but it was not sufficient to bring the lower ports of a line of battle ship under water. The pilot also said that he had not been aware that the *Leopard*'s tompions were out of her guns. Nuttrel said he had seen no sign of cowardice on Barron's part but confessed, "I was too bad scared myself to observe him however, very particularly."[158]

Taylor then recalled Babbitt. He denied attributing Barron's order to the men standing on the guns to fear, but he was forced to admit that Crane probably had that impression from what he had told him, and the same might be true of others.[159]

Taylor also recalled Drayton, who said he thought lieutenants Sidney Smith and Benjamin Smith had been guilty of cowardice. Midshipmen Richard Crump and Wilson each testified that they had heard Babbitt accuse the two lieutenants of this. Taylor also recalled Crane, who said he believed from Babbitt's remarks that Barron "wanted spirit."[160]

On February 2, after a short reexamination of Gordon, Taylor called Tazewell to the stand as a witness. He asked him to read aloud testimony by Gordon at the court of inquiry and the present court and, by inference, accused Gordon of perjury. This centered on Gordon's testimony to the court of inquiry that neither he nor Barron had foreseen a British demand at sea for the return of deserters and his testimony to the opposite effect during the court-martial. The court decided that Gordon's entire testimony at the court of inquiry should be read into the record. No member of the court wanted to discuss the matter of possible perjury; surprisingly, Taylor did not push the matter.[161]

The court now turned to Barron's testimony. Taylor read Barron's lengthy statement, which ran some eighteen thousand words and which even Lieutenant Allen characterized as "elegant."[162]

Barron said he was not guilty of the charge of negligence of duty. Preparing the frigate was Gordon's job; he had been appointed her captain the previous February, and Barron was merely to "proceed in her to take command of the [Mediterranean] squadron. . . ."[163] Barron noted separate regulations governing duties of squadron commanders and captains, including a number of rules for captains. Rule 9 provided: "*At all times whether sailing alone or in a squadron, he shall have his ship ready for an immediate engagement,* to which purpose he shall not permit any thing to be on deck, that may embarrass the management of the guns, and not be readily cleared away." Under Rule 15 a captain was to "*muster the ship's company, at least twice a week, in port or at sea.*" He was also to exercise frequently the ship's company "*in the use of the great guns and small arms*" (Rule 33), and "*He is responsible* for the *whole conduct and good government of* the ship, and for *the due execution of all regulations which concern the several duties of the officers and company of the ship*" (Rule 53).[164]

Barron noted that regulations "prescribed duties for the commodore as chief of a squadron and not as the commander of a particular ship." Captains were "to exercise their respective ships." It did not matter that the *Chesapeake* sailed alone; the *Wasp* was to accompany her and, in the Mediterranean, "several vessels were to be under my command." Barron went on to note:

> If these duties really appertained to me; I alone am responsible for the injury, sustained by the United States, from their non-performance. Yet by a strange perversion, either of judgment, or feeling, the omission is in general terms, imputed to me as an offense; while all the details of omission from specific subjects of accusation against captain Gordon in his approaching trial.[165]

Gordon as captain was responsible for "the subsequent disaster," which was "very materially connected with the want of previous arrangement and discipline in the ship."[166] Barron admitted he had visited the ship only twice before sailing, but Rule 15 of the regulations required only that he muster the crew when he went on board one of the ships in his squadron. He had done more, examining all her decks and some of her storerooms and inquiring into her condition. He had cut short his second visit when he discovered that Gordon "expected a party on board to a ball, and I was unwilling to interrupt his arrangements, although I had previously expressed my disapprobation." On the day before sailing he had ordered the crew mustered, but "I did not go into minute details. Captain Gordon had reported his ship ready for sea; ought I to have doubted the truth of his report[?]"[167]

Regarding the second charge, of failing to clear the ship for action, Barron noted: "On this subject, *you* have the benefit of history; *I* could only speculate." He asked the court to "place yourselves in the situation, in which I was, when these events occurred; and ask of your own minds, whether these circumstances would have led you to conclude, that an attack was probable."[168] The case turned on whether he should have foreseen that the *Chesapeake* might be fired upon, but "I had no suspicion of an attack." He knew deserters from the *Melampus* were on board but believed that matter had been resolved. He did not know of a threat by her captain to recover the men, and he sailed by the enemy squadron without eliciting a sign of hostile intent on its part. The British signals were seen by many, including Gordon, but "all acknowledge that they excited no suspicions." Barron also made much of his sailing instructions, which gave no hint of trouble:

> Being at peace with all the world, our principal objects in sending public vessels of war into the Mediterranean are to protect our commerce and seamen against the predatory dispositions of the Barbary powers,—to keep them at peace with us by a conciliatory deportment. . . . Our interest as well as good faith requires that we should strictly preserve our neutral relations, and that we should cautiously avoid whatever may have a tendency to bring us into collision with any other power.[169]

The *Leopard*'s shadowing maneuvers did not elicit suspicion. When the *Chesapeake* had stood in for land to await the pilot boat, the *Leopard* had followed:

> If the United States had been at war, such a movement, in an unknown ship, would certainly have excited suspicion, in the mind of a vigilant officer. . . . Her subsequent maneuvers were, however, calculated to remove every suspicion which such a movement could have excited in the most cautious mind. We stood in for the land, under easy sail, for half an hour. If such an attack was designed, we were no longer within the limits of the United States; and no respect for our jurisdiction, restrained their operations. Instead of making sail to overtake us, before we had got near the land [and back within territorial waters], she continued to follow us under easy sail.[170]

Barron strongly denied having made the statement at dinner Gordon attributed to him. As proof that Bullus had not heard it, Barron asked whether the doctor "would have been so unmindful of the safety of his wife and children, as to have left them on the gun deck to the latest moment before the attack." Regarding Gordon, Barron noted sarcastically: "It seems difficult to reconcile his subsequent conduct with this representation." Why had Gordon not inspected the gun deck to have the frigate ready for an engagement? And if Barron's suspicions had been "so strongly expressed," why had not Gordon "watched the subsequent maneuvers of the *Leopard*, that he might ascertain the justness of my suspicions?"[171]

Barron went to the heart of the matter regarding Gordon:

It may be said, however, that Captain Gordon is not among the number of my pledged accusers.—most true, a stronger motive operates on him. The web of his destiny is interwoven with mine. My condemnation is the pledge of his acquittal. If it be not proved that the catastrophe resulted from my misconduct, the charge will inevitably revert to that officer, from which neglect of previous discipline and arrangement, the surrender flowed. His examination has unalterably fixed this connexion between us. To the prosecution, his innermost soul is cheerfully unfolded; to me, he is cold as death; and silent as the tomb. Every enquiry of the prosecution, tending to establish my guilt, he has readily answered. To me he refuses all information, on points essential to my defence.[172]

Barron made much of Gordon and the lieutenants testifying that they were certain of a threat from the *Leopard* and yet took no action to prepare for battle. He pointed out the regulation guiding captains that held:

Every commander or other officer who shall, upon signal for battle, or other probability of engagement, neglect to clear his ship for action, or shall not use his utmost exertions to bring his ship into battle, or shall fail to encourage in his own person the inferior officers and men to fight courageously, such officer shall suffer death or such other punishment as a court-martial shall adjudge.[173]

But Barron felt this regulation applied only in case of an existing state of war. Even after receiving Berkeley's order and Humphreys's letter, "I did not believe, that an attack would be made by the *Leopard* upon the *Chesapeake*, in the execution of this order." He based this not on the vagueness of Berkeley's order "although it will be perceived that there is in it, no instructions to use force; and the terms are studiously ambiguous." Rather the men for whom Humphreys was instructed to search were from the six ships mentioned specifically in the order, and the *Melampus* was not among the vessels named.

> It is true that one of the persons afterward taken out, was a deserter from the *Halifax*, which ship was named in the list. But is equally true, that this man had shipped under an assumed name; and I, as well as every other officer of the *Chesapeake*, was then ignorant that such a person was on board. Believing that no persons said to be deserters from the British fleet, were on board, except only the three who had escaped from the *Melampus;* and discovering that the order did not extend to the deserters from that ship, I concluded that no search would be attempted for these men. . . . I did, however, believe that the communication ought to inspire caution on my part. If Captain Humphreys did not rely upon my assurance . . . I imagined that another communication would be made from him, before hostilities commenced, and that abundant time would have been allowed me to make the necessary preparations for battle. . . .[174]

Barron believed that if he had forcibly detained Lieutenant Meade, readied his ship for battle, and an engagement had ensued, he would have been court-martialed for precipitating the battle, especially since the deserters from the *Melampus* had not been specifically mentioned in Berkeley's circular and Secretary Smith had called on him to "strictly preserve our neutral relations, and that we should cautiously avoid whatever may have a tendency to bring us into collision with any other power."[175]

Barron said he

> did not believe an engagement probable, when the British officer departed; although I did deem it proper to be in readiness to guard against every thing which might occur. In execution of this purpose captain Gordon was directed to come to me, the instant the officer left the ship. I immediately communicated to him the object of the application, and my reply, and gave him orders, instantly to prepare the ship for action. . . .[176]

Gordon had represented this as less than an order, but Barron maintained:

> There is no precise form of words, by which an order to prepare for action, is to be given by a commander to an inferior officer. Any

terms sufficiently explicit are, I presume, proper . . . I will not descend to quibble about terms. I confidently affirm, however, that an order was then substantially given to prepare for action. . . .

Having given these orders to Captain Gordon, I repaired to the quarter deck, to watch the movements of the *Leopard;* and then, for the first time, discovered that the tompions were out, and her guns training upon us. On discovering this it was, that I gave the second order to Captain Gordon, to 'hurry his men to quarters'. . . .

I did give the orders to get the men to quarters secretly, and without beat of drum. . . . The order was not only justified, but made necessary by the occasion. . . . While I was desirous to be prepared for any result, it was my duty to pursue such a course as would not provoke hostility, if none was designed, or precipitate it, if intended. . . . [T]he court will judge, if it was possible that a drum could have been beaten, without being heard, at the distance of 50 or 60 yards.[177]

Barron said his bravery had been amply demonstrated:

Wounded by the first broadside, during the whole attack I never quitted the quarter deck. The witnesses concur in saying, that I was in the most exposed situations.—The gangway (which persons unacquainted with naval affairs, would suppose from the charge, to be a place of security and safety,) is the only part of the vessel entirely unsheltered, even from musket balls; and merits the emphatic appellation of the *slaughter house,* given to it by one of the witnesses. . . .

That I hailed the *Leopard* twice, soon after her firing commenced, and said I would send my boat on board, is true. That mind is incapable of either generous or intelligent views, which will not distinguish between a *ruse de guerre,* and an act of cowardice. My antagonists have done me more justice.—They perceived my true motives. . . . [T]hey ascribe my hailing, not as a cowardly disposition to terminate the conflict, but to a wish to gain time to prepare my ship. . . . The beat of the drum in violation of my orders had notified the British commander of my preparations to meet him.

He instantly commenced the attack. My crew, I perceived, were confused and unprepared. A few minutes were all important to my preparations. Was it criminal, or cowardly, by an artifice of this sort, to attempt to amuse my enemy, till I was in condition to repel him?[178]

The "few minutes" necessary to prepare his ship for battle would have made no difference, Barron maintained. Although he was not aware of it at the time, only a few additional guns would have been able to fire. To prepare the ship properly for battle would have taken hours rather than minutes, and this did not include time to drill green crewmen at their battle stations.

Barron defended his surrender of the *Chesapeake*, which he had done to save lives:

> In judging the necessity of this measure, you must ascertain the relative situation of the two ships, at the moment it was adopted. If our situation was such as to furnish no hope of success or escape; if it precluded the expectation of even annoying my antagonist, if it presented no prospect, but the wanton and certain destruction of the crew, . . . there is not on earth a man of sound judgment and correct heart, who will not declare, that the surrender was proper.
>
> My conduct will I hope be tested by the honourable rules of real life, and not by the visionary standard of speculative quixotism. It is admitted that the *Leopard* was a two-decked ship of more than fifty guns, of very superior weight to the *Chesapeake;* the *Chesapeake* a single decked ship, mounted 40 guns. The naval annals of the world, furnish no instance of a capture made by the smaller ship in such a conflict. I mention this disparity, not to justify the surrender; for such disparity of force can never, to a gallant officer, be a reason for yielding without a conflict. I mention it for the purpose of shewing, that in the highest state of discipline, success could not reasonably have been expected. How much this disparity would be increased, by a want of order and discipline in the crew, every man of judgment will at once perceive. My crew was destitute of all order, discipline, and skill. Captain Gordon, who had been in command from February, whose duty I have proved it have been to accustom the men to their quarters, and to the use of the guns, had omitted even to assign them their stations, till a few days before we sailed, and had not once taught them to exercise the guns. . . .
>
> Whatever differences exist in the statements of the witnesses on other points; they all concur in declaring that at *that moment* they were not only unable to *continue,* but even to *commence,* a fire. At that instant there were neither matches, heated loggerheads, powder

horns, cartridges or wads, in any of the divisions, and in some the guns themselves were not entirely prepared. . . .[179]

Barron said only one gun had been fired, and this

after the orders were given to strike the flag. . . . At that time too, the hulls and spars of the ship had suffered materially; twenty of the crew had been killed or wounded; and the residue were dispirited and disheartened. . . . [S]ome of them, actually quitted their quarters, while others were lamenting the useless exposure of their lives. . . . Our antagonist, meanwhile, greatly our superior at the commencement of the attack, was still uninjured, and flushed with the advantage she had acquired over our surprise. . . . The determination to strike the flag, was not however taken till every means had been used to ascertain the state of preparation, and till every hope of repelling the attack had vanished. . . .

Escape was then impossible. No other alternative presented itself, but to sacrifice the lives of my crew or surrender. I adopted the latter.[180]

Barron defended his decision to try to avoid battle:

Was this my duty with the *Leopard?* My duty was defence; not attack—resistance, not assault. It was my duty to use my utmost exertions to keep my ship out of battle, not to bring her to 'battle,' with the ship of a friendly power. Nor did this obligation cease, till the attack commenced.[181]

Barron concluded his defense by saying: "my destiny is in your hands— my life, my honour, the sole patrimony which ten years of service enables me to bestow on my posterity, hand on your decision."[182] The *Norfolk Gazette and Publick Ledger,* in a brief observation on the court-martial, summed up Barron's defense as "eloquent, ingenious, and logical."[183]

The next day, February 4, the court went into private session ashore in Norfolk. Tazewell read the minutes of the proceedings. Over Barron's protest, the court decided to include the findings of the earlier board of inquiry. Someone (possibly Porter) made a motion regretting Tazewell's inclusion of these in the statement of charges, but it was not sustained.[184]

The court rendered its decision on February 8.[185] On the first charge, that of "negligently performing the duty assigned him," it found for Barron. Although the commodore was certainly guilty of remarkable disinterest in his flagship, in assessing responsibility the court held that Captain James Barron . . . was acting under the orders of the honourable the Secretary of the Navy, whereby he was appointed a commodore or commander of a squadron; that by other orders derived from the same source, a master and commander had been appointed to act as captain of this particular frigate under the same James Barron as commodore, and that this acting captain was then on board the ship; the court are of the opinion that it was not the bounden duty of Commodore Barron to examine particularly into her state and condition. . . .[186]

The third charge—that Barron had failed to encourage his men to fight—also was not proven. Barron had exhibited coolness and courage under fire. Ordering his men to quarters secretly without beat of drum

so far from proving him deficient in courage, are considered by the court as strong evidences of his coolness and reflection at that moment. Indeed it would require strong evidence to satisfy this court, that an officer who exposed himself at an open gangway, under a heavy and close fire, who being wounded still remained on his deck during the whole attack, giving his orders coolly and distinctly, and who neither by his words or actions discouraged his crew, or any part of it, could be guilty of this charge.[187]

On the fourth charge, "not doing his utmost to take or destroy the *Leopard*," the court held that, although the *Chesapeake* had not returned fire and the damage sustained did not justify striking the flag, she was in no condition to resist. Boarding the *Leopard* being "impracticable," the only means of repelling the attack was by cannon fire. Had Barron delayed it would only have meant far greater casualties to the crew. Surrender was necessary.[188]

It was the second charge—that Barron had neglected "on the proba- bility of an engagement, to clear the ship for action"—that the court found damning. It concluded that the *Leopard* putting to sea and her triced-up gun ports (in warm weather and a smooth sea) with tompions out did not in themselves indicate hostile intent, but Berkeley's circular "clearly intimated that if certain men were not delivered up he would proceed to use force." This was reinforced by Captain Humphreys's com- munication "that he would take by force, if they could not be obtained by other means, any British deserters that could be found on board. . . ." The court took the position that the intent of Berkeley's order was clear. It determined that it appears to this court from part of the communications of Captain James Barron to the honourable the Secretary of the Navy, and from the evidence of witnesses with whom the said James Barron conversed upon the subject, that he did verily believe from the communication received from the commanding officer of the *Leopard,* that he would take by force, if they could not be obtained by other means, any British deserters that could be found on board the *Chesapeake.*

Despite this, Barron neglected to clear his ship for action.[189]

There was in fact no testimony during the trial that Barron had said that Humphreys was prepared to take the deserters by force. Yet the court found that to be the case, probably as a result of Barron's letter to Smith.

In assessing sentence the court unanimously rejected both death and dismissal from the service. It decided on suspension from service. Terms of eleven and seven years were considered and rejected, and the court sentenced Barron "to be suspended from all command in the Navy of the United States, and that without Pay or official emoluments of any kind, for the period and term of five years" from February 8, 1808. After it was confirmed by the president, Smith formally communicated the sentence to Barron on May 7, 1808.[190]

Barron found the judgment difficult to accept. One of his biographers wrote that he was "now utterly and irretrievably crushed."[191] He remained convinced to the end of his life that he had acted correctly. Barron asked in 1823: "was it my fault that the flag of the *Chesapeake* was disgraced, did I not give the necessary orders, why were they not obeyed, ask a great number of the inhabitants of this town [Norfolk] how the time of that ships officers were spent during her stay in Hampton roads, and the mystery will vanish."[192]

Barron believed the trial had been deliberately orchestrated by the prosecution. He also knew that although he had won acquittal on the most serious charges, in the public mind he would be considered guilty of them as well. Typical of the reaction to the verdict was this comment by a young Oliver Hazard Perry in a letter to his father: "Our officers wait with impatience for the signal to be given to wipe away the stain which the misconduct of one has cast on our flag."[193]

Some thought Barron's sentence too light. Historian Fletcher Pratt summed up the attitude in this quarter when he asserted that James and Samuel Barron were in a sense the "Virginia representatives" in the U.S.

Navy "and thus were somewhat under the special protection of the Virginia presidents, Jefferson, Madison, and (later) Monroe."[194]

Barron's trial had been lengthy: courts-martial of the other three defendants were brief. Gordon's trial began on February 9, and the verdict was announced on February 17.[195] He was charged with "negligently performing the duty assigned him." This revolved around not having prepared the frigate and her crew for the possibility of an engagement before he reported the *Chesapeake* ready for sea.[196]

At the beginning of the trial Tazewell read a statement from Gordon that was for all intents and purposes a frank admission of guilt. Gordon conceded that he had not once exercised the frigate's guns and had called the crew to quarters only three times prior to her sailing. He had not examined her guns to see if they were properly fitted to their carriages and had not seen that matches were primed or in their proper places. Nor had he called for a report from the gunner. Nonetheless, he had reported to Barron that the frigate was ready for sea. Gordon claimed that in making these admissions he was motivated by "conscience." Nevertheless, he expressed confidence that he had acted properly. Gordon said he would not use defense counsel but would rely on the "intelligent officers as my judges." The court then decided to hear additional testimony.[197]

The *Chesapeake*'s lieutenants all rallied behind Gordon. They testified to his vigilance at the Washington Navy Yard and his professional competence during the trip down the Potomac. Crane said that although the men had not been exercised at the guns they were kept busy from "dawn of day until sunset."[198]

Barron also testified. Under questioning by Porter, Barron accused Gordon of having deceived him about the frigate's readiness. The commodore had not inspected the magazines or guns prior to sailing because he considered these Gordon's responsibility. Under Gordon's cross-examination, however, Barron was forced to admit that he had approved of the condition of the frigate, "all but the armament." He also admitted that Gordon had informed him while he was in Hampton of problems encountered in the trip down the Potomac. Gordon also got Barron to concede that it was not normal U.S. Navy practice for guns to be exercised when "coming down the Potomac, with all your guns not aboard and your crew not complete." Barron continued to insist, however, that he was "under an erroneous impression of the state of the ship." Tazewell countered this by reading Barron's letter of June 6 to Secretary Smith, in which he had expressed "pleasure" at her "extreme cleanliness and order."[199]

Barron also admitted, in response to a question from Porter, that the crew could not have been properly trained on the guns before the frigate proceeded to sea. He believed the men should at least have been exercised at the guns but said, "I attributed his not having done so more to the lumbered state of the ship than to any wilful neglect on his part."[200]

Lieutenant Allen attributed the failure to exercise the crew at the guns before the ship sailed to bad weather, "ship's duty," and, on one occasion, to "the lateness of the hour." (In a July letter, however, Allen had been sharply critical of the failure to exercise the men at the guns. He wrote that on June 20 "the men were stationed at their Quarters [and] on the 21st the men were mustered at their quarters and told their stations—*but not exercised!*" The court's Lieutenant Jones asked Allen whether exercising the men at the guns for a half-hour a day would have "materially delayed the ship under the then existing circumstances," and Allen replied, "I do not think it would." He also revealed that the *Chesapeake* had fired salutes of sixteen guns each in passing Mount Vernon and while at Hampton Roads to return a salute from the *Revenge;* no deficiencies had been found on the second occasion, he said.[201]

Midshipman Elliott testified that after the encounter he discovered at least three of the Third Division guns had been defectively mounted and that breechings were too large.[202] At Gordon's request, Decatur countered by testifying that while he had changed the frigate's gun breechings and modified her sponges after taking command, the originals would have given satisfactory service.[203]

With testimony concluded, on February 15 Tazewell read Gordon's lengthy statement defending his actions. He admitted he had never exercised the *Chesapeake*'s guns, but he pointed out that she had only twelve on board before June 6 and that her quarterdeck guns had been mounted only on the fifteenth. Testimony had shown that, because of shoal water, it was not usual for a large ship to carry all her ordnance down the Potomac River. He had been a junior officer during the war with Tripoli and "I know well that the guns of the *New York* in which I sailed under the command of commodore Barron . . . were never exercised until we had got far into the Atlantic."[204]

Gordon had called the crew to quarters only twice, but this was because the crew was not complete. He had left inspection of gun fittings to the gunner and his officers. He also blamed the gunner for not filling the powder horns as ordered. And Gordon said that he had ordered matches kept in the gunner's storeroom to prevent a possible unextinguished match being returned to the magazine and blowing up the ship.[205]

Gordon denied he had ever reported to Barron that the *Chesapeake* was ready for sea; he had said merely that it *would* be ready on a particular day. He had kept Barron closely informed of the status of the vessel and the fact that her guns had never been exercised. Gordon asserted that he had done his duty: "I have the consolation to know too, that the stain the flag of the ship has suffered, did not proceed as a consequence in any degree from my antecedent errors, if such they be."[206]

The court then deliberated Gordon's guilt or innocence on twenty-one specifics of the charge of "negligently performing the duty assigned him." Although it found him innocent of many specifics, he was found guilty of the overall charge. The court rejected death, dismissal from the service, suspension, and public reprimand. It settled on the surprising sentence— little more than a slap on the wrists—of private reprimand by the secretary of the navy "or by such person as he may think proper to appoint for that purpose. . . ." In explaining the sentence, the court held that the untimely death of Lt. Benjamin Smith had inhibited Gordon's defense. He was "certainly guilty of some offence (although a very slight one)." He had not called "upon the Gunner of the said frigate *Chesapeake,* for a regular written report of the state and condition of the guns and all other matters in his Department," and he had not required the same of Captain Hall regarding the marines. But "no evil resulted from any of the neglects of duty charged upon him."[207]

Probably Gordon was saved by political connections. Barron later wrote that Captain Hall had told him that "Tazewell wrote his and Captain Gordon's defence, and I am confident that no man that knew Captain Gordon, will believe that he wrote it, notwithstanding, his declaration to the court when he presented it."[208] Gordon later reportedly made boasts confirming Barron's assertion and subsequently tried to promote Tazewell to be secretary of the navy. It is interesting that Tazewell's fees, approved by the Jefferson administration, were greater than he had requested and equal to the annual pay of a navy captain.[209]

John Hall's trial began on February 18.[210] The captain was charged with negligence of duty: failing to see that his marines were supplied with sufficient cartridges of proper size and not reporting the "exact state and conditions of marines on board" to Captain Gordon.[211] Marine Lt. William Anderson had testified at Gordon's trial that the marines had some four to five hundred cartridges (about ten per man, although each cartouche box could hold twenty-one rounds). The cartridges were indeed "rather small, but the deficiency was so trifling as not to be worth attending to," Anderson said. In trials before going to sea Anderson had found "no sort of defect in them whatsoever. On the contrary, I discovered the ball was carried to a great distance in firing them."[212] Damaging testimony was provided by Marine Sgt. John Otto. He said there were six hundred cartridges available, and testified that he had reported the smallness of them to Hall after sailing and before the encounter with the Leopard. He said they were so small as to fall out of the musket after it was loaded. Hall recalled Otto to the stand and used one of the muskets and a cartridge (identified by Otto) to show the charge would not fall out of the bore.[213] Hall said he had reported the number of cartridges to Gordon but that his superior may have been too busy to take notice; Gordon said he had not. Hall also protested that he, a Marine officer, was being tried by "sea officers only."[214]

The court found Hall guilty "of negligently performing the duty assigned him" but affirmed there were mitigating circumstances and "that no evil has resulted from any of the neglects of duty charged. . . ." Hall was sentenced to be reprimanded by the secretary of the navy, "at such time, and in such manner, as he shall think most proper."[215]

Gunner William Hook was the last to be tried. He had seven years of service with the navy, had been gunner of the Enterprize in the war with Tripoli, and had been in Decatur's party that fired the captured Philadelphia. He was charged with negligence of duty because the Chesapeake's guns were improperly mounted, sponges and wads were not of the proper size, powder horns were unfilled, and matches were not in their proper place. He was also charged with assuming his battle station only after repeated orders and the Leopard had already opened fire.[216] One of the witnesses was Lieutenant Allen. Even allowing for Hook's stammer, Allen was certain that the gunner had told him he had filled seventeen powder horns.[217] After rather cursory testimony from a few witnesses (the February 20 trial could not have taken more than a few hours), Hook rested without formal statement of defense.

The court found Hook guilty on most of the specifications and held that "much of this neglect was wilful." Because of the fatal consequences of the ship's unpreparedness, Hook was dismissed from the service.[218] It was later revealed that Hook had deserted from the Royal Navy. Barron wrote that Hook "first robbed the Chichester, an English 50 gun ship, and then deserted her, he was on board the Chesapeake without my knowledge of his character. What a witness in such a case."[219]

There was another, innocent, victim of the affair: Capt. Samuel Barron. The same day that James Barron was suspended from his command Secretary of the Navy Smith moved against his brother. It appears to be an act of spite because Samuel stood by his brother in his travails. Samuel was "deprived of his employment and put on half pay, $600 per annum."[220] Always in poor health, he died in October 1810 shortly after new Secretary of the Navy Paul Hamilton named him commandant of the Norfolk Navy Yard.[221]

With the trials over, Secretary Smith had reason to be pleased that the honor of the navy was reasonably intact. The chief controversy about the trial is not so much the guilt or innocence of Barron but whether the court protected Gordon and perhaps the frigate's lieutenants. Once Barron was found not guilty of responsibility for the unready state of the *Chesapeake*, only Gordon and his lieutenants could be accountable. Gordon had failed to prepare his ship for a transatlantic voyage, let alone an engagement, and yet Barron had been found guilty of not clearing the *Chesapeake*'s guns for action during the hour between the *Leopard*'s coming alongside and the first shots. The court's conclusion that "no evil" resulted from Gordon's neglect seems inexplicable. The heaviest sentences of the court-martial fell on those at the opposite ends of the rank spectrum, Barron and Hook, while those in between were virtually exonerated.

Aftermath

Stephen Decatur, captain of the *Chesapeake* for the next two years, had hoped he would be the one to avenge the U.S. Navy. He drilled his crew and asserted he would do battle with any British warship on the slightest provocation; in particular, he swore to attack the *Leopard* if he ever encountered her.[1]

After the *Chesapeake-Leopard* Affair the small U.S. Navy expended most of its energies trying to enforce the Embargo. President James Madison, elected in 1808, showed little interest in strengthening the navy. After the 1807 war scare the *Chesapeake* was principally involved in embargo duties. At the end of August 1807 Secretary Smith ordered her into the Chesapeake to look for a pirate schooner that had taken some American merchant vessels in the upper bay.[2] The *Chesapeake*'s departure from Norfolk was delayed by contrary winds and she did not sail until September 2, in company with Gunboats Nos. *58* and *67*. The next morning the frigate passed the Royal Navy's *Triumph* (74), *Cleopatra* (38), and *Halifax* (16), all riding at anchor. On learning that the pirate vessel had been apprehended, Decatur returned to Norfolk.[3]

On January 6, 1808, Decatur wrote Smith to protest the designation of the *Chesapeake* as a 44-gun frigate:

I think it an object of importance not only as respects the Reputation of the officer who may command this ship, but the reputation of the Flag of the United States to have the rate of the *Chesapeake* established, she has been hitherto represented as a 44, this is not the case, she is but an Eight & thirty and mounts but forty guns, the rates of all Frigates are determined by the Number of guns on their main decks, an Eight & thirty carries Twenty eight guns on the main Deck, the *Chesapeake* carries but Twenty Eight & consequently is over rated.

Decatur urged that guns be mounted on the frigate's forecastle: "She is fitted for them & would be much more formidable if she had them, neither would she be attended with any additional expense, for the men who are compelled to station in those parts of the ship, would be sufficient to manage them." Decatur recommended that she carry ten 42-pounder carronades. Smith decided on 32s and directed that ten be shipped from the Washington Navy Yard to Norfolk and mounted on the frigate. They were delivered in early March.[4]

Two months later Smith ordered the *Chesapeake* to St. Mary's, Georgia, to take a small armed vessel presumed to be sailing under a letter of marque and violating the Embargo. Decatur was then to proceed north to Passamaquoddy, Maine, and enforce the trade ban. When the frigate was no longer needed there Decatur was to return to Norfolk. He was admonished not to violate the "acknowledged jurisdiction" of either Spain or Great Britain. The orders were countermanded, however; on July 1, there being no immediate need to sail to St. Mary's, Decatur was ordered to sail to Passamaquoddy, then proceed to St. Mary's. Again the object was to prevent violations of the Embargo. Later that month Smith wrote Decatur to tell him of repeated reports of violations from Rhode Island eastward and ordered Decatur to operate there, with the brig *Argus* and sloop *Wasp* both subject to his orders. The *Chesapeake* got to sea on July 13 and off New England intercepted a number of vessels suspected of embargo violations. The job was a difficult one, made more so by the proximity of Canada and the presence of two Royal Navy ships, the frigate *Squirrel* (32) and brig *Plumper* (18), which stood ready to provide protection to smugglers as soon as they crossed into Canadian waters. The *Chesapeake* cruised in the area from New York to Passamaquoddy until November. Decatur reported that the approach of winter would endanger operations there after the end of the month, and Smith ordered him to proceed to Hampton Roads, where the *Chesapeake* anchored on December 8.[5]

In February 1809 Capt. Isaac Hull succeeded Decatur as captain of the *Chesapeake*; Decatur was transferred to the frigate *United States*.[6] That same month Smith ordered Hull to enter men on two years' enlistment for a cruise. In April Acting Secretary of the Navy Charles Goldsborough authorized the replacement of the frigate's sails and ordered the purchase of necessary provisions. In June the *Chesapeake* was at Boston, and Hull received authorization for a short cruise of several weeks for "exercising" the crew. On her return Secretary of the Navy Paul Hamilton ordered the frigate laid up at Boston. Needed repairs were to be deferred until spring.[7]

Relations with Great Britain continued to worsen, however, and early in 1810 Hamilton appointed a board under captains Tingey and Chauncey to investigate the feasibility of repairing and fitting out the mothballed frigates *Congress, Constellation, Adams,* and *New York*. In June Hamilton sent a letter to captains in which he pointed out "injuries and insults" committed by both France and Great Britain against America. Among these

> stands out most conspicuous the inhuman and dastardly attack on our Frigate *Chesapeake*—an outrage which prostrated the flag of our Country and has imposed on the American people cause of ceaseless mourning. . . . What has been perpetrated may again be attempted. It is therefore our duty to be prepared and determined at every hazard, to vindicate the injured honor of our Navy, and revive the drooping Spirit of the Nation.[8]

It was John Rodgers who avenged the *Chesapeake,* and in circumstances somewhat similar to that ship's encounter with the *Leopard*. The issue sparking the incident was again impressment. The British frigate *Guerrière* had halted an American merchant brig off New York and impressed one John Diggio, a native of Maine. On learning of this, Secretary Hamilton on May 6, 1811, ordered Rodgers to take the frigate *President* (44) to sea. Contrary winds delayed her sailing until the fourteenth, but two days later the *President*'s lookout sighted what was assumed to be a man-of-war northeast of Cape Henry. The latter approached aggressively until her captain realized that the *President* was a U.S. frigate rather than a merchantman. The warship then hoisted the British colors and made all sail south. Feeling—probably hoping—she might be the *Guerrière*, Rodgers ordered a pursuit. The chase continued all afternoon. It was not until after nightfall that the superior sailing qualities of the *President* enabled her to close to within speaking distance. Rodgers claimed he was able to determine neither the size nor power of the other ship.

Three times Rodgers tried to position his ship to windward of his opponent within speaking distance, but the other ship wore and hauled by the wind on different tacks to prevent it. Rodgers claimed that as he was trying to hail the ship she fired a shot at the *President.* One of the American gun crews returned fire without being ordered to do so, and both sides began general fire.

The adversary was the Royal Navy ship sloop *Little Belt* (Capt. A. B. Bingham).[9] Bingham claimed that the Americans had fired first, and even some American sources agreed. Rated a 20-gun ship but actually mounting only eighteen guns, the *Little Belt* sustained considerable damage. Thirteen of her men were killed and another nineteen wounded. The Americans had only a boy wounded in the arm (it required amputation, however). The *President* sustained minor damage to her fore and main masts. The *Little Belt* ceased firing, and Rodgers followed suit. The next morning Bingham declined assistance and the two ships parted company.[10] Both President Madison and Secretary Hamilton immediately approved Rodgers' conduct in the affair, and the commodore found himself hailed as the man who avenged the *Chesapeake.* Later President Madison described Bingham's actions as "a hostile aggression on the flag of the United States."[11]

James Fenimore Cooper wrote that the *President-Little Belt* affair "gave rise to much angry discussion in America, and widened the breach which already existed between the English and American nations." He noted, "In England the account of Captain Bingham was generally believed, and it served to increase a dislike that was so little concealed as to attract general comment." In the United States there was a division of opinion: "A strong feeling existed in the towns, and among a certain portion of the rural population, in favour of what was called the English cause."[12]

The incident was almost repeated. On June 9 the frigate *United States,* under Decatur, sailed from Hampton Roads for New York. On her way to the capes she sighted two British warships, the *Eurydice* (38 guns) and *Atlanta* (24), which stood for the U.S. frigate and reached her at dusk. The captain of the *Eurydice* identified his vessel and informed Decatur that he carried dispatches for the American government. A gun on the *United States* sent a shot in the direction of the British ship. Decatur reported: "I am happy that a pause followed, which enabled me to inform her commander that the fire was the effect of accident." The British captain accepted this, and when a British officer came on board the *United States* Decatur repeated his explanation and learned that no one had been injured on the *Eurydice*.[13]

The British sought redress for the *Little Belt* affair. British Minister Augustus Foster, who arrived in the United States in the summer of 1811, initiated a lengthy correspondence with Secretary of State James Monroe to demand that Rodgers be punished and reparations paid.[14] He contrasted the American response with British conduct in the *Chesapeake* Affair, "when every reparation practicable at the instance the intelligence reached London of the unfortunate event, was made to you, sir, promptly and unasked for." He wrote:

> I feel the more regret, sir, at the course taken by your government in this affair, because I have been necessarily obliged in consequence to suspend carrying into execution that part of my instructions by which I was directed immediately on my arrival here to offer such further reparation for the attack on the *Chesapeake* frigate as would, I am convinced, have proved satisfactory.[15]

Monroe repeatedly assured Foster that there were no orders to frigate captains to attack British warships in order to recover impressed seamen. He also registered "sincere regret . . . that such an encounter took place, and more especially that it should have produced the unfortunate consequence which attended it."[16] But Foster's allusion to the *Chesapeake* affair drew an acid response from Monroe in a letter dated September 14: "It is not seen without surprise that the case of the *Chesapeake* is cited as an example supporting a demand of reparation in the present case. No other remark will be made than that the fifth year is now elapsing without reparation in that case. . . ."[17]

What became of the principals in the *Chesapeake-Leopard* Affair? Both ships were lost during the War of 1812. In 1810 the *Leopard* participated in operations in the Indian Ocean, resulting in the capture of the last remaining French bases there, Mauritius and Reunion. In January 1812 the *Leopard* (then commanded by Capt. William Henry Dillon) and the *Endymion* (40) unsuccessfully chased two French frigates and a brig that had departed Nantes on an Atlantic cruise. On June 18, 1814, the *Leopard*, serving as a troopship and under the command of Capt. Edward Lowther Crofton, was wrecked off Anticosti Island in the St. Lawrence River.[18]

The *Chesapeake* met an even less glorious end. On the outbreak of the war she was in poor repair. Outfitted at Boston and placed under Capt.

Samuel Evans, she set sail into the Atlantic on December 13, 1812. Until April 9, 1813, she cruised from the West Indies to Africa, taking five British merchantmen and managing to escape from a British 74 and a frigate. She returned to Boston on April 18 to be refitted.[19]

On May 20, 1813, Capt. James Lawrence assumed command. Lawrence had been captain of the *Hornet* on February 24, 1813, when she defeated HMS *Peacock,* and he was promoted to captain on the basis of that action. He soon learned that while Charlestown Navy Yard workers had gotten his ship ready, much of her crew was new and untrained. This was in part because of dissatisfaction over pay and prize money, which could be much more lucrative on the many privateers. Of the former officer complement, only twenty-one-year-old 3d Lt. Augustus C. Ludlow remained; Lawrence promptly made him his first lieutenant. Lawrence exercised his crew at the guns six times, but they did not actually fire. The first time the frigate actually got under way under his command was to go into battle.

The Royal Navy had by then established a reasonably complete blockade of the U.S. Atlantic coast. Two British frigates, the *Shannon* and *Tenedos,* maintained close watch off Boston.[20]

Lawrence had been one of the officers in Barron's court-marital, and two years before that he had suffered the humiliation of seeing the British removing seamen from his gunboat (see Chapter 4). These events probably influenced his rash decision to undertake a one-on-one engagement with the *Shannon* (38 guns).[21]

In sharp contrast to the *Chesapeake,* the crew of the *Shannon* was one of the best-trained afloat. Capt. Philip Broke, who had assumed command of the frigate in June 1806, was a key figure in introducing improved gunnery techniques in the Royal Navy and had trained the crew in concentrating fire. (This entailed marking the deck in degrees and directing all guns so their fire converged.) He also spent his own money to equip his ship with the latest aiming devices, and he was a staunch advocate of realistic gunnery training reinforced by frequent drill. Broke was keen to avenge the British warship losses early in the war that had so shocked English public opinion and the Royal Navy.[22]

The *Chesapeake* was slightly larger than the *Shannon,* which was on the design of the *Leda* (38), one of the few classes of frigates of this period with square-tuck sterns. In armament the two ships were equally matched. The *Shannon* mounted fifty-two guns: thirty-three long guns (twenty-eight 18-pounders, four 9s, and one 6) and nineteen carronades (sixteen 32-pounders and three 12s). The *Chesapeake* had fifty guns: twenty-nine long guns, all 18-pounders, and twenty-one carronades (twenty 32-pounders and one 12). The *Chesapeake* shipped about forty more men (*Shannon* 326 men and 23 boys; *Chesapeake* 373 men and 14 boys).[23]

On June 1, 1813, the *Chesapeake* sailed out of Boston harbor. Lawrence chose for action "a smooth sea, a royal breeze, an artillery duel, and a close range."[24] At the onset of the action he missed an opportunity to rake the British frigate. The naval theoretician Alfred Thayer Mahan attributed this to eagerness; Lawrence's friends said it was chivalry. In any case, he discarded tactical advantage in favor of a simple artillery duel.

The difference in the battle was the superior discipline and gunnery of the British. Poor sail handling on the part of the Americans was another factor, as was deteriorated cannon powder that greatly diminished the effectiveness of the *Chesapeake*'s fire. Broadsides from the *Shannon* cut the U.S. frigate's stays and caused her to drift helplessly toward her adversary. The *Shannon* then maneuvered into position and raked her from stem to stern with cannon fire and musketry from her tops, while the *Chesapeake* was unable to reply in kind. Just before the two ships came together Lawrence ordered up a boarding party, but before it could form he was wounded by a musket ball and carried below. Captain Broke and about fifty boarders from the *Shannon* leapt aboard the *Chesapeake*'s quarterdeck. A large majority of the British boarding party was killed or wounded (Broke among the latter), some by their own fire and others by some thirty Americans who rallied at the forecastle; but the British managed to haul down the U.S. flag and take control of the ship.

It was the bloodiest frigate engagement of the War of 1812. The *Shannon* lost thirty-three killed and forty-three wounded; the *Chesapeake* sustained sixty-two killed and eighty-five wounded. Nearly half the *Chesapeake*'s crew and a quarter of the *Shannon*'s were casualties. Lawrence's wounds proved fatal; he died four days later. But his coolness and courage during the battle and his last words ("Don't give up the ship") before being carried from the deck made him an American hero. Lieutenant Ludlow also was mortally wounded; he too had been a member of the court that had condemned Barron.[25] Among those taken prisoner was a Seaman William Martin, perhaps the same William Martin taken off the *Chesapeake* on June 22, 1807, and returned to her on July 10, 1812. There is no record of the other seaman returned, John Strachan, being aboard.[26]

The British sailed the *Chesapeake* to Halifax and took her into the Royal Navy. On August 22, 1814, she sailed for England in company with *La Hogue* (74) and *Orpheus* (36). The three ships carried five hundred prisoners of war. She was paid off at Portsmouth on September 22, 1815, and five years later was sold in the same city to a Mr. Holmes, who broke her up for timber and copper. Much of her wood went for housing, but the greater part of her timbers were used in the construction of a great flour mill, known as the Chesapeake Mill, at Wickham, near Southampton. The mill stands today, some of the timbers still visible.[27]

The subsequent careers of Captain Humphreys and Admiral Berkeley already have been discussed (see Chapter 6). Master Commandant Charles Gordon continued as flag captain of the *Chesapeake.* Nearly nine months after the clash with the *Leopard,* Secretary of the Navy Smith wrote Decatur that "A direct order from me detaching him from the Ship, would be considered as a degradation, under his present circumstances."[28] In February 1809 Gordon took command of the brig *Siren* and sailed her to Lorient, France. On her arrival at that port—ironically, almost on the anniversary of the *Chesapeake-Leopard* affair—French authorities insisted on the right to search the *Siren.* Gordon refused, although he did let the French board without the right to search. On his return Gordon learned that new Secretary of the Navy Paul Hamilton was pleased with his performance; his future in the navy seemed assured.

While the *Siren* was stationed at Baltimore Gordon took umbrage over an article written by Alexander Contee Hanson, vitriolic editor of the Baltimore *Federal Republican,* that disparaged participants in the *Chesapeake-Leopard* Affair. Gordon demanded satisfaction and challenged Hanson to a duel. The duel took place on January 10, 1810; Hanson, a crack shot, badly wounded Gordon in the lower abdomen. He was nursed back to health by his aunt, Hannah Gallatin, but remained partially disabled until 1813.

Although he rejoined the *Chesapeake* at Boston in 1811, Gordon's precarious health led him to petition the Navy Department for a more southerly assignment. In late November 1811 he took command of the Baltimore naval station. In July 1812 he was promoted to captain and ordered to Charlestown, Massachusetts, to take command of the navy yard there and ready the *Chesapeake* for sea. Knowing it would take months to prepare her and that his health might not in any case allow him to command the frigate, Gordon secured permission to remain at Baltimore. It is interesting to speculate what might have happened had it been left to Gordon to avenge the frigate's honor, but it was his friend James Lawrence who took command.

In August 1813 Gordon took command of the frigate *Constellation* at Norfolk. Unsuccessful in two attempts during the winter of 1814 to get her to sea past the British blockade, Gordon spent much of the remainder of the war feuding with Capt. John Cassin and Capt. Joseph Tarbell. Ordered to the Mediterranean in early 1815, Gordon had an unspectacular career commanding the *Constellation* until his death on September 6, 1816, at Messina, Sicily, of complications from his wound five years earlier.[29]

Marine Capt. John Hall left the frigate after his court-martial. He was promoted to major in June 1814 but left the marines in 1817.[30]

William Crane went on to a distinguished naval career. He was promoted to master commandant in March 1813 and to captain in November 1814. Crane commanded the ship *Madison* on Lake Ontario during the War of 1812. Later he was a commodore and chief of the Bureau of Ordnance and Hydrography. Despondent over the 1844 explosion of the "Peacemaker" gun aboard the *Princeton,* which killed the secretary of state, secretary of the navy, and six others, Crane resigned in March 1846, locked himself in his office, and slashed his throat.[31]

John Creighton was promoted to master commandant in July 1813 and to captain in April 1816. He died in October 1838. Sidney Smith was promoted to master commandant in February 1815 and died in May 1827. Midshipman Charles Norton resigned from the service in April 1809. Midshipman Alexander Wadsworth worked his way up to captain; he died in April 1851. Midshipman James Wilson was promoted to lieutenant in May 1812 and last appears in Navy Department records in 1814. Midshipman Glenn Drayton died in September 1814.

The War of 1812 claimed William Henry Allen. Promoted to master commandant in July 1813, he received command of the 18-gun brig *Argus* and was ordered to carry new U.S. Minister William Crawford to France, then raid British shipping in the Channel as part of new Secretary of the Navy William Jones's effort to take the war to the enemy. Fast and nimble, the heavily-armed *Argus* fulfilled Jones's wish. In only a month Allen took twenty British vessels.

On August 14, 1813, Allen sighted the larger 21-gun British brig *Pelican* off Wales. His own vessel was faster and could easily have escaped to continue its raid on British merchant shipping. Allen's biographer says that "common sense and wise judgment should have led him to avoid battle," but Allen chose to fight. The battle went entirely to the British. Five minutes into it, a cannon shot carried off one of Allen's legs. He died four days later at Mill Prison Hospital, Plymouth. The British gave him a splendid funeral, which was attended by all captains then in port.[32]

Henry Babbitt, who made lieutenant in June 1810, also died in action, on January 15, 1815, in the frigate *President.* Taking advantage of bad weather,

Commodore Decatur had the day before taken the *President* to sea from her anchorage off Staten Island. Unfortunately she grounded that same night and was badly damaged before finally getting free ninety minutes later. The delay and damage she sustained allowed four British frigates of the blockading squadron—the *Majestic, Endymion, Potomac,* and *Tenedos*— to come up and cut off her escape. In the resulting battle a 24-pounder shot from the *Endymion* knocked Babbitt down the frigate's after hatch. He died twenty minutes later of a fractured skull. Surrounded, with one-fifth of his crew killed or wounded, Decatur surrendered.[33]

Jesse Elliott played an important role in the War of 1812. On October 9, 1812, he commanded the force on Lake Erie that took the British brigs *Detroit* and *Caledonia.* Although the *Detroit* was subsequently destroyed, the *Caledonia* formed the nucleus of the Lake Erie squadron, and Elliott received deserved acclaim. But his role in the Battle of Lake Erie of September 10, 1813, was controversial. Elliott was captain of the brig *Niagara.* He failed to bring her into action while Commodore Oliver Hazard Perry in the *Lawrence* engaged virtually the entire British squadron. With only nineteen of his 142 men still able to fight, Perry abandoned the *Lawrence* and rowed to the *Niagara.* Perry brought her into the battle, crossed the "T" of the British line, and turned the tide. When British Capt. Robert H. Barclay capitulated, it was the first time a Royal Navy commander had surrendered an entire squadron. After Perry took command of the *Niagara* Elliott rowed to bring up the gunboats, exposing himself to enemy fire, but his previous failure to close grew into bitter controversy. Later there were sharp divisions in the navy between partisans of Perry and Elliott. Decatur was one of Perry's strong defenders.

Elliott continued to court controversy. In May 1840 Elliott, now a commodore, faced misconduct charges based on his Mediterranean service when he had sacrificed crew comfort and ship efficiency to bring home to the United States a considerable collection of ancient artifacts, including two Roman sarcophagi and a half-dozen marble columns, and twenty-one hogs, horses, and jackasses, which he lodged on the *Constitution*'s gun deck. A board found Elliott guilty on five of thirteen counts, including oppression, immorality, and wasting public funds. He was sentenced to four years' suspension without pay, but this was later reduced to two years. Elliott died in 1845, shortly after returning to duty.[34]

Judge Advocate Littleton Tazewell went on to a successful political career, serving as U.S. senator (1824–30) and governor of Virginia (1834–36).[35]

Barron, meanwhile, brooded. He believed the fault for June 22 lay with incompetent and cowardly subordinates, and he blamed Rodgers and Decatur for the court-martial verdict. "Shamed, but proud . . . Barron never again saw the world quite so fair, nor felt the sun so good, the air so sweet to the lungs."[36]

Barron, "suddenly destitute with a large and helpless female family [a wife and five daughters] to support," felt "my only resort was to a nautical proffession [sic]."[37] But with the Embargo in place, opportunities were rare. His brother Samuel offered to help, but he was on half pay. To economize, James moved his family into a small farmhouse on Back River in Hampton.

It was fourteen months before Barron could find work. In April 1809 Robert Cary Jennings of Norfolk offered him command of the small brig *Brazilian* (140 tons), which was to trade with Pernambuco, Brazil. His pay was $40 a month. By late summer he was back in Hampton. Samuel died in November 1810, just after being named commandant of the Gosport Navy Yard, and the next year James Barron's wife, Elizabeth, fell ill. Although she recovered, she remained in poor health the rest of her life.

Barron later wrote that he had "ill success in two voyages." The second began on April 5, 1812, when he sailed as master of the brig *Portia* (170 tons). His brother-in-law, William A. Armistead, a principal in the Norfolk merchant firm of Armistead and Keely, had arranged the command at a pay of $40 a month and 2.5 percent commission on profits. Barron arrived in Lisbon in May, disposed of the cargo, and sent the proceeds as instructed to Armistead's agent in London, withholding enough to buy a load of fruit. He took this to Gothenburg, Sweden, where he arrived in early July. Later that month he sailed to Copenhagen and sold the *Portia*. One of his biographers says he sold her because of the declaration of war between the United States and Britain. But Barron wrote in 1820 that his second voyage "terminated in Denmark, I then contacted acquaintances encouraging me to believe that I could better my situation by improvements in mechances [sic] while at the same time I should increase my knowledge in the line of my profession, and thereby perhaps be again useful to my country. The declaration of war, found me struggling in this pursuit."[38]

The *Portia* brought $7,500. Barron forwarded $7,000 of this to Armistead's agent and kept the remainder for his own living expenses and those of his men, four of whom (including Armistead's brother) were young apprentices. The cargo was confiscated without compensation by the Danish government.[39]

Barron was an inveterate inventor. Earlier in his career he had developed the signals system used by the U.S. Navy. In Denmark he either received patents or obtained rights to a kneading machine for dough, one for spinning hemp into rope, and one that cut cork, plus improved windmill machinery and an elliptical valve water pump. Later he developed an improved plough, a cutting machine for straw, an oil lantern, a washing machine, and a machine to clean and polish leather. In all, he held fifteen U.S. patents for such things as a wind wheel, the washing machine, stoves, fans, a filtering device for liquids, metal blocks and pulleys, and a floating dry dock. One of his most successful inventions was a bellows for ventilating ships. The navy subsequently adopted it, as well as his iron blocks and pulley. In later years he worked on a plan for an unsinkable raft-like vessel to fire shells at enemy ships and a "Marine Catapulta"—an armored steam ram. Henry Wise, in the early 1840s a member of the naval committee of the House of Representatives, wrote that Barron "was continuously urging upon the committee his invention of an impregnable steam propelleter [sic] armed with a pyramidal beak on the water line. He could never obtain appropriation for the experiment. It was deemed visionary." Wise believed the plan led directly to the Civil War CSS *Virginia (Merrimack)*.[40]

Barron's suspension from the navy ended on February 8, 1813. On July 22 he sent two letters from Denmark to Secretary of the Navy Jones (whom he did not personally know). In the first letter he noted the expiration of "the term of my suspension." While he did not actually request a command, he said his object in writing

> is to inform you that the first wish of my heart has always been to render service to my country in an honourable way. If therefore they are wished and will be employed to that end, your commands will be readily obeyed. A letter directed to the care of J. M. Forbes, Esquire, will find me here or in St. Petersburg.

In a longer letter Barron protested his innocence and asked for a "review" of the verdict. Defiance and hurt were evident when he wrote: "I never can, nor never will, acknowledge that the sentence under which I have laboured for these five years was just, or that it was not, the result of malice, and not the sound and disinterested opinion of just and impartial Judges." Barron blamed "Gordon and his officers" for having failed to prepare the frigate for sea during the twenty-two days she lay in Hampton

Roads "with her whole crew on board, and her orders ready." These "dishonorable accusers" sought to "remove the blame to some more important person." Barron added, "my only wish in life is to have an opportunity to prove to the world in general and my Country in particular that I have suffered without just cause for there are circumstances known to those intimately acquainted with the particulars of that affair, that would in my humble opinion convince the world, that I was to say the least of it, cruelly sacrificed."[41]

Jones never replied. Barron's beloved home in Hampton, called Little England, burned with all of its contents, probably during the June 1813 British assault. Meanwhile, Barron eked out a threadbare existence. In Copenhagen he lived in one room and survived on about $15 a month, sufficient to meet expenses except clothing. Finally Barron sold rights to four of his inventions to raise funds to sail home. He arrived at Washington in early December 1818.[42]

Since February 1815 naval affairs had been handled by a Board of Navy Commissioners made up of three post captains. The first commissioners were John Rodgers, Isaac Hull, and David Porter. Hull had been a member of the board of inquiry that had found against Barron; the other two had sat on his court-martial. Rodgers was the president of the board of commissioners, by far its most influential member, and certainly hostile to Barron.[43]

On his return to the United States Barron sought a naval command. He met briefly with the chief clerk of the Navy Department, Benjamin Homans, but received a negative response. In February 1819 he met with Secretary of the Navy Smith Thompson, who restated what Homans had said earlier: that Barron's reinstatement had been blocked by statements about the *Chesapeake* affair Barron had purportedly made in Pernambuco and by his "remaining in a foreign country after the expiration of the term of your suspension and especially during the War with Great Britain. . . ." These actions "were considered improper and requiring explanation before giving you employment."[44]

In March 1819 Barron wrote to President Monroe, pleading the injustice of his sentence and seeking a command.[45] In these efforts Capt. Jesse Elliott was virtually his sole support. Elliott had been Barron's strongest defender during his court-martial, and the two became close friends after Barron's return to the United States. Elliott and Barron also shared a common enemy: Stephen Decatur. Elliott blamed Decatur for the shelving of an inquiry into his feud with Perry after the latter had died at sea in

August 1819. It was Elliott who informed Barron of Decatur's continued criticism of him and who fanned the flames of animosity between the two men.[46]

Decatur was now a member of the Board of Navy Commissioners, and in this position he strongly opposed giving Barron command of the ship of the line *Columbia,* which in the spring of 1819 was fitting out as the flagship of the U.S. Mediterranean squadron. Decatur felt Barron did not deserve consideration by reason of his absence during the War of 1812. (Decatur was not alone in this; virtually all other captains in the navy opposed giving Barron a command.)[47]

Prompted by Elliott, Barron accused Decatur of "ungraciously traducing" his character, and a heated correspondence between the two ensued. While Decatur denied any personal differences with Barron, he wrote him that he did "entertain the opinion that your conduct as an officer since the affair of the *Chesapeake* has been such as ought to forever bar your readmission to the service." He based this on two letters: one of September 7, 1811, from Capt. William Lewis to Chief Clerk of the Navy Department Goldsborough and another corroborating the first, of March 4, 1819, from Thomas P. Goodwin of Baltimore to Secretary Thompson. Lewis had written Goldsborough about a purported conversation between Barron and the British consul at Pernambuco, a Mr. Lyons, in 1809. Lyons told Goodwin about the conversation, and Goodwin told Lewis. Supposedly Barron, in Pernambuco with the merchantman *Brazilian,* told Lyons "that even if the *Chesapeake* had been prepared for action, he would not have resisted the attack of the *Leopard.*" This was because

> he knew (as did our government) there were deserters on board his ship. He said to Mr. Lyon [sic] further, that the President of the U.S. knew that there were deserters on board, and of the intention of the British ships to take them; and that his ship was ordered out under these circumstances with a view to bringing about a contest which might embroil the two nations in a war.[48]

In a heated reply to Decatur demanding satisfaction, Barron denied both the conversation with Lyons and that the *Chesapeake-Leopard* incident was "one of the principal causes of the late war." He also said that he had wanted to return to the United States during the War of 1812 but was prevented by "circumstances beyond my control."[49]

Decatur, afraid he might be branded a coward, rejected a "simple statement of facts" that would have avoided a duel. On March 22, 1820, the two men met at Bladensburg, Maryland. Elliott served as Barron's second, while Commodore William Bainbridge acted in that capacity for Decatur.

Bainbridge measured out a distance between the two men of eight paces, at which range neither was likely to miss, and gave them their pistols. Barron told Decatur "if we meet in the other world, let us hope that we may be better friends." Decatur replied, "I never was your enemy." Under dueling etiquette, such an exchange could be used by the seconds to attempt a last-minute reconciliation, but in this case no one tested the opportunity. Instead, Elliott ordered, "Gentlemen, to your places." Each man aimed at the other's hip; a wound there would disable without killing. They fired simultaneously. Barron dropped to the ground immediately; Decatur remained standing for a moment and then also fell. Both had indeed been shot in the hip. Decatur's shot had glanced off Barron's hip and imbedded in his groin; the ball that struck Decatur severed arteries.

After the duel Porter came up and saw Elliott, perhaps fearing he would be arrested, flee in Barron's carriage. Rodgers also rode up, dismounted, and led his horse to where Barron lay. He stared at him for a few seconds before going to Decatur to inquire about him and offer assistance. A few minutes later Rodgers returned to Barron and asked the extent of his wounds. Barron said he would not answer until Rodgers apologized for their last meeting, when Barron had tipped his hat and Rodgers had refused to respond. Rodgers strode off without a word.

While both men lay wounded, each thinking his wound fatal, they exchanged conciliatory words. Decatur told Barron that he had opposed his reinstatement because Barron had remained abroad during the War of 1812. He then asked Barron why he had not returned, and Barron replied, "because I had not the means."

Decatur was put in a carriage and taken to his Washington residence. As Elliott had not returned with Barron's coach, Porter hailed a passing carriage and lifted Barron in. Just across the district line they encountered Elliott returning at a slow pace, clearly hoping the field would be empty upon his return. Porter insisted Elliott take his place in the carriage with Barron. Apparently Barron's friendship with Elliott did not suffer from this.[50]

While Barron had a long and painful recuperation, Decatur died in great agony that night. Several days later he was accorded an impressive funeral attended by the president, chief justice, delegations from the Senate and House of Representatives, and many high-ranking navy officers.[51]

Barron now had an additional burden to bear within the navy. He was known ever after as "the man who killed Decatur." Publication of the pre-duel correspondence between the two men caused some public opinion to shift to his side, however.[52]

Barron continued to seek active command. He had been restored to the navy roster on February 8, 1813, at half-pay of $600 a year. This continued until February 28, 1819, when he was restored to full pay: he drew this until January 31, 1821.[53] Doubts over his absence from the United States during the War of 1812 prevented his securing a command, however. In April 1820 Barron wrote to President Monroe to request a court of inquiry to clear his name. On March 20, 1821, Secretary Thompson appointed it, under the presidency of Capt. Alexander Murray.[54]

Barron protested to Thompson that his previous requests for active service had been overlooked. He also requested that the court meet in Norfolk instead of New York and that Murray be replaced. In a sharp reply, Thompson noted that the only record of Barron seeking U.S. service was his 1813 letter to Secretary Smith and that there was no record of Barron having called at the Navy Department on his return to the United States or making claim to service prior to their February 1819 meeting. He refused to change the location of the court but offered the schooner *Diligence*, then at Norfolk, for "the conveyance of yourself & counsel," and he agreed to replace Murray with Captain Hull. On April 25 Thompson transferred presidency of the court to Capt. Charles Stewart.[55]

The court of inquiry was held at the New York Navy Yard, beginning on May 10, 1821. Several witnesses testified that Barron had tried to return to the United States during the war but lacked the financial means to do so. Barron denied that he had ever stayed with Lyons, the Pernambuco consul, and stated that the reported conversation was false. The sources of the allegations, Lewis and Goodwin, were both dead. (The court did find Lewis was by all reports of "the strictest honour and integrity" and Good-win was "highly respectable," although "of a very ardent temper, which was particularly manifested when excited by conversation on political subjects.") Barron testified he had not known of Lewis's letter until 1818 and that Jefferson had not wanted war: "It was notorious that he [Jefferson] studiously avoided a war, after the affair of the *Chesapeake*."

Barron's testimony was supported by individuals who had been in Brazil at the time of the alleged remarks, and on July 14, 1821, the court found that the alleged conversation between Barron and Lyons in 1809 "has not been proved." The court found there had been no Navy Department order requiring officers absent from the United States to return there, but it also determined

> that although the evidence produced by Captain Barron establishes his sincere and earnest desire to return to the United States at certain periods, and the difficulty of accomplishing his wishes, yet the court is of opinion, that the evidence of his inability to return sooner than he actually did, is not satisfactory; and it is therefore the opinion of the court, that his absence from the United States, without the permission of the government was contrary to his duty as an officer in the Navy of the United States.[56]

This was certainly less than Barron wanted. He wrote John Myers at Norfolk that the proceedings had exhausted him, but he copied the verdict for Myers to disseminate to friends, including Elliott. Barron said he had shown the opinion "to some men of Celebrity who disdain it to be the most obscure and unjustifiably laconic document, that ever they have seen." He hoped to go to Washington in a few days to "face the Big Fish and learn their further intentions." He also wrote Thompson to "protest against the decision of the court, on the point of criminality alluded to by them," of his absence from the United States during the War of 1812.[57] Elliott wrote Barron that President Monroe "professes himself to be your friend and has promised to have the proceedings of your Court of Enquiry published immediately."[58]

A severe, prolonged illness prevented Barron from pressing his case with Thompson. It was not until May 1822 that he wrote Thompson that he had recovered his health. Barron noted, "The decision of the government respecting my ultimate destiny is to me unknown." He requested a decision and said, "I am ready to execute any order that may be given. It is my wish to render some service to my Country—in compensation for the pay which I receive.[59] That same year Barron learned that President Monroe had allowed the proceedings of his 1807 court-martial to be published.[60]

Although Monroe received Barron at Washington "with the greatest degree of kindness" and promised to see what might be arranged with the Navy Department, nothing was done. By November 1823 Barron was writing about "the subject of my miserable situation" and hinting at intrigues against him.[61] Finally, on July 24, 1824, Barron received command of the Philadelphia Navy Yard. Gen. Andrew Jackson's intercession with the president may have been the deciding factor.[62]

Barron's tenure at Philadelphia was brief. The next May he returned to Norfolk to command the Gosport Navy Yard. This was when the dry dock was established and other important improvements were made to the yard, all of which he supervised.[63] In November 1828 Secretary of the Navy Samuel Southard offered "Commodore" Barron command of the U.S. Navy Pacific squadron off South America with the *Guerrière* as his flagship, but Barron declined because he was trying to establish claims to his father's Revolutionary War bounty lands. (Barron lost the case.)[64] In 1831 Barron again accepted command of the Philadelphia Navy Yard, replacing Bainbridge. He resigned his naval command in 1837 because an officer junior to him was named president of the navy board. Barron tried his hand at farming without success and sought naval command from Presidents Harrison and Tyler. In March 1842 he took command of the Naval Asylum, a home for retired naval personnel, in Philadelphia. In November 1842 Barron retired from that post and moved back to Norfolk, where he contributed a number of articles on his father and brother to the *Virginia Historical Record*. On the death of John Rodgers in 1838, Barron became the senior officer in the navy. He died on April 21, 1851, at the age of eighty-three. The *Chesapeake* was his last U.S. Navy command at sea, but at least Barron had the satisfaction of outliving the other principals in the affair.[65]

The *Chesapeake-Leopard* Affair in Retrospect

B esides revealing what would be a continuing American propensity in times of peace to trust other nations always to follow the rules, the *Chesapeake-Leopard* incident had many aftereffects. It certainly sowed discord in the U.S. Navy. Historian Fletcher Pratt wrote that the practical effect of Barron's trial was "to split the service into two parties," although it "remained at the level of opinion and personal conversation for the most part, and produced few readily visible results."[1] Enmity between naval officers over the affair continued long afterward, although there is no proof this affected the navy in an operational sense.

Another consequence of the encounter was heightened readiness on the part of ship captains. After June 22, 1807, they took care to ensure that their ships were ready for any eventuality immediately upon leaving port; and no U.S. Navy captain would risk letting a British warship get near his own vessel without bringing his crew to quarters for possible action.

The *Chesapeake-Leopard* Affair also sparked national debate about military preparedness. In assessing the 1807 mobilization following the incident the *Norfolk Gazette and Publick Ledger* correctly identified the problem:

Our government relied too much on the *volunteer system,* for both men and money. We do not mean to dilate on this subject *at present,* but we are persuaded that there are not three men of understanding in this part of the country, who would rely on that system of defense. We have had a short but satisfactory lesson on this subject.[2]

Jefferson reconvened Congress in special session in late October as a result of the *Chesapeake-Leopard* Affair. When he addressed it Jefferson was ambivalent regarding military expansion. He noted only that the administration was still considering its course of action. His point of view regarding the navy remained unchanged. As Henry Adams noted, "what Jefferson had so long foreseen took place. He had maintained that the frigates were a mere invitation to attack; that they created the dangers they were built to resist, and tempted the aggressions of Great Britain, which would, but for these ships, find no object to covet."[3]

Jefferson preferred that militia reform take precedence over regular army expansion; and with no administration recommendations forthcoming on the size of the regular military establishment, Congress got bogged down in debate over coast defense, an issue dear to the president. Indeed, the *Chesapeake-Leopard* Affair may actually have encouraged public support for the administration's gunboat program, which was part of the larger goal of improving defenses of harbors and ports. In September 1807 Jefferson wrote Thomas Paine concerning a gunboat model Paine had sent him and observed: "Believing, myself, that gunboats are the only *water* defense which can be useful to us, & protect us from the ruinous folly of a navy, I am pleased with everything which promises to improve them."[4] In December 1808 Congress authorized construction of an additional 188 gunboats.[5]

Gunboats were but part of the coast defense plan. Fortification was another. Under its November 1807 harbor defense plan, Congress spent the remarkable sum of $3 million over the next five years to implement what became known as the Second System defensive works.[6]

The incident also led to the U.S. Navy contracting for an entire new inventory of small arms. For the most part these were new models, supplanting those instituted in 1797. For example, the navy ordered 2,000 new-model cutlasses from Nathan Starr, and Simeon North received a contract for 2,000 improved ship's pistols. The Springfield Armory in Massachusetts also set to work producing a substantial number of new ship's muskets, an improved boarding pike was introduced, and rifles were institutionalized aboard U.S. Navy warships for the first time.[7]

It was not until early 1808 that the administration finally presented to Congress a plan to increase the size of the army. Secretary of War Dearborn proposed adding eight new regiments: five of infantry and one each of riflemen, light artillery, and cavalry. This would triple the size of the army from some 3,000 to 9,000 men (officer strength, included within that number, would go from 200 to over 500). The vote in the House of Representatives in favor of the bill was 95-15, and it was signed into law on April 12, 1808.[8]

What if there had been war in 1807 over the *Chesapeake* Affair? It might have been better for the United States to have fought with Britain in 1807 than five years later. A few weeks after the encounter off the Virginia Capes, France and Russia concluded peace at Tilsit. This arrangement ended the Third Coalition against France and opened the possibility that the Russian and Scandinavian navies might be available to Napoleon. The desperate nature of the British position in 1807 is seen in British Secretary of War Lord Castlereagh's rejection of appeals from Canada for additional troops as "out of the question." Castlereagh hoped that 4,000 British regulars in Canada and another 5,000 in Nova Scotia, plus a revitalized Canadian militia, would be sufficient defense to deter the Americans.[9]

The 1807 British North American Squadron was hardly imposing; three ships-of-the-line, a 50-gun ship, four frigates, and some twenty-seven smaller vessels (including seventeen schooners) spread from Bermuda to Halifax. The Royal navy as a whole was of course the largest naval force in the world. In 1807 there was more than one Royal Navy fighting *ship* for every U.S. Navy *gun*. But with naval operations impending against Denmark, it was unlikely the British would have been able immediately to reinforce their squadron off North America. By late 1812 France and its allies posed no naval threat to Britain and Napoleon's Grande Armeé was deep in Russia, leaving Britain in much better position to send naval assets to America.

The 1807 U.S. Navy was, of course, minuscule. In his report to Congress Secretary Robert Smith gave U.S. navy strength as four frigates rated at 44 guns each, three of 36 guns, and three of 32. There was one ship sloop, four brigs, three schooners, and four bomb ketches. In actual service in November 1807 were only two frigates, a ship sloop, two brigs, a schooner, the four bomb ketches, and sixty gunboats. Another seven gunboats were under construction. Immediately ready to join the active fleet were only two additional frigates, a brig, a schooner, and one gunboat.[10]

The U.S. Army was hardly more ready for war. According to legislation of March 16, 1802, it was fixed at 3,358 men: general and other staff (76), two regiments of infantry (1,614), a regiment of artillery (1,629), and a corps of engineers (39 men). In December 1807 the army was short about 200 privates of even that number. The number of small arms was more than adequate; a December 16, 1807, report from Secretary Dearborn indicates the War Department had 130,000 [13,000?] muskets, 4,500 rifles, and 4,000 pistols. The army also had 261 bronze 3- to 24-pounder cannon and 124 howitzers and mortars. There were sixty-seven mortars (forty 4.5- and 5.5-inch, but Henry Foxall was manufacturing forty additional 10-inch pieces) and one hundred light 9- and 12-pounder field pieces. Much of the army's artillery was in coast defense pieces. There were 1,287 iron siege and fortification pieces, but 927 of the heavier (18- to 42-pounder) guns were intended for fortifications. A total of 692 guns were in specific seacoast locations and the Great Lakes, leaving only 235 for use elsewhere.[11]

True, the U.S. Army was stronger by 1812. In June of that year, while not up to its authorized number of 9,000, the army did have some 7,000 officers and men. But as the 1812 invasion of Canada revealed, it was both poorly trained and miserably led.

The important difference between 1807 and 1812 is not in the military but the political realm. War in 1807 would have seen the country, especially the northeast, more united behind the war effort. It could have been a much more popular and successful war than that of 1812. The Battle of Tippecanoe (1811) had not yet occurred, and the Indians of the northwest, so vital in saving Canada from U.S. invasion in 1812, had not yet been goaded into fury and outright British alliance.

The *Chesapeake-Leopard* incident was of course only one of many causes of the War of 1812. These included impressment and the Orders-in-Council, an economic downturn blamed on the latter, the belief held by many Americans that the British in Canada were goading the Indians to rebel, and the American desire to acquire Canada. Still, the incident brought the United States and Britain to the brink of war.

Each government froze in its official attitudes toward the other in the aftermath of the attack. Private correspondence among the leaders indicates how angry the administration of each nation was toward what it considered the narrow-minded stubborness in the positions taken by the other. In England even the Whig opposition to Perceval's Orders-in-Council could not support Jefferson's insistence that Britain end impressment from American merchantmen as part of the resolution of the incident.[12] And Jefferson's cabinet members became increasingly intemperate when they realized George Rose's mission was not intended to conciliate the most aggravated of American sensibilities.[13] Even though both governments moderated their practices in 1809, each continued fundamental policies and philosophies that the other considered unnecessarily uncompromising. War between the two countries was not inevitable because of the incident itself. But the official reactions to *Chesapeake-Leopard* by both countries backed each government into a corner where diplomatic maneuvering to avoid war became increasingly difficult.

Too late the British made an effort to heal the wounds of the *Chesapeake-Leopard* Affair. In the summer of 1812 London sent emissaries to Washington empowered to make amends. Of the four men removed from the *Chesapeake,* Ratford had already been hanged and one of the three deserters from the *Melampus* had died. War had already been declared when on July 10, 1812, the British schooner *Brim* (Lieutenant Simpson) sailed into Boston harbor from Halifax under a flag of truce. The next day Lieutenant Simpson brought William Martin and John Strachan to the *Chesapeake*'s quarterdeck, where Lt. Jesse Wilkinson met them. Simpson announced that Vice-Admiral Herbert Sawyer had instructed him to return the two seamen "aboard of the *Chesapeake.*" Wilkinson replied, "Sir, I am commanded by Commodore Bainbridge to receive these two American Seamen on the *very* deck from which they were wantonly taken in time of Peace by a vessel of your Nation of superior force." Capt. William Bainbridge then gave a short speech of welcome to the two seamen, one that must have seemed to them scant consolation: "My Lads, I am glad to see you. From this Deck you were taken by British outrage; for your return to it, you owe gratitude to the government of your country. Your country now offers you an opportunity to avenge your wrongs, and I cannot doubt but you will be desirous of doing so on board of this *very* ship. . . ." This was followed by three cheers from "a numerous crowd of people" on the *Chesapeake* and her crew, and from people on boats alongside. After this Bainbridge invited the British captain to lunch.[14]

Notes

PREFACE

1. Adams, *History of the United States,* 929.

ONE. THE ENCOUNTER

1. SecNav to Barron, 17 January 1807. William and Mary College, Earl Greg Swem Library: James Barron Papers [hereinafter cited as JBP]: I, 40. SecNav to Barron, 15 May 1807, in *Proceedings of the General Court Martial Convened for the Trial of Commodore James Barron, Captain Charles Gordon, Mr. William Hook, and Captain John Hall, of the United States' Ship* Chesapeake, *in the Month of January, 1808,* 132–35. [Hereinafter cited as *Court Martial.*]
2. *Chesapeake's* Log, in Barron to SecNav, 23 June 1807, State Department archives, RG45, M125, 8. Also in Dudley, ed., *The Naval War of 1812: A Documentary History,* I, 27.
3. The figure cited is by Purser Robert Goldsborough. It includes a surgeon and surgeon's mate, on board but not attached to the ship. *Court Martial,* 391–92. Gordon testified, "Deserters and discharges had reduced us to Three hundred Seventy odd including fifty three Marines." *Proceedings of a Court of Inquiry, Held at the Navy Yard, Brooklyn, N.Y., Upon Captain James Barron of the United States Navy, in May 1821,* 109. Testimony of Marine Lt. William Anderson, in *Court Martial,* 388. William James, *Naval History of Great Britain,* 4: 254, exaggerates the crew complement to 415, including ten boys and five lieutenants. According to Anthony Steel, James was one of very few English naval historians who even discussed the affair. Steel, "More Light on the *Chesapeake," Mariner's Mirror,* XXXIX (1955), 243. After he took command of the *Chesapeake,* Decatur described the Marines aboard as "the worst detachment I have ever seen—more than four fifths of them are foreigners, they are bad soldiers, turbulent men, & few of them able bodied." Decatur to SecNav, 27 August 1807, M125, 8.

4. Testimony of Capt. John Hall, *Court Martial,* 193.
5. In 1805 Captain Hall, acting under orders from Commodore Samuel Barron, recruited eighteen Sicilian musicians for the American Mediterranean squadron. Hall to SecNav, 28 November 1807, M124, 13. In December 1806, Gaetano Careyo, who claimed to have left the Navy "owing to the ill treatment" he had received from Marine Commandant Lt. Col. Franklin Wharton, asked Smith to provide him and his family passage home to Italy in the *Chesapeake,* and Smith agreed to do so. Careyo to SecNav, 2 December 1806 and February [no day] 1807, M124, 13 and 14. Smith also ordered Gordon to take on board as supernumeraries two marine privates, Silvador Leauria and Gueonio Sardo, "desirous of returning to the Mediterranean." SecNav to Gordon, 2 May 1807, M149, 7. Colonel Wharton wrote Hall on 10 May: "For the purpose of sending home the Italians now of the Band, at their request 10 to go [as their request is to go?], I have added them to your command as music." Appendix D in SecNav to Rodgers, 7 December 1807, M149, 7. A letter to Colonel Wharton, thanking him for passage home on the *Chesapeake,* is signed by seven Italian members of the "U.S. Band of Musicians," M124, 14. A letter of 15 October signed "Francisco Solize & Companions" asked Secretary Smith to grant the "Italian Band" passage "on Board any American armed vessel that may be bound to the Mediterranean." M124, 17.
6. A large part of the crew had been sick. From 1 June to 22 June, the number ranged from seventy-nine to thirty-two men. This is from sick lists of the *Chesapeake,* presented by Gordon at his court-martial. *Court Martial,* 409. This figure, however, differs from that Gordon gave in the unmailed letter to the Secretary of the Navy written on 22 June as the frigate sailed: "During our passage down the river the Crew was uncommonly sickly. We had from 60 to 85 continually on the list, the number is now reduced to 35." "Court of Enquiry," 95. Lt. William Allen said there were nine sick men in hammocks in his second division of the gun deck. "Letters of William Henry Allen, 1807–1813," I, No. 2: 214.
7. Testimony of Gordon, "Court of Enquiry," 59, repeated in *Court Marital,* 230–31 and 263–64; testimony of Surgeon Larkin Griffin, ibid., 409.
8. Barron's testimony at Gordon's court-martial, *Court Martial,* 365. Barron said, "I should never think it proper for a man of war to proceed to sea so lumbered if there was a prospect of meeting with an enemy. But as these had been put on board by order of the government, I considered it necessary to proceed to sea with the first wind. . . ." Ibid., 365–66.
9. Long, *Nothing Too Daring,* 37. Long is perhaps referring to Barron's 23 June report to Secretary Smith: "Yesterday at 6 AM the wind became favorable and knowing your anxiety that the Ship should sail with all possible dispatch, we weighed from our station. . . ." Barron to SecNav, 23 June 1807, M125, 8. Smith did not anticipate action en route to the Mediterranean. When the frigate was being prepared, Smith wrote Barron to ask whether he had examined her powder supply. If Barron thought it unfit for service, Smith wondered if powder could be readily and cheaply obtained at Malta or elsewhere in the Mediterranean. SecNav to Barron, 28 March 1807, M149, 7.
10. Testimony of Barron, *Court Martial,* 180.
11. Barron to SecNav, 23 June 1807, JBP: I, 58; also M125, 8.
12. Captain Humphreys to Capt. John Douglas of the *Bellona,* 22 June 1807. Entered as evidence in the trial of John Wilson: *Trial of John Wilson, alias Jenkin Ratford,* 11. Also in John Marshall, *Royal Naval Biography or Memoirs,* Vol. II, part II, 893.
13. Testimony of Lt. William Allen, *Court Martial,* 44; testimony of Gordon, ibid., p. 100.

14. Barron to SecNav, 23 June 1807, M125, 8. Testimony of Gordon, "Court of Enquiry," 48.

15. *Chesapeake*'s Log, in Dudley, ed., *Naval War of 1812: A Documentary History*, I, 27. Testimony of pilot Charles Nuttrel, *Court Martial*, 195.

16. Barron's testimony at his court-martial, *Court Martial*, 290. Gordon, "Court of Enquiry," 48. Allen, "Court of Enquiry," 128–29.

17. Annex A, SecNav to Capt. John Rodgers, Dec 7, 1807, M149, 7. Testimony of Hall, *Court Martial*, 193.

18. Testimony of Midshipman Glen Drayton, who was on the quarterdeck at the time. Marked "No. 11," E, Box C-L, Special Collections, Swem Library [hereinafter cited as EGSL: SC]. Also, testimony of Gordon before court of inquiry, in *Court Martial*, 231 and 256–57, and testimony of Gordon, "Court of Enquiry," 48–49. Testimony of Lt. William Crane, ibid., 106.

19. Log of the *Leopard* (22 June 1807), PRO, Adm 51/1702.

20. Testimony of Gordon at court of inquiry, in *Court Martial*, 220–21. James says that Humphreys's hail was that he had dispatches from the British commander-in-chief. James, *Naval History of Great Britain*, 4: 250. The reference to the *Wasp* is in Cooper, *History of the Navy*, 2: 14.

21. Testimony of Sailing Master Samuel Brooke, "No. 20," Lot 9, C-L Box, EGSL: SC. Midshipman Drayton confirmed the gun ports were up but was not certain tompions were out of the guns. "No. 11," Lot 11, ibid. Also Annex A, SecNav to Rodgers, 7 December 1807, M149, No. 7. Testimony of Nuttrel, *Court Martial*, 196–97.

22. Barron to SecNav, 23 June 1807, M125, 8. Testimony of Gordon, *Court Martial*, p. 101.

23. Adams, *History of the United States*, 936 and 944.

24. Log of the *Leopard*, 22 June 1807.

25. PRO, Adm 1/497, 220. Also in *Trial of John Wilson*, 19–20.

26. Letter written a few years before Humphreys's death in 1845 and published in a newspaper shortly after Barron's death. Unidentified newspaper clipping in Barron Papers. JBP: I, 82.

27. Humphreys to Douglas, 22 June 1807. Entered as evidence in the trial of Wilson/Ratford, *Trial of John Wilson*, 12. A copy is also enclosed in Barron to SecNav, 23 June 1807, M125, 8; also Marshall, *Royal Navy Biography*, vol. II, part 2, 893–94.

28. Deposition of Dr. Bullus, 27 June 1807, M125, 8.

29. Testimony of Gordon, "Court of Enquiry," 48–49, and *Court Martial*, 101–2.

30. Humphreys to Douglas, 22 June 1807, in *Trial of John Wilson*, 12. Enclosure in Barron to SecNav, 23 June 1807, M125, 8.

31. Cooper, *History of the Navy*, 2: 15.

32. Testimony of Gordon, "Court of Enquiry," 49, and *Court Martial*, 102. Log of the *Leopard* (22 June 1807).

33. Testimony of Gordon, "Court of Enquiry," 50, and *Court Martial*, 102 and 121.

34. Testimony of Gordon at court of inquiry, in *Court Martial*, 222; also testimony at Barron's court-martial, ibid., 103–4, and 121; and Hall, ibid., 88 and 193.

35. Testimony of Hall, "Court of Enquiry," 148.

36. Testimony of Midshipman Glen Drayton, "Court of Enquiry," 43.

37. All four, and Midshipman Jesse D. Elliott, used the identical word, "confusion," in describing their reaction to the halt. Crane, 40; Allen, 50; John Creighton, 70; Gordon, 107; Elliott, 148, all in *Court Martial*.

38. Testimony of Lt. Sidney Smith, ibid., 89.

39. Testimony of Midshipman Glen Drayton, "No. 11," Lot 11, Box C-L, EGSL: SC. Letter of

Allen, 17 July 1807. Lt. William Henry Allen Papers, LC. Testimony of Allen, *Court Martial*, 54. Testimony of Gordon at court of inquiry, in ibid., 234–35. Testimony of Gunner's Mate Thomas Garnet, ibid., 394–95. Midshipman Elliott testified that three guns on the starboard side of his division were incorrectly mounted, and "I should not suppose they would have born [*sic*] more than two fires." Ibid., 397.

40. Testimony of Crane, "No. 15," Lot 12, Box C-L, EGSL: SC. Also *Court Martial*, 39.
41. Allen's testimony, *Court Martial*, 49. Shubrick's testimony, "Court of Enquiry," 35.
42. Testimony of Creighton, ibid., 72; and Midshipman Elliott, ibid., 149.
43. Testimony of Allen, ibid., 65, and Elliott, ibid., 149.
44. Testimony of George Tincombe, *Trial of John Wilson*, 9.
45. See testimony of Tincombe, *Trial of John Wilson*, 9. Sidney Smith corroborated that Barron told Humphreys he did not understand the hail. Testimony of Smith, *Court Martial*, 77; and Creighton, ibid., 67.
46. Humphreys to Douglas, Jun 22, 1807. Entered as evidence in Ratford's trial. *Trial of John Wilson*, 12. Also, Marshall, *Royal Navy Biography*, vol. II, part 2, 894.
47. Testimony of Creighton, *Court Martial*, 67.
48. Humphreys to Douglas, 22 June 1807. Entered in trial of Ratford, *Trial of John Wilson*, 12.
49. Testimony of Tincombe, *Trial of John Wilson*, 10. Log of the *Leopard*, 22 June 1807.
50. Smith said the broadside came "a few seconds" after the warning shot. Hall said it was "almost immediately after." Testimony of Smith, *Court Martial*, 77; Hall, ibid., 85, and Gordon, ibid., 104. See also Crane's testimony in "Court of Enquiry," 113. Log of the *Leopard*, 22 June 1807.
51. Testimony of Crane, "Court of Enquiry," 117.
52. Humphreys to Douglas, 22 June 1807, enclosed in Douglas to William Wellesley Pole, 24 June 1807, Adm 1/1729. Quoted in Perkins, *Prologue to War*, 141.
53. This was the letter written a few years before Humphreys's death in 1845 and published in a newspaper shortly after Barron's death. Unidentified newspaper clipping in Barron Papers. JBP: I, 82.
54. Testimony of Midshipman James Wilson, "Court of Enquiry," 174.
55. Testimony of Wilson (marked "No. 24"), Lot 5, C-L Box, EGSL: SC.
56. Testimony of Hall, *Court Martial*, 85; also Sailing Master Brooke, ibid., 93; Midshipman Glen Drayton, ibid., 127; and Gordon at court of inquiry, ibid., 223.
57. Testimony of Gordon, *Court Martial*, 223. Drayton testified at the court of inquiry that Gordon confronted Hall after the firing began. See Chapter 7.
58. Testimony of Gunner's Mate Thomas Garnet, *Court Martial*, 166.
59. Testimony of Midshipman Alexander Wadsworth, ibid., 156–57.
60. Testimony of Gunner William Hook, ibid., 166–67.
61. Testimony of Midshipman Glen Drayton, ibid., 181.
62. Testimony of Midshipman Muhlenburg, "No. 10," Lot 13. Box C-L, EGSL: SC. Testimony of Brooke in *Court Martial*, 95; and Drayton, ibid., 128. Midshipman Fitz Henry Babbitt testified that all quarterdeck guns were cleared by the time the flag came down, but that they were unable to fire. Ibid., 179.
63. Testimony of Sidney Smith, "Court of Enquiry," 143 and *Court Martial*, 77–78; and Drayton, ibid., 127. Hall said that Barron stood on the aftermost gun of the quarterdeck: ibid., 85. Barron interrupted Elliott's testimony to say that he had hailed twice—once from the gangway and once from abaft. Indeed, other testimony has Barron hailing at least twice.

64. Testimony of Drayton, "No. 11," Lot 11, C-L Box, EGSL: SC; testimony of Wilson, "No. 24," Lot 5, ibid. Also Drayton's testimony in "Court of Enquiry," 41.
65. Barron to Bullus, 3 July 1807, JBP: I, 64.
66. "Court of Enquiry," 184–85. Annex A, SecNav to Rodgers, 7 December 1807, M149, 7. Babbitt provided testimony as to Barron's remark. Court Martial, 171, 173–74. See also testimony of Midshipman Richard Crump, ibid., 206.
67. Testimony of Hall, ibid., 85; testimony of Brooke, ibid., 93 and "Court of Enquiry," 156.
68. Testimony of Hall, "Court of Enquiry," 150; and Court Martial, 85 and 89. Testimony of Wilson, "Court of Enquiry," 174; testimony of Midshipman Robert Steele, ibid., 176.
69. Testimony of Allen, "Court of Enquiry," 131, and Elliott, ibid., 168. Testimony of Creighton, Court Martial, 74; Elliott, ibid., 147; and Norton, ibid., 151–52.
70. Testimony of Gordon, ibid., 105, and Elliott, "No. 23," Lot 4, C-L Box, EGSL: SC. Testimony of Hall, Court Martial, 86. Testimony of Drayton, "Court of Enquiry," 43. Barron said later that he said, "Hall go down on the gun deck and see if you cant get me one Gun fired for the Honor of the Flag before I strike it which I intend to do shortly." Barron to Bullus, 3 July 1807, JBP: I, 64.
71. J. Fenimore Cooper wrote: "This gun was discharged by means of a coal brought from the galley, which was applied by Lieutenant Allen, the officer of the division, with his fingers, after an unsuccessful attempt to make use of a loggerhead." Cooper, History of the Navy, 2: 17. Although Allen testified that he fired the one gun from a coal he took from the galley, he did not say how he transported it. Court Martial, 51 and 59–60. Hall, sent to the gun deck by Barron, later testified: "I observed Mr. Allen attempting to fire a gun, with a loggerhead which was too cold to burn the powder; a man then brought him a coal of fire, with which he fired the gun." Ibid., 86. Also, testimony of Gordon at Court of Inquiry, ibid., 223.
72. Testimony of Allen, Court Martial, 50 and 63, and "Court of Enquiry," 119.
73. Gordon's testimony, "Court of Enquiry," 51.
74. Testimony of Tincombe, Trial of John Wilson, 10. Captain Humphreys stated the firing lasted ten minutes. Humphreys to Douglas, June 22, 1807, in Trial of John Wilson, 12. James says that the Chesapeake fired "a few straggling shot, not one of which struck her opponent." James, Naval History, 4: 250–52. Testimony of Creighton, Court Martial, 75. Gordon said that the "whole time of firing" was about twelve minutes. Ibid., 123. Other testimony was comparable, save that of Crane, who put it at "From seven to ten minutes." "Court of Enquiry," 113. Log of the Leopard, 22 June 1807. Barron to SecNav, 23 June 1807, M125, 8.
75. Extract of log in JBP: I, 52. Also Barron to SecNav, 23 June 1807, RG45, M125, 8.
76. Testimony of Smith, "No. 18," Lot 8, C-L Box, EGSL: SC.
77. Testimony of Brooke, "No. 24," Lot 9, C-L Box, Special Collections, Swem Library. Also, testimony of Quartermaster John Watson, who was at the wheel the entire time, in Court Martial, 190.
78. Testimony of Wilson, Court Martial, 164.
79. Testimony of Drayton, "No. 11," Lot 11, and Muhlenburg, "No. 10," Lot 13, C-L Box, Special Collections, Swem Library. Testimony of Drayton, "Court of Enquiry," 41. Testimony of Gordon, Court Martial, 105–6. Testimony of Drayton, ibid., 126.
80. James, Naval History, 4: 253.
81. Martin, A Most Fortunate Ship, 116–23.
82. Surgeon Joseph Hunt, report of 23 June, in Barron to SecNav, 23 June 1807, M149, 8. Same repeated, but with "Shukly" in Court Martial, 140.

83. Letter of 17 July 1807. LC: Allen Papers.
84. Amendment to report of court martial, "For Page 162," initialled "J.B." JBP: I, 73B. James, *Naval History*, 4: 476–82. Gordon's testimony, "Court of Enquiry," 54; Crane's testimony, ibid., pp. 102–3, 115; Allen's testimony, ibid., 124. Also *Court Martial*, 225–26 and 233.
85. Testimony of Tincombe, *Trial of John Wilson*, 9. Captain Townshend of the *Halifax*, describing deserters from his ship to Admiral Berkeley, noted that Ratford had his name tattooed on his left arm. Townshend to Berkeley, 24 March 1807, PRO: Adm/497: #74. Gordon's testimony, "Court of Enquiry," 53.
86. Testimony of Tincombe, *Trial of John Wilson*, 10. Bradford Perkins asserts they were known deserters, *Prologue to War*, 142. See also "Declaration of Henry Harvey and Thomas Addison late of the United States Frigate *Chesapeake*," in Anthony Steel, "More Light on the *Chesapeake*," *Mariner's Mirror*, 39 (1953): 260–62. Gordon's testimony, *Court of Enquiry*, 53.
87. Humphreys to Douglas, 22 June 1807. Entered in Ratford's trial, *Trial of John Wilson*, 13.
88. James, *Naval History*, 4: 254.
89. Humphreys to Douglas, *Trial of John Wilson*, 18. Also enclosure (which differs slightly) in Barron to SecNav, 23 June 1807, M125, 8.
90. In *Trial of John Wilson*, 13. Also an enclosure in Barron to SecNav, 23 June 1807, M125, 8.
91. Crane's testimony, "Court of Enquiry," 103; Allen's testimony, ibid., 124.
92. *Chesapeake's* Log, in Barron to SecNav, 23 June 1807, M125, 8. Gleaves, *James Lawrence*, 66–68; Anthony, *Decatur*, 169–71; James, *Naval History*, 4: 250–53; Beach, *United States Navy*, 52–65. Testimony of Gordon at court of inquiry, in *Court Martial*, 226.

TWO. THE LION AND THE EAGLET

1. Morris, *The Peacemakers*, 316.
2. Ibid. The definitive Treaty of Paris is included as an appendix, 461–65.
3. Ehrman, *The Younger Pitt*, I: 160.
4. Ritcheson, *Aftermath of Revolution*, Chapter 2.
5. Jarrett, *The Younger Pitt*, 82.
6. A good description of economic problems in this period can be found in Chapter II, "The Challenge of Foreign Trade Restrictions" in Marks's *Independence on Trial*.
7. Dorchester to Secretary of State Sydney, Quebec, 13 June 1787, Public Records Office (London), Colonial Office, 42 Canada 51/11.
8. Sydney to Dorchester, Whitehall, 14 September 1787, CO 42, 51/79.
9. Cottrell, secretary to the Lords of Trade, to Grenville, London, 17 April 1790, British Museum Additional Mss., Liverpool Papers, 38225/173–74.
10. Parrish, "Intrigues of Doctor James O'Fallon," *Mississippi Valley Historical Review*, 17 (Sept. 1930), 230–63.
11. Sydney to Haldimand, Acting governor of Canada, Whitehall, 8 April 1784, C.O. 42, 46/103.
12. The most informative description of Adams's experience in England is in chapters XLVII to LV of Smith, *John Adams*, Vol. 2.
13. Marks, *Independence on Trial*, Chapter IV; McDonald, *Formation of the American Republic*, 202–8.
14. Ritcheson, *Aftermath of Revolution*, 91–92.
15. Reuter, *Trials and Triumphs*, 52.

16. Dorchester to Grenville, 25 Oct. 1789, CO 42.

17. For a more detailed description of Beckwith's often clandestine activities see Reuter, "'Petty Spy' or Effective Diplomat," *Journal of the Early Republic,* 10 (Winter 1990), 472–92.

18. Malone, *Jefferson and the Rights of Man,* 232–33.

19. Wright, *Britain and the American Frontier,* 50.

20. Grenville to Hammond, Whitehall, 2 September 1791; Hawkesbury to Hammond, London, 4 July 1791; No. 2, Grenville to Hammond, Whitehall, 1 September 1791, all in Mayo, ed., *Instructions to the British Ministers,* 14, 7, 18.

21. Washington to Jefferson, Philadelphia, 14 April 1791, in Fitzpatrick, ed., *Writings of George Washington,* 31: 267.

22. Jefferson to British Minister, Philadelphia, 29 May 1792, in Ford, ed., *Works of Thomas Jefferson,* 6: 90–91.

23. Jefferson to U.S. Minister to Gt. Britain, Philadelphia, 11 June 1792, ibid., 104–9; Jefferson to U.S. Minister, Philadelphia, 12 October 1792, ibid., 157.

24. Jefferson to Madison, Philadelphia, 12 May 1793, *Works of Jefferson,* 7: 323.

25. Grenville to Hammond, Whitehall, 13 March 1993, in Mayo, *Instructions to British Ministers,* 38.

26. Secret Orders to Sir Charles Grey, Windsor, 12 November 1793, Prior's Kitchen (Durham, England), Papers of 1st Earl Grey, #175b.

27. Grey to Secretary of War Dundas, Martinque, 3 May 1794, ibid., #2234.

28. *Farmer's Library* (Rutland, Vermont), 29 July 1794.

29. Grenville to Hammond, Whitehall, January 1794, FO 115, 3/1.

30. For a thorough description of how the treaty influenced Republican thinking see Combs, *Jay Treaty.*

31. Still the best discussion of the issues involved in Pinckney's negotiations is Bemis, *Pinckney's Treaty.*

32. Bradford Perkins perhaps overstates the amiability between the two countries but gives interesting details on how it worked out in his *First Rapprochment.*

33. *American State Papers,* Class IV, *Commerce and Navigation,* I, 389.

34. Jackson, "Impressment and Anglo-American Discord," 71.

35. In 1809 Capt. John Shaw reported wages for merchant seamen as high as $30–35 a month. Shaw to SecNav, 20 March 1809. M125, 14.

36. Jackson, "Impressment," 29.

37. Ibid., 11–15 and 51.

38. Chapter One of DeConde's *The Quasi-War* gives an excellent introduction to French attitudes.

39. Grenville to Liston, Downing Street, 8 June 1798, Mayo, *Instructions to British Ministers,* 155–60; Perkins, *First Rapprochment,* 90.

40. Ferling, *John Adams: A Life,* 378–80.

THREE. THOMAS JEFFERSON AND A CHANGING WORLD

1. Richardson, ed., *Compilation of the Messages and Papers of the Presidents,* 1: 323.

2. The *Times* of London, 14 April 1801.

3. Kaplan, *Jefferson and France,* 82–83 and 87–94.

4. Perkins, *First Rapprochement,* 185.

5. Jefferson to King, Washington, 13 July 1802, Lipscomb, ed., *Writings of Thomas Jefferson,* 10: 329–30.

6. Perkins, *First Rapprochement,* 131.
7. King to Madison, London, 30 May 1801, Brugger et al, eds., *Papers of James Madison: Secretary of State Series,* 1: 238; King to Madison, London, 19 May 1801, ibid., 196; King to Madison, London, 1 June 1801, ibid., 250.
8. Madison to King, Washington, 24 July 1801, ibid., 464–70.
9. David Lenox to Madison, London, 25 July 1801, ibid., 478.
10. *Times,* 3 October 1801.
11. *Times,* 6 April 1801.
12. Brown, ed., *Autobiography of James Monroe,* 194.
13. *Times,* 6 October 1801.
14. Thomas Erskine, Sr., to Charles Grey, n.p., 18 March 1798, The Prior's Kitchen (Durham University), Papers of the 2nd Earl Grey-Erskine Correspondence, Box 14, File 2.
15. Rufus King to Madison, London, 20 April 1801, *Papers of Madison,* 1: 105. Rev. William Pinkney, *The Life of William Pinkney* gives a detailed, if somewhat biased, account of his uncle's services as a diplomat.
16. Madison to King, Washington, 28 July 1801, *Papers of Madison,* 1: 485.
17. William Vans Murray to Madison, Hague, 7 May 1801, ibid., 45.
18. Madison to King, Washington, 25 July 1801, ibid., 464–70.
19. Jefferson to Dupont de Nemours, Washington, 1 February 1803, *Jefferson's Letters,* 10: 350.
20. Jefferson to U.S. Minister to France, Washington, 18 April 1802, ibid., 313.
21. DeConde, *This Affair of Louisiana,* 141–46.
22. Ibid., 171–75.
23. Tucker and Hendrickson, *Empire of Liberty,* Chapter 15.
24. Jefferson to Sinclair, Washington, 30 June 1803, *Writings of Jefferson,* 10: 397.
25. Smelser, *The Democratic Republic,* 151–55; Malone, *Jefferson The President, Second Term,* 95–100.
26. Albert Gallatin to Jefferson, New York, 18 August 1803, in Adams, ed., *Writings of Albert Gallatin,* 1: 141.
27. Perkins, *First Rapprochement,* 182–86.
28. "Jefferson to William Short on Mr. & Mrs. Merry," *American Historical Review,* 33 (1928): 823–33.
29. Brown, *Autobiography of Monroe,* 196–97.
30. Monroe to British Secretary of Foreign Affairs, London, 25 September 1805, *American State Papers, Foreign Relations* [hereinafter cited as A.S.P., F.R.], 2: 734–36.
31. Jefferson to Livingston, Monticello, 9 September 1801, *Writings of Jefferson,* 10: 279–80.
32. King to Madison, London, 14 July 1801, *Papers of Madison,* 1, 410.
33. Admiral George C. Berkeley to William Marsden, Bermuda, 23 March 1807, Public Records Office (London), Adm 1/497, 72–73; Captain Townsend to Berkeley, Bermuda, 7 March 1807 with enclosures, ibid., 74, 83.
34. Gallatin to Jefferson, Washington, 16 April 1807, *Writings of Gallatin,* 1: 335–36.
35. Steele, "Anthony Merry and the Anglo-American Dispute about Impressment, 1803–1806," *Cambridge Historical Journal,* IX, no. 3 (1949): 348.
36. Jefferson to Madison, Monticello, 15 August 1804, *Writings of Jefferson,* 11: 46.
37. Tucker, *The Jeffersonian Gunboat Navy,* Chapter 2, "The Jeffersonian Program."
38. Ben-Atar, *Origins of Jefferson Commercial Policy,* 169–72.
39. Nettels, *Emergence of a National Economy,* 230–42.
40. Steele, "Anthony Merry," pp. 342–43.

41. Zimmerman, *Impressment of American Seamen,* 255.

42. Mackenzie, *Life of Stephen Decatur,* 146. This was undoubtedly picked up by Anthony, *Decatur,* 168. Beach, *United States Navy,* p. 60.

43. Jefferson to Gallatin, Monticello, 8 September 1804, *Writings of Jefferson,* 11: 48.

44. "Memorial of the Merchants of the City of New York," 28 December 1805, *A.S.P., F.R.,* 2: 737–39; "From the Merchants and Traders of Philadelphia," n.d., ibid., 740–41.

45. Tucker and Hendrickson, *Empire of Liberty,* 191–92; Perkins, *Prologue to War,* 78.

46. Madison to Monroe, Washington, 5 January 1804, *A.S.P., F. R.,* 730–32.

47. Monroe to Secretary of Foreign Affairs, London, 23 September 1805, ibid., 734–36.

48. Perkins, *Prologue to War,* 45–46.

49. Jefferson to Madison, Monticello, 27 August 1805, *Writings of Jefferson,* 11: 87.

50. Lascelles, *Life of Charles James Fox,* chapters 4 and 15; Rose, "The Contest with Napoleon," chap. 3 in volume 1 of *Cambridge History of British Foreign Relations, 1783–1919.*

51. Jefferson to Monroe, Washington, 4 May 1806, *Writings of Jefferson,* 11: 109–11.

52. Fox to Merry, Downing Street, 7 April 1806, in Mayo, *Instructions to British Ministers,* 221.

53. Perkins, *Prologue to War,* 116–17.

54. *Times,* 21 February 1806.

55. Quoted in Horsman, *Causes of the War of 1812,* 77.

56. Perkins, *Prologue to War,* 107–8.

57. Fox to Merry, Downing Street, 6 June 1806, Mayo, ed., *Instructions,* 223; Howick to George III, Admiralty, 8 June 1806, (Prior's Kitchen) Papers of the 2nd Earl Grey—George III Correspondence, Box 17, File 1, #21.

58. Merry to Fox, Washington, 3 August 1806, Papers of 2nd Earl Grey, Box 56, File 5A.

59. Lester, *Anthony Merry Redivivus,* 55.

60. Phineas Bond to Fox, Philadelphia, 7 September 1806, and Bond to Fox, Philadelphia, 29 September 1806, and Thomas Barclay to Fox, New York, 29 September 1806, Papers of 2nd Earl Grey, Box 56, File 5A.

61. Grenville to Auckland, Downing Street, 8 August 1806, Auckland, ed., *Journal and Correspondence of Lord Auckland,* 4: 284.

62. For a most critical analysis of the Grenville ministry's failures to contain French influence, see Rose, "The Contest with Napoleon," in vol. 1 of *The Cambridge History of British Foreign Relations.*

63. Howick [Grey] to Erskine, Downing Street, 24 September 1806, Mayo, *Instructions,* 226–27.

64. Merry to Fox, Washington, 3 August 1806, Papers of 2nd Earl Grey, Box 56, File 5A.

65. Howick to Monroe, Downing Street, 22 October 1806, 2nd Earl Grey Papers—Correspondence with James Monroe, Box 41, File 9, #2; Lord Landsdowne to Howick, Straton Place, 9 October 1806, 2nd Earl Grey Papers—Correspondence with Landsdowne, Box 38, File 10.

66. Merry to Fox, Lancaster, Pa., 31 August 1806, 2nd Earl Grey Papers, Box 56, File 5A.

67. Henry Richard, Lord Holland, *Memoirs of the Whig Party,* 2: 98–103.

68. Quoted in Steele, "Anthony Merry. . . ," 539; Grey to Sir John Nicole, Admiralty, 14 June 1806, 2nd Earl Grey Papers—Promiscuous, vol. B/3A: 31.

69. Auckland to Howick, Palace Yard, 30 December 1806, 2nd Earl Grey Papers, Box 5, File 5. Chap. 4 of Perkins's *Prologue to War* provides a good summary of the Monroe—Pinkney negotiations with Auckland and Holland.

70. Howick to Baring, London, 2 December 1806, 2nd Earl Grey Papers—Baring correspondence, Box 6, File 5; Howick to George III, 1 January 1807, 2nd Earl Grey Papers—Correspondence with George III, Box 17, File 1.
71. *Times,* 7 December 1806; Perkins, *Prologue to War,* 134.
72. King to Baring, New York, 30 September 1806, 2nd Earl Grey Papers—Baring Correspondence, Box 6, File 5, #4.
73. Jefferson to Monroe, Washington, 21 March 1807, *Writings of Jefferson,* 11: 167–70.
74. Madison to Monroe and Pinkney, Washington, 20 May 1807, *A.S.P., F. R.,* 3: 166–73.
75. Gallatin to Jefferson, Washington, 13 April 1807, *Writings of Gallatin,* 1: 332–35.
76. Madison to Erskine, Department of State, 29 March 1807, *A.S.P., F. R.,* 3: 159; Erskine to Howick, Philadelphia, 3 June 1807, PRO: FO, 5/52.
77. Erskine to Howick, Washington, 6 January 1807, and Erskine to Howick, Washington, 1 February 1807, ibid.
78. Erskine to Howick, Washington, 28 March and 22 April 1807, Ibid.
79. Monroe to Howick, Portland Place, 26 March 1807, 2nd Earl Grey Papers—Correspondence with Monroe, Box 41, File 9, #5.
80. Thomas Erskine, Sr., to Howick, n.p., 15 March 1807, 2nd Earl Grey Papers—Erskine Correspondence, Box 14, File 2, #11.

FOUR. THE *LEOPARD* AND THE ROYAL NAVY

1. "Remarks," in *Trial of John Wilson,* 26.
2. Perkins, *First Rapprochement,* 92–105.
3. Briggs, *Doctrine of Continuous Voyage,* 11–40; Perkins, *Prologue to War,* 72.
4. "Sentence of the Vice-Admiralty Court of Nassau, New Providence in the case of the Brig *Essex,* Joseph Orne Master." *The Naval War of 1812. A Documentary History,* 1: 17–18.
5. The test studies of impressment are Jackson, "Impressment," and Zimmerman, *Impressment of American Seamen.*
6. Robert Liston to William Wydham Greenville, 12 May 1797, in Mayo, *Instructions to the British Ministers,* 135n.
7. Jackson, "Impressment," 2–5.
8. Evan Nepean to George Hammond, 2 Apr 1799, FO 5/27; Lords of the Admiralty to Carmarthen, 12 December 1786, Adm 2/374; both in Jackson, "Impressment," 5.
9. Secretary of the Admiralty to Adm. Edward Vernon, 11 October 1745, quoted in Jackson, "Impressment," 2.
10. William Stevens stated that seamen in the U.S. Navy could be given only twelve lashes, while Royal Navy regulations allowed a hundred or more. He also wrote there was no evidence in the U.S. Navy of "flogging through the fleet" or "keelhauling." Stevens, *Affair of Honor,* 37. This is not entirely correct. The *Chesapeake*'s log of September 24, 1807, states: "At Meridian fired a Gun & Made Signal. . . . John Williams was flogged through the fleet & Recd. 168 lashes Agreeable to a Sentence of a Court Martial, heald [*sic*] on board the U.S. Frigate *Chesapeake* on Thursday Seper. 17th. 1807." The same log also noted on November 25, 1807: "Punished Isaac Watson, & Jno Williams for Desertion, with 2 doz. Each." For punishment in the U.S. Navy see McKee, *A Gentlemanly and Honorable Profession,* 233–67.
11. Jackson, "Impressment," 27–30, 72–75, 118, and 123.
12. Berkeley to Marsden, 23 March 1807, PRO: Adm/497: #72. Jackson, "Impressment," 27–

30 and 73–74. For Gallatin's view of British seamen in the U.S. merchant marine see Gallatin to Jefferson, Washington, 16 April 1807, in *Writings of Gallatin,* 1: 335–36.

13. Gaines, "Outrageous Encounter," p. 155.

14. Jackson, "Impressment," 17–18.

15. Ibid., 53.

16. Ibid., 54.

17. Mowat to Robert Liston, 27 March 1797, Adm 1/493, in Jackson, "Impressment," 407.

18. James, *Naval History,* 4: 245–47.

19. Jackson, "Impressment," 57.

20. Ibid., 78–79.

21. Ibid., 258.

22. Rose to Canning, FO 5/56, 27 December 1807, in Steel, "More Light on the *Chesapeake,*" 254.

23. Cooper, *History of the Navy,* 1:167–173; Palmer, *Stoddert's War,* 61–63.

24. Jackson, "Impressment," 137.

25. Beach, *United States Navy,* 57. Stevens, *Affair of Honor,* 31.

26. Jackson, "Impressment," 138. Loring was reprimanded and relieved of his command.

27. Cooper, *History of the Navy,* 1: 161.

28. Palmer, *Stoddert's War,* 89–91. Beach, *United States Navy,* 57–58.

29. Zimmerman, *Impressment of American Seamen,* 135.

30. Order of 12 July 1805, M125, 2.

31. A full account of the incident is in Tucker, *Jeffersonian Gunboat Navy,* 79–80.

32. *Norfolk Gazette and Publick Ledger,* 8 September 1806 and 13 April 1807.

33. Ibid., 18 September 1806.

34. Goldsborough to S. Barron, 6 October 1806, M149, 7.

35. *Norfolk Gazette and Publick Ledger,* 13 April 1807.

36. David Erskine to Admiral Sir George Cranfield Berkeley, private, 11 December 1806, George Cranfield Berkeley MSS, Public Library of Toronto, Toronto, Canada; Erskine to Madison, 4 January 1807, and Madison to Erskine, 7 January 1807, enclosed in Erskine #3 to Charles Grey, Viscount Howick, 1 February 1807, PRO: FO 5/52; Erskine to Berkeley, 16 January 1807, Berkeley MSS. Cited in Jackson, "Impressment," 258–59.

37. Capt. John Douglas to John Hamilton, copy, 18 December 1806, Berkeley MSS. Cited in Jackson, "Impressment," 259–60.

38. Ibid., 260.

39. Verbal instructions from the British government are in unsigned Berkeley memorandum, n.d. [late 1807], Berkeley MSS, fols. 126–34; Berkeley to William Marsden, 2 February 1807, Adm 1/497. All in Jackson, "Impressment," 261.

40. Ibid., 262.

41. Testimony of Sgt. Richard Frodsham of the Royal Marines, in *Trial of John Wilson,* 14–15. James, *Naval History,* 4: 72–73. *Norfolk Gazette & Publick Ledger,* 14 September 1807.

42. *Norfolk Gazette and Publick Ledger,* 2 March 1807, in Emmerson, *The* Chesapeake *Affair,* 5.

43. Barron to SecNav, 7 April 1807, M125, 7. Hamilton to Decatur, 6 March 1807, M125, 7. For accounts of this see James, *Naval History,* 4: 326–28; Adams, *History of the United States during the Administration of Jefferson and Madison,* 4: 1–2; and Steel, "More Light on the *Chesapeake,*" *Mariner's Mirror,* 39 (1953), 244–48. Strachan's name appears with variant spellings. See Barron to SecNav, 7 April 1807, M125, 7.

44. Letter from Captain Townshend to Admiral Berkeley, 24 March 1807, PRO: Adm/497,

#75; also his testimony and that of Lieutenant Carter and Midshipman Turner at Ratford's trial, *Trial of John Wilson*, 4 and 6. See also James, *Naval History*, 4: 473–74.

45. Townshend to Berkeley, 21 March 1807, PRO: Adm 1/497, #74. Lowell, *Peace without Dishonour*, 10. Perkins, *Prologue to War*, p. 141.

46. Lowell, *Peace without Dishonour*, p. 10.

47. Ibid., 12.

48. Hamilton to Decatur, 6 and 7 March 1807, M125, 7. Hamilton to Sinclair, 9 March 1807, ibid.

49. Letter of Townshend to Admiral Berkeley, 15 August 1807, and testimony at Ratkin's trial, *Trial of John Wilson*, 4 and 6.

50. Hamilton to Captain Decatur, 6 and 7 March 1807; Decatur to Hamilton, 7 March, 1807; Lieutenant Sinclair to Hamilton, 8 March 1807; Hamilton to Sinclair, 9 March 1807; Hamilton to Parker, 10 March 1807; Parker to Hamilton, 14 March 1807, FO 5/52. All in Jackson, "Impressment," 262. See also Steel, "More Light on the *Chesapeake*," 246.

51. Hamilton to Erskine, 17 March 1807; Erskine #21 to George Canning, 17 July 1807, FO 5/52. In Jackson, "Impressment," 264.

52. SecNav to Barron, 6 April 1807, M149, 7.

53. Barron to SecNav, 7 April 1807, M125, 7. Barron's report says five men escaped in the gig. Hamilton named Ware, Martin, Strachan, and John Little. Hamilton to Decatur, 6 March 1807, M125, 7.

54. Report signed by Creighton dated 11 August 1807, in Erskine to Canning, 1 September 1807, PRO: FO 5/22. Cited in Steel, "More Light on the *Chesapeake*," 250.

55. Crofts to Gallatin, 7 August 1807, enclosed in Thomas Barclay (British consul general in New York) to Canning, 2 September 1807, PRO: FO 5/53. The full report is in Steel, "More Light on the *Chesapeake*," 250–51.

56. Barron to SecNav, 7 April 1807, M125, 7. "Remarks" in *Trial of John Wilson*, 24–27.

57. Erskine to Berkeley, 9 April 1807, Berkeley MSS. See Jackson, "Impressment," 264.

58. After the *Chesapeake-Leopard* Affair the Norfolk paper printed a story about the action of June 1, 1794. Berkeley was said to have received "a scratch to the head, so very slight, that a midshipman would have been ashamed to have mentioned it to the standers by during such an engagement." Nonetheless, he insisted on going to the cockpit to have it attended. The lieutenant left in charge saw this as an opportunity for promotion. He soon brought the ship into position where it was engaged by three French ships of the line, one of which was able to rake the *Marlborough*. Seeing this, Adm. Richard Howe asked his captain, Sir Roger Curtis, what was "wrong with the *Marlborough*." After looking at the *Marlborough* by telescope Curtis replied "I don't know my Lord, but I should imagine from the conduct of the *Marlborough* that Captain Berkeley has been killed." *Norfolk Gazette and Publick Ledger*, 31 July 1807.

59. Jackson, "Impressment," 282. *Dictionary of National Biography*, 2: 358–59; Gaines, "Outrageous Encounter," 22–30.

60. Perkins, *Prologue to War*, 140–41.

61. Berkeley to Marsden, 31 May and 10 April 1807, Adm 1/497. In Gaines, "Outrageous Encounter," 34.

62. Capt. Townshend to Berkeley, 7 and 24 March, 1807, PRO: Adm 1/497, #75. Hamilton to Berkeley, 21 March, 1807; Capt. Douglas to Berkeley, 15 April 1807; Erskine to Berkeley, 9 April 1807. Berkeley MSS. All in Jackson, "Impressment," 265 and Gaines, "Outrageous Encounter," 42.

63. Berkeley to Marsden, 23 March and 28 April 1807, PRO: Adm 1/497; also in Jackson, "Impressment," pp. 265–66.

64. Berkeley to Marsden, 28 April 1807, Adm 1/497; Douglas to Berkeley, 1 June 1807, Berkeley MSS. See Jackson, "Impressment," 266; log of the *Leopard*; Gaines, "Outrageous Encounter," 48–49.

65. Dumas Malone, *Jefferson the President: Second Term*, 416.

66. Berkeley to Marsden, 31 May 1807, Adm 1/497, in Jackson, "Impressment," 267. Gaines, "Outrageous Encounter," 49–51. For the Charleston incident see *The Peoples Friend and Daily Advertiser*, 12 May 1807.

67. PRO, Adm 1/497, 158.

68. Jackson, "Impressment," p. 267.

69. Berkeley to Humphreys, 1 June 1807, enclosed in Berkeley to Marsden, 4 July 1807. Admiralty Papers, Public Record Office, Adm 1/497. In Perkins, *Prologue to War*, 141, and Adams, *History of the United States*, 4: 3. Also, Jackson, "Impressment," 267–68.

70. Clowes, *The Royal Navy*, 5: 68; Marshall, *Royal Naval Biography*, vol. II, Part 2, 897; Colledge, *Ships of the Royal Navy*, 200.

71. James, *Naval History*, 4: 253–54. John Marshall, *British Naval Biography*, vol. II, Part 2, 897.

72. Marshall, *British Naval Biography*, vol. II, Part 2, 897. Statement of J. E. Douglas of the *Bellona* to Capt. James Barron, 10 July 1807, JBP: I, 65.

73. Letter of 17 July 1807. LC: Lt. William Henry Allen Papers.

74. Marshall, *British Naval Biography*, vol. II, Part 2, 896–97.

75. Ibid., 891–92; O'Byrne, *Naval Biographical Dictionary*, 265.

76. *The Herald* (Norfolk), 27 June 1807.

77. Log of the *Leopard*, 6–21 June 1807, PRO, Adm 51/1702; James, *Naval History*, 5: 247–50.

78. Jackson, "Impressment," 269. Adams, *History of the United States of America During the Second Administration of Thomas Jefferson*, 2: 14–15.

FIVE. BARRON, THE *CHESAPEAKE*, AND THE U.S. NAVY

1. For Federalist advocacy of the navy see "No. 11," *The Federalist*, ed. Cooke, 68–70.

2. See the diary of Sen. William Maclay of Pennsylvania for February 1, 1791. *Journal of William Maclay*, 383.

3. *Writings of Thomas Jefferson*, 15: 397, 400–403. *Annals of Congress, 1789–1824*, 4: 433. [Hereinafter cited as *Annals*.]

4. Harold and Margaret Sprout, *Rise of American Naval Power*, 33–34. Congress, *American State Papers, Naval Affairs* [hereinafter cited as *A.S.P., N.A.*], 1: 6, 8, 17, and 19.

5. Harold and Margaret Sprout, *Rise of American Naval Power*, 28–32.

6. Cross, *The* Chesapeake, 17.

7. Letter from Tyrone Martin to Spencer Tucker, March 5, 1995.

8. U.S. Navy Department, *Register of Officer Personnel*, 69. Howard I. Chapelle gives slightly different dimensions: 152'6" between perpendiculars; 40'11" extreme beam, and 13'9" depth in hold. Chapelle, *American Sailing Navy*, 135 and 535. Cross, *The* Chesapeake, 21–24. *Dictionary of American Fighting Ships*, vol. 2, 95.

9. Clowes, *Royal Navy*, 5: 15. Chapelle, *American Sailing Navy*, 135. Cooper, *History of the Navy*, 2: 18. Capt. Stephen Decatur to SecNav, 1 September 1808, M125, 12. Cross, *The* Chesapeake, 24.

10. The 38-gun rating is by the court of inquiry into the affair with the *Leopard*. SecNav to

Rodgers, 7 December 1807, Annex A, M149, 7. James gave her armament as twenty-eight long 18-pounders on her main deck, fourteen 32-pounder carronades (leaving an empty port on each side) on her quarterdeck, and two 32-pounder carronades and two long 12s (leaving three vacant ports on each side) on her forecastle, for a total of forty-six guns. James, *Naval History*, 4: 253. The same figures are given by Marshall in *Royal Navy Biography*, vol. II, Part 2, 897.

11. Rees, *Cyclopedia*, vol. 6:, n.p. See "Cannon" entry.

12. See Tucker, *Arming the Fleet*, 120–30.

13. *Dictionary of American Fighting Ships*, 2: 95.

14. Cross, *The* Chesapeake, 25–41. SecNav to Barron, 22 April 1806, JBP: I, 32.

15. SecNav to Barron, 26 May 1806, JBP: I, 32.

16. SecNav to Stewart, lieutenants and midshipmen, 28 April 1806, M149, 7. Tingey to SecNav, 27 March, 1807, M125, 7. SecNav to Barron, 26 May 1807, LC: BFP, I, 32, and SecNav to Barron, 29 May 1806, JBP: I, 32.

17. SecNav to Barron, 17 January 1807, JBP: I, 40.

18. Stevens, *Affair of Honor*, 1–14.

19. Ibid., 183 and 185.

20. JBP: I, 8.

21. Stevens, *Affair of Honor*, 15–32. Long, *Ready to Hazard*, 33. Maxwell, ed. *Virginia Historical Register, and Literary Note Book*, 4, no. 3 (July 1851): 161–62.

22. Stevens, *Affair of Honor*, 37–38. Long, *Ready to Hazard*, 33.

23. The quote from Rodgers is in Jay D. Smith, "Commodore James Barron: Guilty as Charged?" *United States Naval Institute Proceedings*, VIIC (November 1967): 80. That from Barron is in Stevens, *Affair of Honor*, 33–49.

24. Stevens, *Affair of Honor*, 49–53; Long, *Ready to Hazard*, 71, 99–100.

25. Long, *Ready to Hazard*, 100. *Register of Officer Personnel*, 3. SecNav to Barron, 29 May 1806, JBP: I, 32; XIII, 3.

26. *Virginia Historical Register and Literary Note Book*, 4: no. 3 (July 1851): 165. Also Stevens, *Affair of Honor*, 55.

27. See Smith, "Barron: Guilty as Charged?" 79.

28. SecNav to Barron, JBP: I, 39. On 19 March 1807, Secretary Smith lifted the prohibition ordering Rodgers to remain at Havre de Grace, Md. SecNav to Rodgers LC: RFP, IIIB, 3 (#4789).

29. Maloney, *Captain from Connecticut*, 121. See exchange of letters between Rodgers and Barron, JBP: I, 36 and 38. Also Stevens, *Affair of Honor*, 55–57, and Long, *Ready to Hazard*, 110.

30. Anthony, *Decatur*, 172. On the 1806 incident see Stevens, *Affair of Honor*, 57. On Susan Wheeler see also Emmerson, *The* Chesapeake *Affair*, 174–75.

31. SecNav to Barron, 17 January 1807, JBP: I, 40.

32. Cooper, *History of the Navy*, 2: 21.

33. SecNav to Barron, 17 January 1807; Gordon, 21 January and 23 February 1807, M149, 7. Gordon's testimony in *Court Martial*, 211. Cooper identified Gordon as the youngest master commandant. Cooper, *History of the Navy*, 2: 12.

34. Smith, "Barron: Guilty as Charged?" 80.

35. Long, *Ready to Hazard*, 110. Morris L. Radoff, "Captain Gordon of the *Constitution*," *Maryland Historical Magazine* 67 (1972): 389. Herbert Baird Simpson, "Charles Gordon: Jacobite and Loyalist," *South Atlantic Quarterly* 28, no. 4 (October 1928): 390–404. Calderhead, "A Strange Career," *Maryland Historical Magazine* 72 (Fall 1977): 373–75.

Register of Officer Personnel, 21. Naval Historical Center, ZB Files. Martin, *Most Fortunate Ship,* 76.

36. Naval Historical Center, ZB Files. Adams, *History of the United States of America During the Second Administration of Thomas Jefferson,* 2: 5. Calderhead, "Strange Career," 376. Captain Murray to SecNav, 20 September, 1805; 12 and 20 January 1806, in M125, 4.

37. Amendments to report of court-martial, initialed "J.B.," JBP: I, 73B.

38. SecNav to Gordon, 23 February 1807, Ridgely, 18 February; and Sinclair, 20 February 1807, M149, 7.

39. Sinclair to Barron, 12 March 1807. JBP: I, 42.

40. SecNav to Tingey, 24 January and 24 February 1807, M149, 7. Tingey to SecNav, 23 February 1807, M125, 7.

41. *Register of Officer Personnel,* 69. Letters from Tingey have Barron at the yard on 23 February and 27 March. Tingey to SecNav, same dates, M125, 7. A letter from Barron has him at the yard on 7 April. Barron to SecNav, same date, M125, 7. *Court Martial,* 362.

42. Barron later tried to use this in his defense. The copy of this correspondence in his papers has the endorsement on the back, "*Chesapeak's* powder, an important paper." JBP: I, 40.

43. SecNav to Tingey, 27 March 1807, M149, 7. Two weeks earlier, in a letter to Capt. John Rodgers, Tingey apologized for the delay: "I have been so much engaged at the yard, with the outfit of the *Chesapeake* and *Wasp.*" Tingey to Rodgers, 11 March 1807, LC: RFP, IIIA, 1 (#47359).

44. Tingey to SecNav, 27 March 1807, M125, 7.

45. SecNav to Surgeon E. Cutbush and Lt. A. Sinclair, both 3 March 1807; to Barron, 27 March 1807; to Lawrence, 26 April 1807; to Gordon, 9 May 1807, M149, 7. SecNav to Barron, 23 February 1807, JBP: I, 40. Navy Agent George Harrison, Philadelphia, to SecNav, 28 March 1807, M124, 15.

46. "Letters of William Henry Allen, 1800–1813," 1, no. 2: 206–8.

47. SecNav to Barron, 17 January 1807, JBP: I, 40; and SecNav to Barron, 10 April 1807, M149, 7.

48. SecNav to Tingey, 26 February 1807, M149, 7. Guttridge and Smith, *The Commodores,* 122. (The letter to Tingey omits beef and pork.)

49. *Court Martial,* 10.

50. Stevens, *Affair of Honor,* 63.

51. Barron to Gordon, 1, 10, and ? May 1807, *Court of Enquiry,* 69–71; reprinted in *Court Martial,* 239–42.

52. Testimony of Master Commandant Gordon, *Court Martial,* 111. Lieutenant Allen says she had only four guns on board, but he must be referring to the period of a few days later when, in order to lighten the frigate, eight of her guns were removed. Letter of July 17, 1807, LC: Lt. William Henry Allen Papers.

53. Abstract of *Chesapeake's* log taken for Gordon. JBP: I, 72. Testimony of Lt. William Crane, *Court Martial,* 402.

54. Testimony of Allen, *Court Martial,* 403. Gordon's unfinished letter to SecNav, 22 June 1807, *Court of Enquiry,* 93–95.

55. Letter of Allen, 17 July 1807. LC: Allen Papers; abstract of *Chesapeake's* log taken for Captain Gordon in 1808, JBP: I, 72. Testimony of Purser Robert W. Goldsborough, *Court Martial,* 301. *Norfolk Gazette and Publick Ledger,* 5 June 1807.

56. Testimony of Gordon, "Court of Enquiry," 95.

57. *Register of Officer Personnel,* 50.

58. Lowell, *Peace without Dishonour,* 10.

59. Ibid., 15.

60. Ibid., 12.

61. Testimony of Purser Robert Goldsborough, *Court Martial,* 391–92.

62. Beach, *United States Navy,* 52–53.

63. Capt. Thomas Tingey to Capt. John Rodgers, 27 June 1807, LC: RFP, IIIB, 3 (#4794).

64. Barron to SecNav, 22 July 1813, M125, 30.

65. "Conclusions of Board of Inquiry," Annex A, SecNav to Rodgers, 7 December 1807, M149, 7.

66. Testimony of Crane, *Court Martial,* 24; Allen, Ibid., 48 and 56; and Gordon, Ibid., 99–112. Also Gordon's testimony, "Court of Enquiry," 55, repeated in *Court Martial,* 227–28. LC, *Chesapeake* Log. Navy Agent at Norfolk Daniel Bedinger to SecNav, 11 June 1807, M124, 15.

67. "Court of Enquiry," 56–57.

68. Barron to SecNav, 6 June 1807, M125, 8. There is some dispute as to the length of Barron's first visit, but the log states he came aboard "at 1/2 past 10" and departed at "11." Abstract of *Chesapeake*'s log taken for Captain Gordon, 1808, JBP: I, 72. For Barron's subsequent testimony as to the state of the frigate see *Court Martial,* 364–74.

69. Testimony of Allen, *Court Martial,* 59.

70. Abstract of *Chesapeake*'s log, taken for Captain Gordon, 1808. JBP, I, 72. Testimony of Crane, court-martial of Captain Gordon, in *Court Martial,* 358–59.

71. In "Court of Enquiry," 74, and *Court Martial,* 209, 364–65.

72. Abstract of *Chesapeake*'s log, taken for Captain Gordon, 1808, JBP: I, 72. Ibid., *Court Martial,* 309.

73. Testimony of Allen at Gordon's court-martial, based on his journal, in *Court Martial,* 377–78; also 113 and 244. Gordon's unfinished letter to SecNav of 22 June 1807, is in ibid., 261. *Chesapeake*'s log, in ibid., 400.

74. Gordon to Barron, 17 June 1807, in "Court of Enquiry," 75.

75. Testimony of Crane, "Court of Enquiry," 104; testimony of Allen, ibid., 125.

76. "Court of Enquiry," 75–76.

77. Testimony of Allen in *Court Martial,* 378. *Chesapeake*'s log, ibid., 400–1.

78. Barron to SecNav, 21 June 1807, M125, 8. Gleaves, *James Lawrence,* 66–67. Testimony of Allen at Gordon's court-martial, in *Court Martial,* 378.

79. SecNav to Barron, 15 May 1807, *Court Martial,* 132–35. For more on Smith's instructions, see Barron's court-martial in Chapter Seven.

80. This request was in a letter of 12 March 1807. Barron subsequently noted on the back, "From that infamous Hypocrite, T. Jefferson" and "no consequence." JBP: I, 43.

81. Gordon to SecNav, 22 June 1807, read at court of inquiry, in *Court Martial,* 261.

SIX. THE THREAT OF WAR

1. Cooper, *History of the Navy,* 1: 22.

2. James, *Naval History,* 4: 255.

3. "Letters of William Henry Allen," vol. 1, no. 2: 212.

4. Long, *Nothing Too Daring,* 38.

5. Dye, *Fatal Cruise of the* Argus, 67.

6. Lieutenants of the *Chesapeake* to SecNav, M125, 8. They sent a copy of the letter to Barron and he acknowledged it the same day. JBP: I, 50, 51.

7. Letter of Allen to his father, June 24, 1807, "Letters of William Henry Allen," vol. 1, no. 2: 215–16.

8. Letter from the *Chesapeake* (addressee unknown), 17 July 1807. LC, Lieutenant William Henry Allen Papers.

9. SecNav to lieutenants, 26 June 1807, M149, 7.

10. Guttridge and Smith, *The Commodores*, 133.

11. *Gazette and Publick Ledger,* 24 June 1807, in Emmerson, *The* Chesapeake *Affair,* 13.

12. *Gazette and Publick Ledger,* 26 and 29 June, 1807.

13. Decatur to SecNav, 29 June 1807, M125, 8. Letter from Committee at the Exchange Coffee House, Hampton to Decatur, 28 June 1807; Decatur in reply, same date, in Emmerson, *The* Chesapeake *Affair,* 34.

14. Hamilton to George Canning, 27 June 1807, PRO, FO 5/53, 262–63. Captain Douglas to Vice Admiral Berkeley, 27 June 1807, PRO, Adm 1/497, 221.

15. SecNav to Lt. Benjamin F. Read, Barron, and Decatur, all 26 June 1807, M149, 7. Also excerpt from the *Chesapeake*'s log, JBP: I, 52.

16. Cabell's letter to Mathews of 2 July 1807 is reproduced in Emmerson, *The* Chesapeake *Affair,* 39a–b. See Gaines, "The *Chesapeake* Affair" 131–42. Hamilton to Brig. Gen. Thomas Mathews, 26 June 1807, PRO, FO 5/53, 260.

17. General Mathews to Governor Cabell, 8 July 1807, in Emmerson, *The* Chesapeake *Affair,* 60. *Norfolk Gazette and Publick Ledger,* 13 July 1807.

18. Tingey also said that command might have gone to Rodgers, "if it had been conceived that it would have been agreeable to you. I have said I presume it would not." Captain Tingey to Captain Rodgers, 27 June 1807, LC: RFP, Series IIIB, 3 (#4794).

19. Tingey to Rodgers, 24 October 1807, LC: RFP, IIIB, 4 (#4883?)

20. Campbell to SecNav, 15 August 1807, M125, 8.

21. *Naval Documents related to the United States Wars with the Barbary Powers,* 4: 546–47. Maloney, *Captain from Connecticut,* 123.

22. Log of the *Chesapeake,* 1 July 1807.

23. Printed in *Gazette and Publick Ledger,* 3 July 1807.

24. Damage report by lieutenants Benjamin Smith and Sidney Smith and Sailing Master Samuel Brooke, in Barron to SecNav, 23 June 1807, M125, 8. Decatur to SecNav, 4 July 1807, ibid.

25. Decatur's testimony at court-martial of Gordon, in *Court Martial,* 410. *Norfolk Gazette and Publick Ledger,* 3 July 1807. For a report on repair of the *Chesapeake* see Josiah Fox to Tingey, 7 July 1807, Josiah Fox Papers, Peabody Museum, Letter Book [LB] II, 180–81. Fox to Decatur, ibid., LB IV, 188.

26. *Gazette and Publick Ledger,* 3 July 1807.

27. Decatur to SecNav, 4 July 1807, M125, 8. Douglas's letter to Mayor Richard Lee of Norfolk is in Emmerson, *The* Chesapeake *Affair,* 44. But when Littleton Tazewell met with Douglas, the latter denied he had in any way threatened Norfolk. See Tazewell's letter to Lee, in ibid., 46–50.

28. Perkins, *Prologue to War,* 142.

29. Berkeley to William Marsden, 4 July 1807. PRO, Adm 497, 213–14.

30. Berkeley to Earl Bathurst, 13 and 17 August 1807. Binkley, ed., *The Bathurst Manuscripts,* 63–65.

31. This letter and response to it were printed in large type in the *Gazette and Publick Record*

on 6 July, the only such time this was done during the crisis. Decatur to SecNav, 4 July 1807, M125, 8. John Cunningham, a pilot, told Decatur that he had overheard the first lieutenant of the *Bellona* say that she, the *Leopard,* and the *Melampus* had been lightened (forty tons of bread were moved from the *Triumph* and her ballast was shifted) "for the purpose of lessning [*sic*] her Draft as much as possible" in order to come up to Norfolk. Affidavit on board the *Chesapeake,* 8 July 1807, in Decatur to SecNav, 8 July 1807, ibid.

32. Frank Owsley, "Robert Smith," 85–86. Decatur to SecNav, 29 June, 4 and 11 July, 1807, M125, 8. See 8 July letter for Decatur's sketch of dispositions.

33. SecNav to Decatur, 3 July 1807, M149, 7. Decatur to SecNav, 8 July 1807, M125, 8.

34. SecNav to Lieutenant Elbert, and Captains Decatur and Hull, all 3 July 1807. Also 6 July 1807 to lieutenants Perry and Blodget; and 7 July to Master Commandant John Shaw; 8 July to Commodore Samuel Barron, M149, 7. Decatur to SecNav, 8 July 1807, M125, 8. SecNav to Preble, 17 July 1807, LC: Preble Papers, #4370.

35. SecNav to Barron and Decatur, 8 July 1807, M149, 7. Barron to SecNav, 15 July 1807, M125, 8.

36. *Gazette and Publick Ledger,* 6 July 1807.

37. Adams, *Administrations of Thomas Jefferson,* 949. Secretary of War Henry Dearborn to Governor Cabell, 6 July 1807, in Emmerson, *The* Chesapeake *Affair,* 59.

38. *Gazette and Publick Ledger,* 8 July 1807.

39. M124, 16.

40. "Nat Ingraham & Son" to SecNav, 15 July 1807, M124, 16.

41. SecNav to Rodgers, 9 July 1807, M149, 7.

42. John ? to Dearborn, 6 July 1807, M124, 16.

43. M. Cluff to SecNav, 30 August 1807, M124, 17.

44. Jefferson to Dearborn, 7 July 1807. Ford, ed., *Writings of Jefferson,* 9: 101. Jefferson to Cabell, 8 July 1807, ibid., 9: 88, n. 1.

45. Dearborn to Cabell, 6 July 1807, in Emmerson, *The* Chesapeake *Affair,* 59. For a lengthy discussion of Governor Cabell's activities and the organization of the defenses in Virginia, see Gaines, "Outrageous Encounter," 74–97.

46. *Gazette and Publick Ledger,* 8 July 1807.

47. SecNav to Decatur, 8 July 1807, M149, 7.

48. *Gazette and Publick Ledger,* 10 July 1807.

49. *Gazette and Publick Ledger,* 13 July 1807. Decatur to SecNav, 15 July 1807, M125. 8.

50. See editorials on the occasion of Hamilton's return to Britain in 1815 and on his death, in Emmerson, *The* Chesapeake *Affair,* 171–73.

51. Malone, *Jefferson,* 5: 433.

52. Clowes, *The Royal Navy,* 5: 452, 499, and 555. Colledge, *Ships of the Royal Navy,* 200.

53. Erskine to Douglas, 8 July 1807, and Hardy to Hamilton, 15 July 1807, Berkeley MSS. In Jackson, "Impressment," 274–75.

54. *Gazette and Publick Ledger,* 10 July 1807, and Decatur to SecNav, 11 July 1807, M125, 8.

55. SecNav to Decatur, 11 July 1807, M149, 7.

56. Decatur to SecNav, 12, 14, 15, and 31 July, M125, 8.

57. *Gazette and Publick Ledger,* 27 July, 1807.

58. Berkeley to William Marsden, 27 July 1807, PRO: Adm/497, #250.

59. *Gazette and Publick Ledger,* 27 July 1807.

60. Decatur to SecNav, 5 August 1807, M125, 8. *Gazette and Publick Ledger,* 3 August 1807.

61. Decatur to SecNav, 19 August 1807, M125, 8.

62. This was apparently not regarded with any seriousness, either by Rowe or Rodgers.

Rowe did not report the incident to Rodgers until 8 September, and Rodgers did not inform the Navy Department. The letter from Rowe to Rodgers is in LC: RFP, IIIB, 4 (#4849).

63. Rodgers to SecNav, 5 September 1807, M125, 8. Paullin, *Commodore John Rodgers*, 188–90.

64. There may have been only two incidents, although the different numbers suggest three. *Gazette and Publick Ledger*, 20 July and 3 August 1807; Emmerson, *The* Chesapeake *Affair*, 64 and 70. Also, Berkeley to Marsden, 27 July 1807. PRO: Adm/497, #250. Decatur to SecNav, 14, 15, and 19 July, 19 and 27 August, and 19 November 1807, and Hull to SecNav, 31 July, 1807, M125, 8 and 9. Winfield Scott, *Memoirs*, 1: 19–20.

65. *Gazette and Publick Ledger*, 27 July 1807.

66. Ibid., 27 July and 5 August 1807. Taylor's cavalry troop was discharged on 27 August. Ibid., 28 August 1807. The two remaining artillery and infantry companies were deactivated at the beginning of November. Ibid., 4 November 1807.

67. Ibid., 5 August 1807.

68. Ibid., 7 August 1807.

69. Flournoy, ed., *Calendar of Virginia State Papers*, 9: 591.

70. Decatur to SecNav, 27 August 1807, M125, 8.

71. SecNav to Decatur, 3 November 1807, M149, 7. Gosset, *Lost Ships of the Royal Navy*, 54.

72. Ratford's testimony, *Trial of John Wilson*, 15. *Gazette and Publick Ledger*, 16 September 1807.

73. PRO, Adm 1/5383.

74. James, *Naval History*, 4: 255. Mahan, *Sea Power*, 1: 255. "Receipt for Return of Men aboard *Chesapeake*," Adm. 1/502.

75. Marshall, *Royal Navy Biography*, vol. 2, part 2, 893.

76. Berkeley to Humphreys, 4 July 1807, in Marshall, *Royal Naval Biography*, vol. 2: Part 2, 895–96.

77. *Gazette and Publick Ledger*, 14 September 1807.

78. First Secretary of the Admiralty W. W. Pole to Berkeley, 24 August 1807, Adm 2/1365, 10–13. Berkeley's successor was Sir John B. Warren. *Gazette and Publick Ledger*, 11 December 1807.

79. Berkeley to William Cole, 4 October 1807, replying to letter of 24 August [?], 1807, PRO: Adm/497 #378.

80. *Gazette and Publick Ledger*, 11 December 1807.

81. *Dictionary of National Biography*, Stephen, 2: 358–59. Admiralty to Berkeley, 26 December 1808, ADM 2/1367, 74–78.

82. Jackson, "Impressment," 282; Marshall, *Royal Naval Biography*, vol. 2, part 2, 596; O'Byrne, *Naval Biographical Dictionary*, 165–66; and newspaper clipping (unidentified) in JBP: I, 82. O'Byrne wrote that Humphreys acted "pursuant to the orders of his Commander-in-Chief" and that his "conduct throughout the whole transaction met with the warm approval of Vice Admiral Berkeley."

83. Gore, *Nelson's Hardy and His Wife*, 40–41. Gore notes that "Lady Hardy never forgot the miseries of the first months of her marriage. She used to tell her grandchildren how the ship was kept always ready for action and no fire was ever allowed in her cabin."

84. *Gazette and Publick Ledger*, 26 October and 16 December 1807.

85. James, *Naval History*, 4: 255–56. Decatur to SecNav, 5 December 1807, with enclosures, M125, 9. *Gazette and Publick Ledger*, 4, 7, and 18 December 1807.

86. "Remarks" (afterward) in *Trial of John Wilson*, 24.

87. SecNav to Decatur, 16 July 1807, M149, 7.
88. "Declaration of Henry Harvey and Thomas Addison late of the United States Frigate *Chesapeake*," in Steel, "More Light," 260–61; "Affidavit of William Brown," ibid., 263.
89. "Affidavit of William Brown," in Steel, "More Light," 263.
90. In Erskine to Canning, 3 December 1807, PRO: FO 5/52. Quoted in Steel, "More Light," 253–54.
91. Log of *Chesapeake*, 16 November 1807.
92. Decatur to SecNav, 27 November 1807, M125, 8. Madison to Erskine, 24 November 1807, in Erskine to Canning, 3 December 1807, PRO: FO 5/52, in Steel, "More Light," 253–54. Also, "Declaration of Henry Harvey and Thomas Addison late of the United States Frigate *Chesapeake*," ibid., 262.
93. SecNav to Decatur, 10 and 25 November 1807, M149, 7.
94. Circular letter from SecNav to Decatur (Norfolk), Captain Chauncey (New York), Lieutenant Elbert (Charleston), Lieutenant Lawrence (New Orleans), 14 December 1807, M149, 7; and Decatur to SecNav, 27 December 1807, M125, 9.
95. Steel, "More Light," 254–55.
96. Bromley to Hamilton (2 letters), 9 January 1808, in Steel, "More Light," 255.
97. Decatur to Hamilton, 10 January 1808, Ibid.
98. Ibid., 261–63.
99. Ibid., 255–58.
100. In a letter of 25 January 1808, Smith approved Decatur's actions in not discharging three seamen as requested by Bromley: "Consequently with our National Honor we cannot recognize a right on the part of the Commanding Officer of any foreign armed Vessel, to make such a demand upon the Commanding Officer of any Public Vessel of War of the United States, and especially within our own Territory." M149, 8. Bromley claimed that Decatur had sent Henry Henning and Thomas C—[?], two seamen "lately discharged from the *Chesapeake*," to Baltimore on Gunboat No. 5 although they had asked to be discharged at Norfolk to join HMS *Statira*, and that there were two hundred British subjects still on board U.S. vessels at Norfolk. Bromley to Erskine, 28 March 1808, enclosed in SecNav to Decatur, 12 April 1808, M149, 8.
101. Smith to Decatur, Chauncey, and Elbert, 8 January 1808, M149, 8.
102. McKee, "Foreign Seamen," 384–93.
103. SecNav to Decatur, Chauncey, Master Commandant Dent (Charleston), and Lieutenant Leonard (New Orleans), 18 and 29 February 1808, M149, 8. Decatur to SecNav, 27 December 1807, M125, 9.
104. SecNav to Sailing Master Thomas N. Gautier, 4 June 1808, M149, 8. Letters to other commanders are similar.
105. McKee, "Foreign Seamen," 392.
106. "Declarations of Henry Harvey and Thomas Addison late of the United States Frigate *Chesapeake*," reprinted in full in Steel, "More Light," 260–62.
107. "Affidavit of William Brown," in ibid., 263.
108. Decatur to SecNav, 13 April 1808, M125, 11.

SEVEN. PRESIDENT JEFFERSON'S DILEMMA

1. *Times* of London, 20 August 1807.
2. Adams, *History of the United States of America During the Second Administration of Thomas Jefferson,* 27–33.

3. Jefferson to James Bowdoin, 10 July 1807, *Writings of Jefferson*, 11: 268–70.

4. Erskine to Canning, 1 July 1807, PRO (London), FO 5/52.

5. Hamilton to Canning, 26 June 1807, FO 5/53 (Consular Reports).

6. Bond to Canning, 1 July 1807, FO 5/53.

7. Burton Spivak, *Jefferson's English Crisis*, 74–78.

8. *Times* of London, 27 July 1807.

9. Ibid., 6 August, 1807.

10. Jefferson to Henry Dearborn, 25 June 1807, and to Gallatin, 25 June 1807, *Writings of Jefferson*, 11: 255.

11. Jefferson to Dearborn, 7 July 1807, ibid., 4: 260–61.

12. Jefferson to Cabell, 8 July 1807, ibid., 11: 262.

13. Gallatin to Joseph Nicholson, 17 July 1807, Adams, ed., *Writings of Albert Gallatin*, 1: 338.

14. Gallatin to Jefferson, 25 July 1807, ibid., 1: 340–41.

15. "Proclamation," 2 July 1807, A.S.P., F.R. 3: 23–24.

16. Jefferson to Cabell, Washington, 29 June 1807, *Writings of Jefferson*, 11: 256.

17. Spivak, *Jefferson's English Crisis*, 82.

18. Madison to Monroe, 6 July 1807, A.S.P., F.R., 3: 183–85.

19. Jefferson to John Taylor, 1 August 1807, *Writings of Jefferson*, 11: 304–5.

20. Ibid.

21. Jefferson to Bowdoin, Washington, 10 July 1807, ibid., 11: 268.

22. Jefferson to Armstrong, 17 July 1807, ibid., 11: 283–85; to Dupont de Nemours, 14 July 1807, ibid., 11: 274–75; to the Marquis de LaFayette, 14 July 1807, ibid., 11: 276.

23. Jefferson to Cabell, 16 July 1807, ibid., 11: 280–81; to Dearborn, ibid., 11: 284–85.

24. Erskine to Madison, 13 July 1807, FO 5/52.

25. Erskine to Douglas, 8 July 1807, FO 5/52.

26. Erskine to Berkeley, 16 August 1807, and Erskine to Berkeley, 20 August 1807, FO 5/52.

27. Circular of Capt. J. E. Douglas to the Mayor of Norfolk, 3 July 1807, FO 5/52 #259.

28. Berkeley to Erskine, Halifax, 1 September 1807, FO 5/52.

29. Erskine to Canning, 2 July 1807, and to Canning, 17 July 1807, FO 5/52.

30. Erskine to Canning, Washington, 31 July 1807, FO 5/52.

31. Bond to Canning, Philadelphia, 2 August 1807, FO 5/53.

32. Canning to Monroe (private), Foreign Office, 25 July 1807, A.S.P., F.R., 3: 187.

33. Monroe to Madison, 4 August 1807, A.S.P., F.R., 3: 186.

34. Hamilton to Berkeley, 21 March 1807; Berkeley to Marsden, 23 March 1807; Douglas to Berkeley, 15 April 1807; and Berkeley to Marsden, 1 May 1807, PRO: Adm 1/497.

35. The *Times*, 28 July 1807.

36. Canning to Monroe, Foreign Office, 3 August 1807, A.S.P., F.R., 3: 188.

37. Monroe and Pinkney to Madison, 22 October 1807, A.S.P., F.R., 3: 196–97.

38. Canning to Lord Boringdon, n.p., 30 September 1807, in Aspinal, ed., *Later Letters of George III*, 4: 630.

39. The *Times*, 5 August 1807.

40. The *Times*, 8 August 1807.

41. Ibid., 10 August 1807; Jefferson to Clinton, 6 July 1807, *Writings of Jefferson*, 11: 257.

42. *Political Register*, 15 August 1807.

43. *Political Register*, 5 September 1807.

44. *Gentlemen's Magazine*, LXXVIII, Pt. 2, August 1807.

45. *Political Register*, 30 October 1807; Perkins, *Prologue to War*, 190.

46. Castlereagh to Lord Chatham, Brighton, 3 December 1807, Marquess of Londonderry, ed., *Letters and Dispatches of Lord Castlereagh*, 101–2, 104–7.
47. Cookson, *The Friends of Peace*, 43; The *Times*, 24 August and 16 September 1807.
48. *Political Register*, 16 October 1807; The *Times*, 18 October 1807; Adams, *History*, 76–77.
49. Canning to Monroe, Foreign Office, 23 September 1807, A.S.P., F.R., 3: 199–201.
50. Monroe to Madison, 10 October 1807, ibid., 3: 191–93.
51. Adams, *History*, 72–76.
52. Instructions to George H. Rose, Foreign Office, 24 October 1807, FO 5/56, #1.
53. Rose to Canning, 27 and 31 December 1807, FO 5/56.
54. Adams, *History*, 78–80.
55. *Diary of John Quincy Adams*, 48.
56. Gallatin to Jefferson, Washington, 21 October 1807, *Writings of Gallatin*, 1: 360.
57. Report to the House of Representatives by James Madison, 12 November 1807, A.S.P., F.R., 3: 8–9.
58. Bond to Canning, 1 December 1807, and Barclay to Canning, 12 December 1807, FO 5/53.
59. Perkins, *Prologue*, 151–60; Malone, *Jefferson the President*, 479–90.
60. Rose to Canning, Washington, 8 January 1808, FO 5/56; Rose to Madison, Washington, 26 January 1808; A.S.P., F.R., 3: 212; Rose to Canning, Washington, 25 February 1808, FO 5/56; Madison to Rose, Department of State, 5 March 1808, A.S.P., F.R., 3: 214–16; Brant, *James Madison*, 409–18.
61. For an interesting discussion of how Jefferson's schemes to acquire the Floridas created division among congressional Republicans, see Chapter 5, "Attempts to Purchase Florida," in Carson, "Congress in Jefferson's Foreign Policy, 1801–1809." Unpublished Ph.D. dissertation, Texas Christian University, 1983.
62. Rose to Canning, Washington, 4 March 1808, FO 5/56; Rose to Madison, Washington, 17 March 1808. A.S.P., F.R., 3: 217.
63. Jefferson to Gallatin, Washington, 19 April 1808, *Writings of Jefferson*, 12: 30; Gallatin to Jefferson, Washington, 23 May 1808, *Writings of Gallatin*, 1: 390; Adams, *History*, 249–52.
64. Ibid., 271–73; Carr, *Coming of War*, 251–55.
65. Horsman, *Causes of the War of 1812*, 135.
66. Carr, *Coming of War*, 255.
67. Frankel, "The 1807–1809 Embargo," 304.
68. Pinkney to Madison, London, 4 August 1808, A.S.P., F.R., 3: 225–26.
69. Pinkney to Madison, London, 21 September 1808. A.S.P., F.R., 3: 228–30; Pinkney to Canning, Great Cumberland Place, 28 December 1808, ibid., 240.
70. Frankel, "The 1807–1809 Embargo," 307–8, concludes "the evidence points toward greater economic suffering on the part of Britain than the United States."
71. Adams, *History*, 277–84.
72. Jefferson to Thomas Mann Randolph, Washington, 7 February 1809, *Writings of Jefferson*, 12: 248; Jefferson to Gen. John Armstrong, Washington, 15 March 1809, ibid., 261.
73. Malone, *Jefferson the President*, 262–68.

EIGHT. ASSESSING THE BLAME

1. Barron to Bullus, 3 July 1807, JBP: I, 64.
2. Cooper, *History of the Navy*, 19.
3. Adams, *History of the United States of America During the Second Administration of Thomas Jefferson*, 2: 21.

4. Letter from Allen to his father, written on board the *Chesapeake*, "Letters of William Henry Allen," 2: 225.

5. Barron to SecNav, 23 June 1807, JBP: I, 54.

6. Testimony of Barron at Gordon's court-martial, *Court Martial*, 365. Barron said: "I should never think it proper for a man of war to proceed to sea so lumbered if there was a prospect of meeting with an enemy. But as these had been put on board by order of the government, I considered it necessary to proceed to sea with the first wind. . . ." Ibid., 365–66.

7. Barron to Bullus, 3 July 1807, JBP: I, 64.

8. Gordon's testimony at court of inquiry, in *Court Martial*, 230. Crane, in ibid., 361; testimony of Lt. John Orde Creighton, ibid., 386; Barron to Bullus, 3 July 1807, JBP: I, 64.

9. Barron to Bullus, 3 July 1807, JBP: I, 64. Amendment to report of Court-Martial, "For page 162," initialled "J.B." JBP: I, 73B.

10. Ibid.; Dye, *Fatal Cruise of the Argus*, 38.

11. Barron to Bullus, 3 July 1807. JBP, I: 64.

12. Ibid. Also Guttridge and Smith, *The Commodores*, 134.

13. Stevens, *Affair of Honor*, 77. Also, Anthony, *Decatur*, 172.

14. SecNav to Decatur, 26 October 1807, M149, 7. Decatur to SecNav, 19 November 1807, M125, 9.

15. Excerpt from letter of August 27, 1808, from Allen to his father, written on board the *Chesapeake*. "Letters of William Henry Allen," 1, no. 2, 226–27.

16. SecNav to Preble, Hull, and Chauncey, 26 June; to Barron and Decatur, 27 June; to Hull, 11 July 1807; and to Murray, 12 September 1807, M149, 7. Preble to SecNav, 2 July 1807, M125, 8. *Norfolk Ledger and Gazette*, 26 August 1807. Guttridge and Smith, *The Commodores*, 144. Amendments to report of the court-martial, "page 15." Initialled "J.B." JBP, I, 73B. See also Chapter 5. The navy's practice of hiring civilians to act as judge advocates continued until after the Civil War.

17. Tazewell to SecNav, 6 October 1807, M124, 17. For background on Tazewell see Peterson, *Littleton Waller Tazewell*, 1–52.

18. Barron wrote Bullus on 3 July that his wound made it impossible to sit up. JBP: I, 63. See also Capt. Samuel Barron to Captain Murray, 4 October; Richard Rush to Capt. S. Barron, 5 October; Capt. S. Barron to Rush, 6 October 1807, JBP and "Court of Enquiry," 20–23.

19. Tazewell to SecNav, 8 October 1807, M124, 17; Log of the *Chesapeake* (10 and 14 October, 1807); *Norfolk Gazette and Publick Ledger*, (14 October 1807); SecNav to Decatur, 26 October 1807, M149, 7.

20. "Court of Enquiry," 23. Peterson, *Tazewell*, 51.

21. Tazewell to SecNav, 8 October and 6 November 1807, M124, 17; to Barron, 8 October 1807, JBP: I, 65.

22. In his letter to Rodgers, Smith had added, "which surrender was made . . . without the defense having been made, which might have been expected from the known valor of Americans. . . ." Annex A in orders from SecNav to Rodgers, 7 December 1807, M149, 7. Grant, *Isaac Hull*, 159. "Court of Enquiry," 23.

23. Muhlenburg identified those on the quarterdeck as Barron, Gordon, Lieutenants Benjamin and Sidney Smith, Marine Captain Hall; and Midshipmen Wilson, Babbitt, Drayton, Crump, Davis, Pearce, and himself. "Court of Enquiry," 27–34.

24. Shubrick's testimony, "Court of Enquiry," 34–40.

25. Drayton's testimony, "Court of Enquiry," 40–45.

26. Ibid., 45–47.

27. Gordon's testimony is in "Court of Enquiry," 47–98, 108–12.

28. Gordon's testimony, "Court of Enquiry," 55–56.

29. Ibid., 57–59.

30. Ibid., 60–61.

31. Ibid., 61.

32. Ibid., 60–61.

33. Ibid., 61–63.

34. Ibid., 63–68.

35. Gordon's testimony, "Court of Enquiry," 52.

36. Ibid., 76–80.

37. Ibid., 80–81.

38. Ibid., 81–82.

39. Ibid., 85.

40. Ibid., 86.

41. Ibid., 88–89.

42. Ibid., 89–90.

43. Ibid., 93–95.

44. Ibid., 96–97.

45. Ibid., 110.

46. Ibid., 110–11.

47. Ibid., 112.

48. Crane's testimony is in ibid., 99–108 and 113–17.

49. Ibid., 99.

50. Ibid., 99–108.

51. Ibid., 107–15.

52. Allen's testimony, "Court of Enquiry," 118–33.

53. Ibid., 119.

54. Ibid., 120

55. Ibid., 122. Allen wrote in July 1807 that "it had been reported a long time before that they intended to take the men from us." During the passage down the Potomac Bullus had told him that the *Melampus*'s captain "had said he intended to take the men out of us, and asked whether I thought they would attempt it." Allen, letter of 17 July 1807, LC: Lt. William Henry Allen Papers.

56. *Court Martial,* 122.

57. Letter of 17 July 1807. LC: Lt. William Henry Allen Papers.

58. "Court of Enquiry," 123–28.

59. Ibid., 127.

60. Ibid., 127–29.

61. Ibid., 129–33.

62. Creighton's testimony, "Court of Enquiry," 133–42.

63. Ibid., 135–37.

64. Ibid., 138–39.

65. Ibid., 138–42.

66. Ibid., 139.

67. Ibid., 140–41.

68. Smith's testimony, "Court of Enquiry," 143–47.

69. Ibid., 142–46.
70. Hall's testimony is in "Court of Enquiry," 147–54.
71. Ibid., 148–49.
72. Ibid., 150–52.
73. Ibid., 152–54.
74. Brooke's testimony, "Court of Enquiry," 154–59.
75. Ibid., 155.
76. Ibid., 156–57.
77. Hook's testimony, "Court of Enquiry," 159–64.
78. Ibid., 159–61.
79. Ibid., 161–62.
80. Ibid., 162.
81. Ibid., 162–63.
82. Babbitt's testimony is in "Court of Enquiry," 164–67.
83. Ibid., 164–65.
84. Ibid., 165–66.
85. Elliott's testimony, "Court of Enquiry," 167–71.
86. Ibid., 167.
87. Ibid., 168–69.
88. Ibid., 169–70.
89. Ibid., 171.
90. Wilson's testimony, "Court of Enquiry," 171–74.
91. Ibid., 172.
92. Ibid., 172–74.
93. Steele's testimony is in "Court of Enquiry," 174–76.
94. Ibid., 175.
95. Broom's testimony is in "Court of Enquiry," 176–77.
96. Ibid., 176.
97. Ibid., 179.
98. See "Court of Enquiry," 179–87.
99. Ibid., 181.
100. Ibid., 182–83.
101. Ibid., 183–84.
102. Ibid., 184.
103. Ibid., 184–85.
104. Ibid., 185.
105. Ibid., 186.
106. Ibid., 186.
107. Ibid., 187. The court's findings are also in Annex A, SecNav to Rodgers, 7 December 1807, M149, 7, and Tazewell to SecNav, 27 November 1807, M124, 17.
108. SecNav to Rodgers, 7 October 1807, LC: RFP, IIIB, 4 (#4866); and 13 November 1807, M149, 7.
109. Ap C. Jones, *Exceptions to the Illegal Organization*, 14.
110. *Court Martial*, 3.
111. Stevens, *Affair of Honor*, 80.
112. "Letters of William Henry Allen," no. 2: 221.
113. Anthony, *Decatur*, 172.
114. Decatur to SecNav, 17 December 1807, M124, 9.

115. SecNav to Decatur, 26 December 1807, M149, 7.

116. Anthony, *Decatur,* 172.

117. Amendments to report of court-martial. "Page 267." Initialled "J.B." JBP: I, 73B.

118. Long, *Ready to Hazard,* 111. On 19 November 1798 Bainbridge surrendered the schooner *Retaliation,* the only U.S. Navy warship lost in the Quasi-War. From September 1800 to January 1801 he was forced to undergo the humiliation of hoisting the Algerine flag on his frigate and allow her use as a floating zoo/embassy for the Dey of Constantinople. Two years later he surrendered the *Philadelphia* after she ran aground off Tripoli.

119. Guttridge and Smith, *The Commodores,* 179–80.

120. The full specifications are in SecNav to Rodgers, 7 December 1807, M149, 7.

121. Tazewell to SecNav, 6 and 7 October, 27 November and 10 December 1807, M124, 17 and 18. SecNav to Tazewell, 12 October 1807, M209, 3. Peterson, *Tazewell,* 53.

122. Peterson, *Tazewell,* 54.

123. "In consideration of Dr. Bullus's late absence from the Country, of the situation in which he found his family on his return to it, and of his earnest entreaties to be excused from attending the Court. . . ." SecNav to Rodgers, 27 January 1808, M149, 8.

124. Tazewell to SecNav, 11 January 1808, M124, 19.

125. *Court Martial,* 24–25.

126. Ibid., 44–47.

127. Long, *Nothing Too Daring,* 38.

128. Watson, *Tragic Career,* 24.

129. Crane's testimony is in *Court Martial,* 24–43.

130. Guttridge and Smith, *The Commodores,* 155.

131. Allen's testimony is in *Court Martial,* 43–65.

132. Guttridge and Smith, *The Commodores,* 156–57.

133. Ibid., 123–24.

134. Smith's testimony is in *Court Martial,* 75–84.

135. Hall's testimony is in *Court Martial,* 84–92.

136. Brooke's testimony is in *Court Martial,* 92–98.

137. Gordon's testimony is in *Court Martial,* 98–125. Guttridge and Smith, *The Commodores,* 157.

138. Gordon's testimony, *Court Martial,* 115–18.

139. Ibid., 119.

140. Ibid., 123–24 and 233.

141. Drayton's testimony is in *Court Martial,* 125–31.

142. *Court Martial,* 131 and 143; Guttridge and Smith, *The Commodores,* 158–59.

143. Guttridge and Smith, ibid.

144. Elliott's testimony is in *Court Martial,* 145–50.

145. Norton's testimony is in *Court Martial,* 151–54.

146. Wadsworth's testimony is in *Court Martial,* 155–60.

147. Wilson's testimony is in *Court Martial,* 160–65.

148. Garnett's testimony is in *Court Martial,* 165–67.

149. Bullus deposition, in Emmerson, *The* Chesapeake *Affair,* 132.

150. *Court Martial,* 170.

151. Guttridge and Smith, *The Commodores,* 160.

152. Gibson, "John Bullus," *The Historical Review of Berks County* 9 (April 1944) 3: 76–77; SecNav Smith to Bullus, 17 June and 5 September 1806, M149, 7; and Stephen Decatur,

Junr. Papers, Historical Society of Pennsylvania. William Dunn graciously supplied the authors with his file on Bullus.

153. Testimony of Babbitt, *Court Martial*, 171–80; also C-L Box, Lot 3, EGSL: SC.

154. Sinclair's testimony is in *Court Martial*, 180–81.

155. Ibid., 183. Elliott's recall to the stand is in ibid., 181–84.

156. Their testimony is in *Court Martial*, 185–92.

157. Hall's testimony is in *Court Martial*, 192–95.

158. Nuttrel's testimony is in *Court Martial*, 195–99.

159. *Court Martial*, 199-202.

160. *Court Martial*, 202–8

161. Tazewell's testimony is in *Court Martial*, 212–15.

162. Barron's testimony is in *Court Martial*, 267–327. Allen to his father, 5 February 1808, "Letters of William Henry Allen," 1, no. 2: 225.

163. *Court Martial*, 269.

164. Ibid., 271. Emphasis in original.

165. Ibid., 276–77.

166. Ibid., 278.

167. Ibid., 279–80.

168. Ibid., 281.

169. Ibid., 282–88.

170. Ibid.

171. Ibid., 293–94.

172. Ibid., 296.

173. Ibid., 332.

174. Ibid., 300–1.

175. Ibid., 301–2.

176. Ibid., 304.

177. Ibid., 304–7.

178. Ibid., 308–9.

179. Ibid., 313–15.

180. Ibid., 314–18.

181. Ibid., 325.

182. Ibid., 326.

183. *Norfolk Gazette and Publick Ledger*, 4 February 1807.

184. *Court Martial*, 327.

185. For the verdict, see ibid., 328–50.

186. Ibid., 338

187. Ibid., 342–46.

188. Ibid., 346–49.

189. Ibid., 338–42.

190. Ibid., 323–36. SecNav to Barron, 7 May 1808, M149, 8.

191. Watson, *Tragic Career*, 43.

192. Barron to Hon. Thomas Newton, 27 November 1823, JBP: VI, 16.

193. Stevens, *Affair of Honor*, 94.

194. Pratt, *Preble's Boys*, 53.

195. Trial proceedings are contained in *Court Martial*, 351–454.

196. The full charges are in ibid., 10–12.

197. Ibid., 351–56.

198. Ibid., 362.

199. Ibid., 364–72.

200. Ibid., pp. 373–74.

201. In the letter cited Allen incorrectly gave the month as May rather than June. Letter of 27 July 1807, LC: William Henry Allen Papers. Allen's testimony is in *Court Martial*, 374–83.

202. *Court Martial*, 398.

203. Ibid., 410

204. Ibid., 419–20. Gordon's whole statement is in ibid., 433–36.

205. Ibid., 424–28.

206. Ibid., 430–35.

207. Ibid., 453–54. The full charges are in SecNav to Rodgers, 7 December 1807, M149, 7. The court's conclusion and sentences are in *Court Martial*, 442–54; also SecNav to Decatur, 21 May 1808, M149, 8.

208. "For page 21," part of amendments to report of court-martial, signed "J.B." JBP: I, 73B.

209. Amendment to report of court-martial, "For Page 212[?]," initialed "J.B." JBP: I, 73B. Guttridge and Smith, *The Commodores*, 170.

210. For Hall's trial see *Court Martial*, 454–79.

211. Full specifications in *Court Martial*, 13–14.

212. Anderson's testimony at Gordon's trial is in *Court Martial*, 388–89; at Hall's trial it is in ibid., 457–58.

213. Otto's testimony is in ibid., 459–63 and 464–65.

214. Gordon's testimony is in ibid., 465. Hall's short statement to the court is in ibid., 470–72.

215. The full specifications of charges are in SecNav to Rodgers, 7 December 1807, M149, 7. The court's conclusion and sentences are in SecNav to Decatur, 21 May 1808, M149, 8; and *Court Martial*, 473–76.

216. See *Court Martial*, 12–13, and 479–96.

217. Ibid., 486.

218. SecNav to Rodgers, 7 December 1807, M149, 7. SecNav to Decatur, 21 May 1808, M149, 8. Guttridge and Smith, *The Commodores*, 168.

219. Amendments to report of court-martial, "Page 13," initialed "J.B." JBP: I, 73B.

220. Amendment to report of court-martial, initialed "J.B." JBP: I, 73B.

221. Guttridge and Smith, *The Commodores*, 171.

NINE. AFTERMATH

1. Beach, *United States Navy*, 69.

2. Decatur to SecNav, 27 August 1807, M125, 8.

3. Decatur to SecNav, 29 August 1807, M125, 8. Log of *Chesapeake*, 2–3 and 11 September 1807.

4. Decatur to SecNav, 1 June 1808, M125, 11; SecNav to Decatur, 16 January 1808, M149, 8. Log of the *Chesapeake*, 7 March 1808.

5. SecNav to Decatur, 6, 7, and 16 June; 1 and 19 July; 2 August and 10 November 1808, M149, 8. Log of the *Chesapeake*, 12 June, 13 July, 8 December 1808. Decatur to SecNav, 13 July; 8, 10, 13, 15, 26, and 29 August; 6 and 30 September; 3 November 1808, M125, 12 and 13.

6. SecNav to Decatur, 2 February 1809, M149, 8.

7. SecNav to Hull, 27 February and 17 April 1808 and 5 August 1809, M149, 8. SecNav to Bainbridge, 19 July 1809, ibid.

8. Fowler, *Jack Tars and Commodores,* 158.

9. The ship is always referred to in American sources and even most British as *Little Belt,* although according to William Gilkerson she was the *Lille Belt.*

10. For the two different accounts of the encounter see Rodgers to SecNav, 23 and 31 May and 16 July 1811, M125, 21 and 22; and Capt. A. B. Bingham to Vice Admiral Herbert Sawyer, 21 May 1811, in Dudley, ed., *Naval War of 1812,* 1: 42. For the U.S. Navy court of inquiry see *The Weekly Register,* 21 September and 30 November 1811.

11. Monroe to Augustus Foster, 11 October 1811, in *The Weekly Register,* 16 November 1811.

12. Cooper, *History of the Navy,* 2: 28–29.

13. Decatur to SecNav, 10 June 1811, M125, 22.

14. Foster to Monroe, 3 July and 5 September 1811, in *The Weekly Register,* 6 November 1811.

15. Foster to Monroe, 24 July 1811, *The Weekly Register,* 16 November 1811.

16. Monroe to Foster, 18 July 1811, *The Weekly Register,* 16 November 1811.

17. Monroe to Foster, 14 September 1811, *The Weekly Register,* 16 November 1811.

18. Clowes, *Royal Navy,* 5: 452, 499 and 555. Colledge, *Ships of the Royal Navy,* 200.

19. *Dictionary of American Fighting Ships,* vol. 2, 95.

20. Cross, *The* Chesapeake, 64.

21. Letter of Broke to Lawrence in Cross, *The* Chesapeake, 69. There are a number of books on the engagement. See Pullen, *The* Shannon *and the* Chesapeake and Padfield, *Broke and the* Shannon.

22. Tucker, *Arming the Fleet,* 48. The British losses were the *Guerrière* to the *Constitution, Frolic* to *Wasp, Macedonian* to *United States, Java* to *Constitution,* and *Peacock* to *Hornet.* On Broke, see Pullen, *The* Shannon *and the* Chesapeake, 41–42.

23. Pullen, *The* Shannon *and the* Chesapeake, 50.

24. Mahan, *Sea Power,* 2: 145. For the action, see 134–47.

25. Pullen, *The* Shannon *and the* Chesapeake, 52–63. See also Mahan, *Sea Power,* 2: 134–47, and Cooper, *History of the Navy,* 2: 102–7. Tucker, *Arming the Fleet,* 25–26.

26. Pullen, *The* Shannon *and the* Chesapeake, Appendix F, 147.

27. Gates, *The Portsmouth that has Passed,* 239. Cross, *The* Chesapeake, 77. Pullen, *The* Shannon *and the* Chesapeake, 76.

28. SecNav to Captain Decatur, 5 March 1808, M149, 8.

29. SecNav to Captain Decatur, 1 June 1808, M149, 8. SecNav to Gordon, 27 February 1809, M149, 8. Radoff, "Captain Gordon," 389; Calderhead, "A Strange Career in a Young Navy," 379–86. Tucker, *Jeffersonian Gunboat Navy,* 106, 119, 122–23, 126, 130, 137, and 166. Naval Historical Center, ZB Files.

30. SecNav to Decatur, 30 May and 1 June 1808, M149, 8. *Register of Officer Personnel,* 687.

31. Ibid., 137.

32. Dye, *Fatal Cruise of the* Argus, 261–90.

33. Guttridge and Smith, *The Commodores,* 262–66.

34. Stevens, *Affair of Honor,* 113, 193–95; Martin, *Most Fortunate Ship,* 211–12.

35. Stevens, *Affair of Honor,* 113, 193–95; Captain Decatur, 1 June 1808, M149, 8; Morris I. Radoff, "Captain Gordon," 389; *General Navy Register. List of Officers of the U.S. Navy and Marine Corps.* Tucker, *Jeffersonian Gunboat Navy,* 106, 119, 122–23, 126, 130, 137, 166; McKee, *Gentlemanly and Honorable Profession,* 224; K. Jack Bauer, "George Bancroft," in *American Secretaries of the Navy,* 1: 223; Mahon, *War of 1812,* 90–91 and 172–75;

Roosevelt, *Naval War of 1812*, 157, 159–69, 218, 246, and 253; Emmerson, *The* Chesapeake *Affair*, 195; also Peterson, *Littleton Waller Tazewell*.

36. Anthony, *Decatur*, 174.

37. Barron to President Monroe, April 1820, JBP: III, 43.

38. Stevens, *Affair of Honor*, 55, 95–99. See letters to his daughter during this period, JBP: III. Also *Proceedings of a Court of Inquiry, Held at the Navy Yard, Brooklyn, New York, Upon Captain James Barron of the United States' Navy, in May, 1821*.

39. Stevens, *Affair of Honor*, 99; *Proceedings of a Court of Enquiry*.

40. Stevens, *Affair of Honor*, 100, 173–82. Stevens quotes Wise's *Seven Decades of the Union*, (Philadelphia: J. B. Lippincott, 1871). See also Barron's letters to his daughter Jane, JBP, III.

41. Barron to SecNav, 22 July 1813, M125, 30; and JBP: II, 20 and 21, and IV, 4.

42. Stevens, *Affair of Honor*, 104–8, 115.

43. Paullin, *Paullin's History of Naval Administration*, 166–69.

44. Stevens, *Affair of Honor*, 116 and 158. JBP: IV, 9.

45. Barron to Decatur, November 1819, in Watson, *Tragic Career*, 71. Barron to Monroe, 6 March 1819. JBP: III, 26.

46. Stevens, *An Affair of Honor*, 121.

47. Long, *Ready to Hazard*, 229–31; Mackenzie, *Life of Stephen Decatur*, 306–7.

48. See *Proceedings of a Court of Inquiry*, 5–8. Correspondence between Barron and Decatur covering the period June 1819 to March 1820 is in JBP: III, 20 (19 items). The full letter from Lewis to Goldsborough is in ibid., II, 4. See also Mackenzie, *Life of Stephen Decatur*, 307–26 and Appendix. Also Stevens, *Affair of Honor*, 119–30. Goodwin was a friend of Decatur.

49. Barron to Decatur, 23 October 1819; Decatur to Barron, no date. JBP: III, 30.

50. Letter of Elliott to John Myers, 30 March 1820, JBP: III, 34. Bainbridge provided a different, and unflattering, version. He reported Decatur as saying "Will you please tell me why you did not return to this country during the war?" Barron supposedly replied with evident embarrassment, "I will tell you what I never expected to tell a living soul. I was in an English prison for debt." Barnes, *Yankee Ships and Yankee Soldiers*. (Barnes was the great grandson of Bainbridge.) Linda Maloney has charged that Bainbridge "helped to foment the fatal duel between Decatur and James Barron, acting as Decatur's second and refusing to permit a reconciliation between the duelists," and that Elliott played a similar role as "one of the engineers" of the fatal duel. Maloney, *Captain from Connecticut*, 315 and 335. On Bainbridge's role see also Long, *Ready to Hazard*, 232–36. Some thirty years after the affair Decatur's widow Susan wrote a memorial to Congress stating that Decatur "never had any personal misunderstanding with the author of his death! The whole affair was gotten up through malice and cowardice on the part of one of the seconds, Captain Elliott, and accomplished through envy and jealousy on the part of the other, Commodore Bainbridge." Zabriskie, "The *Chesapeake* Affair," 16. For the duel see Long, *Ready to Hazard*, 236–39; and Stevens, *Affair of Honor*, 135–48.

51. Watson, *Tragic Career*, 77–79. Also letter from Elliott to John Myers at Norfolk, 30 March 1820, JBP, III, 34.

52. Augustus Fleming in New York to Barron, 9 April 1820, JBP: III, 41.

53. *Proceedings of a Court of Inquiry*, 96.

54. JBP, III, 43.

55. Ibid., IV, 9.

56. See *Proceedings of a Court of Inquiry*, 93 and 96. JBP: XIII, 1. Affidavit of Robert Jennings on 10 May 1821, in ibid., IV, 12. Also Stevens, *Affair of Honor*, 152–59.

57. Barron to John Myers of Norfolk, 2 August 1821, and to Thompson, 4 August 1821. JBP: IV, 29 and 31.
58. Elliott to Barron, 1 March 1822, JBP: V, 9.
59. Barron to Thompson, 2 May 1822, JBP: V, 15.
60. Hugh Nelson and Thos. Newton to SecNav, 8 March 1822, M124, 92.
61. Barron to Honorable Thomas Newton, 27 November 1823, JBP: VI, 16.
62. Stevens, *Affair of Honor,* 166.
63. SecNav Samuel Southard to Barron, 2 May 1825, JBP: VII, 19.
64. SecNav to Barron, 5 November 1828, and Barron to SecNav, 6 November 1828, JBP: VIII, 17, 18. See Stevens, *Affair of Honor,* 167–68.
65. Watson, *Tragic Career,* 81–84. Stevens, *Affair of Honor,* 168–72, 191. The flat-topped Barron tomb may still be seen in the churchyard of Trinity Episcopal Church, Portsmouth, Virginia.

TEN. THE *CHESAPEAKE-LEOPARD* AFFAIR IN RETROSPECT

1. Pratt, *Preble's Boys,* 53.
2. *Norfolk Gazette and Publick Ledger,* 5 August 1807, in Emmerson, *The* Chesapeake *Affair,* 71.
3. Adams, *History of the United States of America During the Second Administration of Thomas Jefferson,* 2: 24.
4. *Works of Jefferson,* 10: 492–93. Charles Goldsborough believed that the *Chesapeake-Leopard* Affair actually led to greater gunboat construction. See Goldsborough, *United States Naval Chronicle,* 1: 324–25.
5. *A.S.P., N.A.* 1: 68–69.
6. Lewis, *Seacoast Fortifications,* 25.
7. Letter from William Gilkerson to Spencer Tucker, April 4, 1995. For more information on this see Gilkerson, *Boarders Away. With Steel-Edged Weapons and Polearms* and *Boarders Away. II. Firearms of the Age of Fighting Sail.*
8. Crackel, *Mr. Jefferson's Army,* 162–63, 169–70.
9. Castlereagh to the Earl of Chatham, 31 December 1807, in *Correspondence, Dispatches, and Other Papers of Viscount Castlereagh,* 8: 104.
10. Letter from SecNav Robert Smith to House of Representatives, 16 November 1807, in *A.S.P., N.A.* 1: 168–69.
11. Report of General Dearborn, 19 November and 2 December 1807, in response to a request from the Speaker of the House of Representatives, in *American State Papers, Class V: Military Affairs,* 1: 217–23.
12. Grenville to Grey, Camelford House, 28 April 1809, Grey Papers—Grenville Correspondence, Box 21, File 2.
13. Madison to Gallatin, Montpelier, 31 August 1808, *Writings of Gallatin,* 1: 411.
14. *The War* (New York newspaper), July 25, 1812, reprinted in vol. 1 of Samuel Woodworth, *The War: Being a Faithful Record of the Transactions Between the United States . . . and . . . Great Britain;* Mahon, *War of 1812,* 42; also, Bainbridge to SecNav, 11 July 1812, M125, 24.

Glossary

Abaft. Toward the stern of the vessel; rearward.

Abeam. In direction at right angles to fore-and-aft line of a vessel.

Bomb. Exploding shell. Also term for bomb vessels, warships carrying one or two mortars to bombard shore installations.

Bower anchor. Ship's largest anchor.

Bowsprit. Spar projecting forward from bow of sailing vessel to which headsails were secured. Projecting still further from it are the jib boom and flying jib boom.

Breeching. Stout rope to limit recoil of gun and its carriage.

Brig. A two-master, square-rigged ship.

Cannon. A muzzle-loading large gun of medium to long range.

Cap square. Metal pieces securing the trunnions (lugs) of a gun to the brackets of a carriage. Cap squares were hinged to permit easy removal of the gun.

Captain. Highest rank in the American sailing navy. Also courtesy title for commander of a vessel.

Careen. To haul a vessel down on her side for cleaning or repair.

Carronade. Short, light-for-caliber, chambered, muzzle-loading gun of short range and low velocity. Naval carronades had no trunnions; they were attached to the carriage by a lug underneath.

Cartridge. Cylinder, usually made of flannel, containing the gunpowder charge for the gun. A cartridge prevented overcharging and caking of loose powder.

Cockpit. An area in a ship usually below the waterline, used by the surgeon in attending the wounded.

Commander. Individual in charge of vessel. Later designation of master commandant, rank between lieutenant and captain.

Commodore. Title for captain in command of a squadron of vessels. As a courtesy, captains who so served were generally referred to as commodores after they were no longer in that capacity.

Cutter. A single-masted, fore-and-aft-rigged vessel.

Ensign. National flag flown by warships in commission.

Frigate. Square-rigged ship (each mast had crossyards), with a single covered gun deck. Large frigates carried 50 to 60 guns, small ones 26 to 38.

Full-rigged. Three-masted sail rig with yards running at right angles ("square rigged") to the keel.

Gun deck. A frigate's main deck, carrying its battery of heavy long guns.

Handspike. Heavy iron rods used, among other things, to lever the carriages and cannon in aiming.

Heel. To lean over to one side in response to wind pressure.

Ketch. Fore-and-aft-rigged sailing vessel. Tall mainmast and smaller mizzen-mast.

Larboard. The left or port side of a vessel.

League. Horizontal distance of three nautical miles.

Lee and leeward. The downwind side of a vessel.

Lieutenant. Rank immediately below master commandant.

Linstock. A wooden staff about 2.5 feet long that held the match. It had a pointed metal end and was stuck upright in the wooden match tub.

Lock. Firing device, analogous to flintlocks for small arms. In use for cannon in U.S. Navy in the Barbary Wars. These were aboard but not installed on the guns during the June 22 encounter.

Loggerhead. Heavy iron bar, which, when heated in the galley, was used to melt pitch or fire off a gun.

Master commandant. Rank between lieutenant and captain (later known as commander).

Match. Rope impregnated with saltpeter that ignited the priming powder in the vent of a gun.

Port. The left side of a vessel; the later term for "larboard."

Powder horn. Polished horn used to hold priming powder for the cannon.

Quarters. Battle station. When a crew was called to quarters, the men reported to their battle stations. "Quartering" a crew prior to battle was essential in order that each man know his station and duties in time of battle.

Rake. To cannonade the length of a ship, either from bow or stern.

Rate. An indication of the firepower of a warship. Smaller numbers meant more guns: 1st rates had 100 or more; 6th rates 20 to 29.

Rigging. The ropes needed to support the masts (standing) or work yards and sails (running).

Ship. A three-masted, full-rigged vessel.

Ship of the line. A two- to four-decked three-master, full-rigged ship that carried 64 to 120 guns. The U.S. Navy had no ships of the line in active service until 1815.

Ship sloop. Any warship with its guns on a single deck, but full-rigged. Also termed a "corvette."

Sloop. A single-masted, fore-and-aft-rigged vessel.

Spring. When anchoring on a spring, a rope is passed from a stern-port forward, where it is made fast to the anchor ring. Once the vessel is anchored, it may be swung in either direction by means of shortening the spring rope.

Stanchion. Post or support.

Taffrail. Railing surrounding quarterdeck area.

Tompion. Watertight plug placed in the muzzle of cannon to keep out sea water and debris. Removing tompions would be an indication that cannon were being readied to fire.

Trunnion. Lugs on either side of the gun, by which it was supported in its carriage. True carronades did not have trunnions but were secured by means of a navel ring at the bottom of the piece.

Wear. To put a vessel on the other tack by turning her away from the wind.

Weather gauge. Position upwind of another ship in battle.

Windward. Toward the wind.

Bibliography

PRIMARY SOURCES

British Museum:
  Thomas Grenville Papers
  Liverpool Papers
Durham University (Durham, England)
  Prior's Kitchen: Earl Grey Family Records
Huntington Library and Art Gallery, San Marino, Calif.:
  William Henry Allen Papers: letters from Allen to his father, Gen. William
    Allen, and journal kept aboard the *Chesapeake.*
Library of Congress, Manuscript Division, Washington, D.C.:
  Thomas Jefferson Papers
  Lt. William Henry Allen Papers
  Log of the *Chesapeake* (May 9, 1807 to February 21, 1809).
  Joseph Hopper Nicholson Papers
  William Plumer Papers
  Rodgers Family Papers: Series III. [Cited as LC: RFP]
Maine Historical Society:
  Journal kept by Midshipman Alexander Wadsworth aboard the *Constitution.*
National Archives, Washington, D.C.:
  Department of State, Notes to Great Britain, 1807.
  RG45, Series 464, Box 328, Folder "0-1859 NO-Courts of Enquiry":
    "Chesapeake-Leopard Court of Inquiry." 1807. Handwritten "Minutes of
    the Proceedings of the Court of Enquiry . . . concerning the causes of the

surrender of The *Chesapeake,* a frigate of the United States. . . ."

RG45, M124, Misc. Letters received by the Secretary of the Navy. Rolls 13–19, 90, 92.

RG45, M125. Letters received by the Secretary of the Navy: Captain's Letters, 1807. Rolls 7–9.

RG45, M149. Letters sent by the Secretary of the Navy to Officers, 1807. Rolls 7–8.

RG24, M209. Miscellaneous letters sent by the Secretary of the Navy, 1807. Roll 3.

RG217. Bureau of Construction. 1813 Plan of *Chesapeake.*

New York Historical Society:

Albert Gallatin Papers

Peabody Museum of Salem, Mass.:

Josiah Fox Papers

Public Records Office (London):

Log book of the *Leopard* (January 28, 1807 to August 16, 1807). Admiralty Papers. Adm51/1702

Admiralty Records 1/476 to 2/1365.

Colonial Office Records

Foreign Office. FO5/53.

Toronto Public Library, Toronto, Canada:

Admiral George Berkeley Letters

William and Mary College, Earl Greg Swen Library:

James Barron Papers, Boxes I-XIII. [Cited as JBP.]

Also 300 manuscript pages of court-martial records of *Chesapeake-Leopard* Affair.

PRINTED DOCUMENTS

Adams, John Quincy. *The Diary of John Quincy Adams, 1794–1845.* Edited by Allan Nevins. New York: Scribner's, 1951.

———. *Writings of John Quincy Adams.* Edited by Worthington Chauncey Ford. 7 vols. New York: Macmillan, 1913–17.

American State Papers, Class I: Foreign Relations. Vols. 2 and 3. Washington, D.C.: Gales and Seaton, 1832.

American State Papers, Class IV: Commerce and Navigation. Vol. 1. Washington, D.C.: Gales and Seaton, 1832.

American State Papers, Class V: Military Affairs. Vol. 1. Washington, D.C.: Gales and Seaton, 1832.

American State Papers, Class VI: Naval Affairs. Vol. 1. Washington, D.C.: Gales and Seaton, 1834.

Auckland, Lord. *Journal and Correspondence of Lord Auckland.* 4 vols. London:
Privately printed, 1861–63.

The Bathurst Manuscripts. Edited by Francis Binkley. Vol. 76 of Historical
Manuscript Commission Reports. London: HMSO, 1923.

*Correspondence, Dispatches, and Other Papers of Viscount Castlereagh, Second
Marquess of Londonderry.* Edited by Charles William Vane. 8 vols. London: H.
Colburn, 1853.

The Federalist. Edited by Jacob E. Cooke. Middletown, Conn.: Wesleyan
University Press, 1961.

Flournoy, Henry W., ed. *Calendar of Virginia State Papers and Other
Manuscripts from January 1, 1799, to December 31, 1807.* Vol. 9. Richmond, Va.:
R. F. Walker, 1893.

Fox, Charles James. *Memorials and Correspondence of Charles James Fox.* Edited
by Lord John Russell. 4 vols. London: Richard Bentley, 1853–57.

Gallatin, Albert. *The Writings of Albert Gallatin.* Edited by Henry Adams. 3 vols.
New York: Antiquarian Press, 1960 (reprint of 1879 edition).

Holland, Lord. *Memoirs of the Whig Party.* 2 vols. London: Longman, Brown,
Green, 1844.

Instructions to the British Ministers to the United States, 1791–1812. Edited by
Bernard Mayo. American Historical Association Annual Report, 1936.
Washington, D.C.: Government Printing Office, 1941.

Jay, John. *The Correspondence of John Jay.* 4 vols. New York: Burt Franklin
Reprint, 1970.

Jefferson, Thomas. *The Papers of Thomas Jefferson.* Edited by Julian P. Boyd.
21 vols. Princeton: Princeton University Press, 1950–.

——. *Thomas Jefferson: Writings.* Edited by Merrill D. Peterson. New York:
Library of America, 1984.

——. *The Works of Thomas Jefferson.* Edited by Paul Leicester Ford. 12 vols.
New York: Knickerbocker Press, 1904.

——. *Writings of Thomas Jefferson.* Edited by Andrew A. Lipscomb and Albert
E. Bergh. 20 vols. Washington, D.C.: Thomas Jefferson Memorial Association
of the United States, 1903–4.

King, Rufus. *The Life and Correspondence of Rufus King.* 6 vols. New York:
DeCapo Press Reissue, 1971.

The Later Letters of George III. Edited by A. Aspinal. 5 vols. Cambridge:
Cambridge University Press, 1962–70.

*List of Officers of the Navy of the United States and of the Marine Corps from
1795 to 1900.* Edited by Edward W. Callahan. New York: Haskell House, 1969
(reprint of 1901 edition).

Maclay, William. *Journal of William Maclay.* Edited by Edgar S. Maclay. New
York: D. Appleton and Co., 1890.

Madison, James. *The Papers of James Madison.* Edited by W. T. Hutchinson, et al. Chicago: University of Chicago Press, 1962.

———. *The Papers of James Madison.* Edited by Robert Brugger, et al. 2 vols. Secretary of State Series. Charlottesville, Va.: University of Press of Virginia, 1986–93.

Messages and Papers of the Presidents, 1789–1897. Vol. 1: 1789–1817. Edited by James D. Richardson. Washington, D.C.: Government Printing Office, 1896–99.

Monroe, James, *The Autobiography of James Monroe.* Edited by Stuart Gerry Brown. Syracuse, N.Y.: Syracuse University Press, 1959.

Naval Chronicle. Vol. 18. London: Bunney & Gold, 1807.

Naval Documents Related to the United States Wars with the Barbary Powers. Vol. 6: Naval Operations Including Diplomatic Background from May 1805 through 1807. Washington, D.C.: U.S. Office of Naval Records and Library, GPO, 1944.

The Naval War of 1812: A Documentary History. Vol. 1. Edited by William S. Dudley. Washington, D.C.: Naval Historical Center, GPO, 1985.

Proceedings of a Court of Enquiry, Held at the Navy Yard, Brooklyn, N.Y., upon Captain James Barron of the United States Navy, in May 1821. Washington, D.C.: Jacob Gideon, Jr. 1821.

Proceedings of the General Court Martial Convened for the Trial of Commodore James Barron, Captain Charles Gordon, Mr. William Hook, and Captain John Hall, of the United States Ship Chesapeake, *in the Month of January 1808.* Published by Order of the Navy Department. Washington, D.C.: Jacob Gideon, Jr., 1822.

St. Vincent, Earl of. *Letters of Admiral of the Fleet, the Earl of St. Vincent.* Edited by David Bunner Smith. 2 vols. London: Navy Records Society, 1927.

The Trial of John Wilson, alias Jenkin Ratford, for Mutiny, Desertion and Contempt: To which are subjoined, a Few Cursory Remarks. Boston: Snelling and Simons, 1807.

United States Congress. *American State Papers: Documents, Legislative and Executive, of the Congress of the United States.* 38 vols. Washington, D.C.: Gales & Seaton, 1832–61.

———. *The Debates and Proceedings in the Congress of the United States, 1789–1824.* 42 vols. Washington, D.C.: Gales & Seaton, 1834–56.

Washington, George. *The Writings of George Washington.* Edited by John C. Fitzpatrick. 39 vols. Washington, D.C.: Government Printing Office, 1931–44.

NEWSPAPERS

Farmers Library (Rutland, Vt.), July 29, 1794.

National Intelligencer (Washington, D.C.), 1807.

Norfolk Gazette and Publick Ledger (Norfolk, Va.), September 1806—July 1807.
Times (London), 1796–1807.
The War (New York), July 25, 1812.
The Weekly Register (Baltimore), September—November 1811.

SECONDARY SOURCES

Adams, Henry. *History of the United States of America during the Administrations of Thomas Jefferson.* 2 vols. New York: Library of America, 1986 (reprint of 1931 edition).
———. *History of the United States of America during the Administrations of James Madison.* New York: Library of America, 1986 (reprint).
———. *The Life of Albert Gallatin.* Philadelphia: J. B. Lippincott & Co., 1880.
Adams, Mary P. "Jefferson's Military Policy with Special Reference to the Frontier, 1805–1809." Ph.D. diss., University of Virginia, 1958.
Allen, Gardner W. *Our Naval War with France.* Boston: Houghton Mifflin, 1909.
Allen, Harry C. *Great Britain and the United States: A History of Anglo-American Relations.* New York: St. Martin's Press, 1969.
American Secretaries of the Navy. 2 vols. Edited by Paolo E. Coletta. Annapolis, Md.: Naval Institute Press, 1980.
Anthony, Irvin. *Decatur.* New York. Charles Scribner's Sons, 1931.
Ap C. Jones, Thomas. *Exceptions to the Illegal Organization, Proceedings, Findings, and Sentence, &c., of the Naval Court Martial in the Case of Commodore Thos. Ap C. Jones. July, 1851.* Washington, D.C.: Gideon and Co., 1851.
Barnes, James. *Yankee Ships and Yankee Sailors: Tales of 1812.* New York: Macmillan, 1928 (reprint of 1897 edition).
Barrow, Clayton R. J., comp. and ed. *America Spreads Her Sails: U.S. Seapower in the Nineteenth Century.* Annapolis, Md.: Naval Institute Press, 1973.
Beach, Edward L. *The United States Navy: 200 Years.* New York: Henry Holt and Co., 1986.
Bemis, Samuel Flagg. *The Jay Treaty: A Study in Commerce and Diplomacy.* 2d ed. New Haven: Yale University Press, 1962.
———. *Pinckney's Treaty.* Baltimore: Johns Hopkins University Press, 1926.
Ben-Atar, Doran S. *The Origins of Jeffersonian Commercial Policy and Diplomacy.* New York, St. Martin's Press, 1993.
Brant, Irving. *James Madison, Secretary of State, 1800–1809.* Indianapolis: Bobbs-Merrill Co., 1953.
Briggs, Herbert W. *The Doctrine of Continuous Voyage.* Baltimore: Johns Hopkins University Press, 1926.

"The British and American Navies." *Edinburgh Review* 71 (1840): 120–70.

Brown, Roger H. *The Republic in Peril: 1812.* New York: Columbia University Press, 1964.

Burt, A. L. *The United States, Great Britain, and British North America from the Revolution to the Establishment of Peace After the War of 1812.* New Haven: Yale University Press, 1940.

Calderhead, William R. "A Strange Career in a Young Navy: Captain Charles Gordon, 1778–1816." *Maryland Historical Magazine* 72 (Fall 1977): 18–41.

Cambridge History of British Foreign Policy, 1783–1919. Cambridge: Cambridge University Press, 1939.

"The Career of Commodore Barron." *Virginia Historical Register and Literary Note Book* 14.4 (July 1852): 161.

Carr, Albert Z. *The Coming of War: An Account of the Remarkable Events Leading to the War of 1812.* Garden City, N.Y.: Doubleday & Co., 1960.

Carson, David. "Congress in Jefferson's Foreign Policy, 1801–1809." Ph.D. diss., Texas Christian University, 1983.

Chapelle, Howard I. *The History of the American Sailing Navy.* New York: W. W. Norton, 1949.

Clauder, A. C. *American Commerce as Affected by the Wars of the French Revolution and Napoleon, 1793–1812.* Philadelphia, 1932.

Clowes, William Laird. *The Royal Navy, a History: From the Earliest Times to the Present.* Vol. 5. London: Simpson Low, Marston and Co., 1900.

Colledge, James Joseph. *Ships of the Royal Navy.* Annapolis, Md.: Naval Institute Press, 1987.

Combs, Jerald A. *The Jay Treaty: Political Battleground of the Founding Fathers.* Berkeley: University of California Press, 1970.

Cookson, J. E. *The Friends of Peace: Anti-war Liberalism in England, 1793–1815.* Cambridge: Cambridge University Press, 1982.

Cooper, James Fenimore. *History of the Navy of the United States of America.* 3d ed., 2 vols. Cooperstown, N.Y.: H. & E. Phinney, 1848.

Crackel, Theodore J. *Mr. Jefferson's Army: Political and Social Reform of the Military Establishment, 1801–1809.* New York: New York University Press, 1987.

Cross, Charles B., Jr. *The* Chesapeake: *A Biography of a Ship.* Chesapeake, Va.: Norfolk County Historical Society, 1968.

DeConde, Alexander. *The Quasi-War: The Politics and Diplomacy of the Undeclared War with France, 1797–1801.* New York: Scribner's, 1966.

———. *This Affair of Louisiana.* New York: Scribner's, 1976.

Dictionary of American Fighting Ships. Vol. 2. Washington, D.C.: U.S. Navy, History Division, GPO, 1936.

Dictionary of National Biography. Edited by Sir Leslie Stephen and Sir Sidney Lee. Vol. 2. London: Oxford University Press, 1921.

Dye, Ira. "Early American Merchant Seafarers." *American Philosophical Society Proceedings* 120 (1976): 331–60.

———. *The Fatal Cruise of the* Argus: *Two Captains in the War of 1812.* Annapolis, Md.: Naval Institute Press, 1994.

Ehrman, John. *The Younger Pitt.* (2 vols.) New York: Dutton, 1969.

Emmerson, John Cloyd. *The* Chesapeake *Affair of 1807: An Objective Account of the Attack by HMS* Leopard *upon the U.S. Frigate* Chesapeake *off Cape Henry, Va., June 22, 1807, and Its Repercussions.* Portsmouth, Va.: 1954.

Ferling, John. *John Adams: A Life.* Knoxville: University of Tennessee Press, 1992.

Forester, Cecil S. "Bloodshed at Dawn." *American Heritage* 15, no. 6 (October 1964): 40–45, 73–76.

Fowler, William M., Jr. *Jack Tars and Commodores: The American Navy, 1783–1815.* Boston: Houghton Mifflin, 1984.

Frankel, Jeffrey A. "The 1807–1809 Embargo Against Great Britain." *Journal of Economic History* 42 (June 1982): 291–308.

Gaines, Edwin Metcalf. "The *Chesapeake* Affair: Virginians Mobilize to Defend National Honor." *Virginia Magazine of History and Biography* 64 (April 1956): 131–42.

———. "Outrageous Encounter: The *Chesapeake-Leopard* Affair of 1807." Ph.D. diss., University of Virginia, 1975.

Gardiner, Leslie. *The British Admiralty.* Annapolis, Md.: Naval Institute Press, 1968.

Gates, William G. *The Portsmouth That Has Passed, with Glimpses of God's Port: Panorama of a Thousand Years.* Edited by F.J.H. Young. Portsmouth, England: Charpentier, 1946.

Gibson, James, E. "John Bullus—Reading Physician and Naval Surgeon." *Historical Review of Berks County* (Reading, Pa.) 9, no. 3 (April 1944): 77.

Gilkerson, William. *Boarders Away: With Steel-Edged Weapons and Polearms.* Lincoln, R.I.: Andrew Mowbray, 1991.

———. *Boarders Away II: Firearms of the Age of Fighting Sail.* Lincoln, R.I.: Andrew Mowbray, 1991.

Gleaves, Albert. *James Lawrence: Captain, United States Navy. Commander of the* Chesapeake. New York: G. P. Putnam's Sons, 1904.

Goldsborough, Charles W. *The United States Naval Chronicle.* Vol. 1. Washington, D.C.: James Wilson, 1824.

Gore, John. *Nelson's Hardy and His Wife.* London: John Murray, 1935.

Gosset, W. P. *The Lost Ships of the Royal Navy, 1793–1800.* London: Mansell Publishing Ltd., 1986.

Grant, Bruce. *Isaac Hull, Captain of Old Ironsides: The Life and Fighting Times of Isaac Hull and the U.S. Frigate* Constitution. Chicago: Pellegrini and Cudahy, 1947.

Guttridge, Leonard F., and Jay D. Smith. *The Commodores.* New York: Harper and Row, 1969.

Hanson, Alexander Contee. *Reflections upon the Late Correspondence between Mr. Secretary Smith and Francis James Jackson.* Baltimore: Published for the author, 1910 (originally published in the *Federal Republican* of Baltimore).

Heath, Phoebe Anne. *Napoleon I and the Origins of the Anglo-American War of 1812.* Paris: Henri Didier, 1929.

Henrich, Joseph G. "The Triumph of Ideology: The Jeffersonians and the Navy, 1779–1807." Ph.D. diss., Duke University, 1971.

Horsman, Reginald. *The Causes of the War of 1812.* Philadelphia: University of Pennsylvania Press, 1962.

Jackson, Scott Thomas. "Impressment and Anglo-American Discord, 1787–1818." Ph.D. diss., University of Michigan, 1976.

James, William. *The Naval History of Great Britain: From the Declaration of War by France in 1793, to the Accession of George IV.* Vols. 4 and 6. London: Macmillan and Co., 1902.

Jarrett, Derek. *The Younger Pitt.* New York: Scribners, 1974.

Jones, Wilbur D. *The American Problem in British Diplomacy.* Athens: University of Georgia Press, 1971.

Kaplan, Lawrence S. *Entangling Alliances with None: American Foreign Policy in the Age of Jefferson.* Kent, Ohio: Kent State University Press, 1987.

———. *Jefferson and France: An Essay on Politics and Political Ideas.* New Haven: Yale University Press, 1967.

Lafeber, Walter. "Jefferson and an American Foreign Policy." No. 12 in *Jeffersonian Legacies,* edited by Peter S. Onuf. Charlottesville: University Press of Virginia, 1993.

Lester, Malcolm. *Anthony Merry Redivivus: A Reappraisal of the British Minister to the United States, 1803–1806.* Charlottesville, Va.: University of Virginia Press, 1978.

"Letters of William Henry Allen, 1800–1813." *Huntington Library Quarterly* 1, nos. 1 and 2 (October 1937 and January 1938): 101–32, 203–43.

Lewis, Emanuel Raymond. *Seacoast Fortifications of the United States: An Introductory History.* Washington, D.C.: Smithsonian Institution Press, 1970.

Lewis, Michael. *A Social History of the Navy, 1793–1815.* London: George Allen, 1960.

List of Officers of the Navy of the United States and of the Marine Corps from 1795 to 1900. Edited by Edward W. Callahan. New York: Haskell House, 1969 (reprint of 1901 edition).

Long, David F. *Nothing Too Daring: A Biography of Commodore David Porter, 1780–1843.* Annapolis, Md.: Naval Institute Press, 1970.

———. *Ready to Hazard: A Biography of Commodore William Bainbridge, 1774–1833.* Hanover, N.H.: University Press of New England, 1981.

Lowell, John. *Peace without Dishonour—War with Hope: Being a Calm and Dispassionate Enquiry into the Question of the* Chesapeake, *and the Necessity and Expediency of War.* Boston: Greenough and Stebbins, 1807.

Mahan, Alfred Thayer. *Sea Power in Its Relations to the War of 1812.* 2 vols. Boston: Little, Brown, 1918.

Mahon, John K. *The War of 1812.* Gainesville: University of Florida Press, 1972.

Malone, Dumas. *Jefferson and the Rights of Man.* Boston: Little, Brown, 1951.

———. *Jefferson the President: Second Term, 1805–1809.* Boston: Little, Brown, 1974.

Maloney, Linda. *The Captain from Connecticut: The Life and Times of Isaac Hull.* Boston: Northeastern University Press, 1986.

Marks, Frederick W. III. *Independence on Trial: Foreign Affairs and the Making of the Constitution.* 2d ed. Wilmington, Del.: Scholarly Resources, 1986.

Marshall, John. *Royal Naval Biography or Memoirs of the Services of all the Flag-Officers superannuated Rear Admirals, Retired-Captains, Post Captains and Commanders.* Vol. 2. Part 2. London: Longman, Hurst, et al., 1825.

Martin, Tyrone G. *A Most Fortunate Ship: A Narrative History of "Old Ironsides."* Chester, Conn.: Globe Pequot Press, 1982.

McDonald, Forrest. *The Formation of the American Republic, 1776–1790.* Baltimore: Penguin, 1965.

McKee, Christopher. "Foreign Seamen in the United States Navy: A Census of 1808." *William and Mary Quarterly,* 3d series, 42 (July 1985): 383–93.

———. *A Gentlemanly and Honorable Profession: The Creation of the U.S. Naval Officer Corps, 1794–1815.* Annapolis, Md.: Naval Institute Press, 1991.

———. *Edward Preble: A Naval Biography, 1761–1807.* Annapolis, Md.: Naval Institute Press, 1972.

MacKenzie, Alexander Slidell. *Life of Stephen Decatur: A Commodore in the Navy of the United States.* Boston: Little, Brown, 1846.

McLeod, Julia. "Jefferson and the Navy: A Defense." *Huntington Library Quarterly* 8 (February 1945): 153–84.

Moore, John Bassett. *Digest of International Law.* Vol. 2. Washington D.C.: Government Printing Office, 1906.

Morison, Samuel Eliot. *The Oxford History of the American People.* New York: Oxford University Press, 1965.

Morris, Richard B. *The Peacemakers: The Great Powers and American Independence.* New York: Harper & Row, 1965.

Nettels, Curtis P. *The Emergence of a National Economy, 1775–1815.* New York: Harper & Row, 1962.

O'Byrne, William R. *A Naval Biographical Dictionary: Comprising the Life and Services of Every Living Officer in Her Majesty's Navy, From the Rank of Admiral of the Fleet to that of Lieutenant, Inclusive.* London: John Murray, 1849. Ann Arbor, Michigan: University Microfilms, 1976.

Padfield, Peter. *Broke and the* Shannon. London: Hodder and Stoughton, 1968.

Palmer, Michael A. *Stoddert's War: Naval Operations during the Quasi-War with France, 1798–1801.* Columbia: University of South Carolina Press, 1987.

Parrish, John C. "The Intrigues of Doctor James O'Fallon." *Mississippi Valley Historical Review* 17 (September 1930): 230–63.

Paullin, Charles O. *Commodore John Rodgers.* Annapolis, Md.: Naval Institute Press, 1909.

———. *Paullin's History of Naval Administration, 1775–1911.* Annapolis, Md.: Naval Institute Press, 1968.

Perkins, Bradford. *The Causes of the War of 1812: National Honor or National Interest?* New York: Holt, Rinehart and Winston, 1962.

———. *The First Rapprochement: England and the United States, 1795–1805.* Philadelphia: University of Pennsylvania Press, 1955.

———. "George Canning, Great Britain, and the United States, 1807–1809." *American Historical Review* 63 (October 1957): 1–22.

———. *Prologue to War: England and the United States, 1805–1812.* Berkeley: University of California Press, 1961.

Peterson, Norma Lois. *Littleton Waller Tazewell.* Charlottesville: University Press of Virginia, 1983.

Pinkney, Rev. William. *The Life of William Pinkney.* New York: Da Capo Press, 1969 (reprint).

Pool, Eugene H. *The Frigate* Chesapeake. Providence, R.I.: Mariner, 1930.

Poolman, Kenneth. *Guns off Cape Ann: The Story of the* Shannon *and the* Chesapeake. London: Evans Brothers Ltd., 1961.

Pratt, Fletcher. *Preble's Boys: Commodore Preble and the Birth of American Sea Power.* New York: William Sloane Associates, 1950.

Pratt, Julius W. *Expansionists of 1812.* New York: Macmillan, 1925.

Pullen, Hugh Francis. *The* Shannon *and the* Chesapeake. Toronto: McClelland and Stewart, 1970.

Radoff, Morris I. "Captain Gordon of the *Constellation.*" *Maryland Historical Magazine* 67 (1972): 389–418.

Rees, Abraham. *The Cyclopedia, or, Universal Dictionary of Arts, Sciences, and Literature.* Vol. 6. Philadelphia: Samuel F. Bradford and Murray, Fairman, 1810.

Reuter, Frank T. "'Petty Spy' or Effective Diplomat: The Role of George Beckwith." *Journal of the Early Republic* 10 (Winter 1990): 472–92.

———. *Trials and Triumphs: George Washington's Foreign Policy.* Fort Worth: Texas Christian University Press, 1983.

Ritcheson, Charles R. *Aftermath of Revolution: British Policy Toward the United States, 1783–1795.* Dallas: Southern Methodist University Press, 1969.

Roosevelt, Theodore. *The Naval War of 1812.* New York: G. P. Putnam's Sons, 1882.

Savage, Carleton, ed. *The Policy of the United States Toward Maritime Commerce in War*. 2 vols. Washington, D.C.: Government Printing Office, 1934–36.

Scott, Winfield. *Memoirs of Lieut.-General Scott, LL.D.* Vol. 1. New York: Sheldon & Co., 1864.

Sears, Louis M. *Jefferson and the Embargo*. Durham, N.C.: Duke University Press, 1927. Reprint, New York: Octagon Books, 1966.

Simpson, Herbert Baird. "Charles Gordon: Jacobite and Loyalist." *South Atlantic Quarterly* 27, no. 4 (October 1928): 390–404.

Smelser, Marshall. *The Democratic Republic, 1801–1815*. New York: Harper and Row, 1968.

Smith, Gene A. *"For the Purposes of Defense": The Politics of the Jeffersonian Gunboat Program*. Newark, Del.: University of Delaware Press, 1995.

Smith, Jay D. "Commodore James Barron: Guilty as Charged?" U.S. Naval Institute *Proceedings* 93 (November 1967): 79–85.

Smith, Page. *John Adams*. Vol. 2. Garden City, N.Y.: Doubleday, 1962.

Spivak, Burton. *Jefferson's English Crisis: Commerce, Embargo, and the Republican Revolution*. Charlottesville: University Press of Virginia, 1979.

Sprout, Harold, and Margaret Sprout. *The Rise of American Naval Power, 1776–1918*. Princeton: Princeton University Press, 1939. Reprint, Annapolis, Md.: Naval Institute Press, 1980.

Stevens, William Oliver. *An Affair of Honor: The Biography of Commodore James Barron, USN*. Norfolk, Va.: Norfolk County Historical Society of Chesapeake, Virginia, in cooperation with the Earl Gregg Swem Library of the College of William and Mary in Virginia, 1969.

Symonds, Craig L. *Navalists and Antinavalists: The Naval Policy Debate in the United States, 1785–1827*. Newark, Del.: University of Delaware Press, 1980.

Steel, Anthony. "Anthony Merry and the Anglo-American Dispute about Impressment, 1803–1806." *Cambridge Historical Journal* 9, no. 3 (1949): 331–51.

———. "Impressment in the Monroe-Pinkney Negotiation, 1806–1807." *American Historical Review* 57 (1951–52): 352–370.

———. "More Light on the *Chesapeake*." *Mariner's Mirror* 39 (1953): 243–65.

Tucker, Robert W., and David C. Hendrickson. *Empire of Liberty: The Statecraft of Thomas Jefferson*. New York: Oxford University Press, 1992.

Tucker, Spencer C. *Arming the Fleet: U.S. Navy Ordnance in the Muzzle-loading Era*. Annapolis, Md.: Naval Institute Press, 1989.

———. *The Jeffersonian Gunboat Navy*. Columbia, S.C.: University of South Carolina Press, 1993.

U.S. Navy Department, Office of Naval Records and Library. *Register of Officer Personnel, United States Navy and Marine Corps, and Ships' Data, 1801–1807*. Edited by Edward W. Callahan. Washington, D.C.: Government Printing Office, 1945.

Updike, Frank A. *The Diplomacy of the War of 1812*. Gloucester, Mass.: Peter Smith, 1965.

Virginia Historical Register, and Literary Note Book. Edited by William Maxwell. Vol. 4, no. 3 (July 1851). Richmond, Va.: Macfarlane & Ferguson.

The Voice of Truth, or Thoughts on the Affair between the Leopard *and the* Chesapeake. *In a Letter from a Gentleman of New-York to his Friend.* New York: Printed for J. Osborn, 1807.

Watson, Paul Barron. *The Tragic Career of Commodore James Barron, U.S. Navy (1769–1851).* New York: Coward-McCann, Inc., 1942.

Wendt, Lt. Col. William R. "At Loggerheads in a 'Cold' War." U.S. Naval Institute *Proceedings* 76 (May 1950): 519–25.

Woodworth, Samuel. *The War: Being a Faithful Record of the Transactions Between the United States . . . and . . . Great Britain.* Vol. 1. New York: S. Woodworth and Co., 1813–15.

Wright, J. Leitch. *Britain and the American Frontier, 1783–1815.* Athens: University of Georgia Press, 1975.

Zabriskie, George A. "The *Chesapeake* Affair." *New-York Historical Society Quarterly Bulletin* (October 1944), 1–16.

Zimmerman, James Fulton. *Impressment of American Seamen.* New York: Columbia University Press, 1925.

Index

About the Authors

Spencer C. Tucker is professor of European and military history at Texas Christian University and chair of the history department. He has written two books on naval history—*Arming the Fleet: U.S. Navy Ordnance in the Muzzle-Loading Era* and *The Jeffersonian Gunboat Navy*.

Frank T. Reuter is a professor emeritus at Texas Christian University. A specialist in U.S. diplomatic history, he is the author of *Trials and Triumphs: George Washington's Foreign Policy*.